Glimmers of Hope

Glimmers of Hope

Toward the Healing of Painful Life Experiences
through Narrative Counseling

Edited by
TAPIWA N. MUCHERERA

WIPF & STOCK · Eugene, Oregon

GLIMMERS OF HOPE
Toward the Healing of Painful Life Experiences through Narrative Counseling

Wipf & Stock
An Imprint of Wipf and Stock Publishers
199 W. 8th Ave., Suite 3
Eugene, OR 97401

www.wipfandstock.com

ISBN 13: 978-1-62032-467-7

Manufactured in the U.S.A.

Contents

Contents

Preface

MANY OF US TEACHERS can attest that there are times when we have learned much more from the life experiences students bring to the classroom than from the textbook knowledge. As editor of this book, it has been a blessing to teach graduate students because many of them are second career people. Many of these students bring challenges/questions to the theories we explore in class, and/or confirm and provide practical integration to the theory. In other words, the classroom becomes a place not only of learning about theory but a laboratory, a place where the integration of theory and practice come alive. The contributors are diverse; Americans (USA), Africans, Caribbean, and Asian by birth.

This book is mainly based on personal problematic life stories written for the Narrative Counseling Course they took from me. Having learned the theory in class and mastered it, some of the students wrote their final papers based on how a counselor worked with them on a problem using the Narrative Approach. Thus demonstrating they were now able to understand and apply the approach the counselor used on them, they integrated it with what they had learned in class. Eureka! They connected the dots. Others, as they role-played their real life experiences, used these role-plays as a place to integrate theory into practice while resolving their problem. While others mastered the theory, and then reflected and retraced how they resolved a particular problem by applying the Narrative Approach. They discovered there was a theory behind what they were doing. The class helped flesh out the concepts and processes of the theory and how to apply it more clearly to their problem. Still there were a few who took case scenarios they observed and then applied the Narrative Approach to those cases.

As you read the chapters of the contributors, I'm assured you will connect at some level with some of their stories. Human experiences have a way to connect people, whether those experiences are joyous or painful ones. The stories and experiences contained in this book vary from adoption coupled with identity issues, abortion, physical and sexual abuse, bullying, fear, suicidal thoughts (cutting), people pleasing, grief, infertility, recovering from colonization experiences, and the hope experienced by children in child-headed families orphaned by the HIV/Aids pandemic. The setting and beginnings of these stories are sad and painful. It is, however, through the work of using the Narrative Approach that these bleak and painful stories are brought back to hope fulfilled. They are truly stories of 'glimmers of hope.' The life journey of the people in this book continues, but life circumstances may call them to remember, re-author, and revisit these experiences. However, because they've applied the Narrative Approach they will be equipped with better skills.

Tapiwa Mucherera, PhD
Professor of Pastoral Counseling,
Asbury Seminary.

Acknowledgments

THIS WORK COULD HAVE not come about without the influence of Dr. Edward P. Wimberly, Alice Morgan, and the late Michael White, who is one of the founders of Narrative Counseling or Conversations. It is clear that the voices of many of the founders of Narrative Therapy/Counseling echo in this book. I want to thank the students who volunteered to work hard in transforming their final semester papers into chapters. Further still, I want to thank those students who volunteered to share their heartbreaking personal experiences, overcoming the pain, and putting it in writing with the hope that these stories will help those facing similar circumstances. What kept each person in these stories from giving up was not a guarantee that the bleak circumstances they found themselves would suddenly vanish, but it was *"glimmers of hope"* experienced through the caring and sharing with others when they needed it the most. The ultimate hope was in holding on to their faith in a God who loved them, reading scriptures, and believing in a future with hope. Thank you for sharing how these *small rays of hope* carried you through these treacherous life moments.

To Cheri Cowell, our editor, what a wonderful piece of work you helped us put together. Thanks for tirelessly working through the manuscript, especially in helping all of us to shape it from a mere end of semester paper to a true academic piece. Your work with each and everyone is greatly appreciated. You are a very patient person who pushes for deadlines in a very gentle way. Thanks.

Lisa Yarelys Perez, you are such a great gift and truly well organized. Without your help we could not have been coordinated to meet the deadline. You are always "on top of your game" in following through and following up with information. You were such a gift to all of us as we worked through putting together the manuscript.

The greatest honor and praise goes to our God who gave us lives and gives us strength to face a future with Hope. Without God, none of the stories contained in this book would have been possible. It is God through Christ and the Holy Spirit that we have abundant life now and look to a future of living with Him forever. Read the stories for yourself and see what God can do—resurrecting bleak stories to stories of Hope!

Contributors

Tapiwa N. Mucherera, PhD. Professor of Pastoral Care and Counseling—Asbury Theological Seminary; Ordained Elder—United Methodist Church Zimbabwe/ Florida Annual Conferences.

Trisha L. Kraal, BA, MAC. Korean-born adoptee raised in Michigan; BA Social Work—Asbury University; (MAC) Asbury Theological Seminary, Wilmore, Kentucky.

Benjamin M. Lovell, BSc, MDiv. MDiv—Asbury Theological Seminary; Chaplain Residency at Deaconess Hospital.

Jim Berlau, BA, MDiv. MDiv—Asbury Theological Seminary; BSc—Communications and Theater Arts, Frostburg State University Baltimore, MD; Ten years ministry service.

Debbie Daley-Salinger, BS, MSc, MDiv, MAPC cand. A native of Jamaica, W.I.; BS Computer Science; M.Sc. Computer and Information Systems—Phoenix University; MDiv & MAPC—Asbury Theological Seminary; Elders' orders—United Methodist Church.

Adena Bowen, BS, (MAMH & MA Youth Ministry cand). BS (Biology)—University of Georgia; Master's of Art's in Youth Ministries and Mental Health Counseling—Asbury Theological Seminary.

Kari D. Romero, BA, M.Ed, & MDiv. MDiv—Asbury Theological Seminary, Union University; (M. Ed) Adjunct faculty—Southeastern University; High school English teacher—Tennessee; Ordained—children, youth & college ministries.

CAROL VODVARKA, BA, MAMH CAND. Mental Health Counseling—Asbury Theological Seminary; AA Paralegal Studies—Wesley College Dover, Delaware; BA Psychology—Wilmington University, New Castle, Delaware; Facilitates grief and loss support groups.

KRIS ANDREWS BONDERENKO, BA, MAC CAND. Founder of Passionate Life Solutions; MAC—Asbury Theological Seminary; Author ebook, "Sassy Single Mom's Guide to Living a Life She Loves by Honoring the Essence of Who She Is" (2011).

LORA GREGORY, BS, MAC CAND. B. Sc Music Education and Applied Violin—Indiana Wesleyan University; MAC—Asbury Theological Seminary; Leads summer mission trips for teens to Africa and Europe.

SÈGBÉGNON MATHIEU GNONHOSSOU, MA. DMIN, PHD CAND. PhD candidate—University of Manchester/Nazarene Theological College; Language and Communication Sciences—University of Abomey, Calavi, Republic of Benin, West Africa; M.A—Intercultural Mission, Fresno Pacific Biblical Seminary, Fresno, California; DMin—Asbury Theological Seminary, Wilmore, Kentucky.

JEANNIE CHAPMAN, BA, M.S. ED, MAPC CAND. MAPC—Asbury Theological Seminary. M.S.—Edu Troy State University; B. S. Music—Georgia Southwestern State University (1992); Director of Worship and Music—Clayton 1st United Methodist Church, Clayton, Georgia.

ERIKA A. MAYERS, BSC, MAC CAND. MAC—Asbury Theological Seminary; Experience in the medical and healthcare insurance industries.

MARCI HANNAH BOURLAND, BSC, MA, MDIV CAND.—MDIV.—Asbury Theological Seminary; MA—Leadership for Evangelism & Discipleship—Columbia Biblical Seminary & Graduate School of Missions; BSc—Psychology—Georgia Southern University; Licensed minister—Maranatha Ministerial Fellowship International; Local pastor and Elder's order candidate—South Georgia Annual Conference, United Methodist Church; 7 years ministry service.

INTRODUCTION

Bringing Bleak Stories to Life through Narrative Counseling

Tapiwa N. Mucherera

It is not surprising you will find elements of your own life story intertwine with the many true and personal stories presented in this book. True, isn't it, that sometimes hope is nestled in a person enduring through suffering, even though we all want to avoid pain at all cost. This opening chapter introduces the whole book and gives a synopsis of each the following chapters. I begin with a few key concepts and terms used in Narrative Counseling, such *as Internalized and Externalized Conversations, Deconstruction, Re-authoring or storying, Re-membering, etc.,* so the reader is familiarized with the language of narrative before reading the many stories presented.

NARRATIVE THERAPY: AN INTRODUCTION

"Narrative Therapy is a form of psychotherapy, pioneered in Australia and New Zealand in the 1980s, that emphasizes the importance of story and language in the development and expression of interpersonal and intrapersonal problems."[1] Through questioning, Narrative Therapy helps clients to recognize and reflect on the differing but positive elements of their current problem-focused presentation of their lives empowering

---

1. Shapiro, *Applications of Narrative Theory*, 96–100.

them to recreate a more positive outlook on life. Alice Morgan simplified what Narrative Therapy is by describing it as "a respectful, non-blaming approach to counseling and community work giving emphasis to the concept that people are empowered to be the experts in their own lives. Using the practice of Narrative Therapy people come to understand and live their lives through a process of 'Re-authoring or 'restoring' conversations, which makes telling stories the central vehicle of understanding the works of Narrative Therapy."[2] As much as the New Zealand and Australian conference is said to have marked the beginnings of the Narrative Therapy approach, Narrative Counseling practices, however, have been present in many indigenous and oral cultures, since story is the way of life.[3]

Within the process of Narrative Therapy there are certain concepts and techniques that help the counselor host the therapeutic conversation and guide it in a positive direction, all while staying within the parameters of the client's agenda. The first concept the counselor pays attention to is *Internalized Conversations*. In this phase, the problem is inward focused. The stories told about the problem or of the problem are inwardly focused making the person the problem.[4] The next phase is to work toward moving the problem from internal to being external to the client by Naming the Problem. Naming the Problem furthers the process of externalizing the problem as it helps the client to see the problem as a separate entity and themselves as more than their problem. According to Morgan, *Externalized Conversations* are conversations that place the problem outside of the person, meaning the person is no longer the problem—the *problem* is the problem.[5] Once the problem is named and separated from the person the counselor can explore the meaning of the problem and the social or systemic beliefs that maintain the problem. This helps to thicken the story from a thin description story of the problem to a more enriched story with thicker meaning. The counselor may have to help the client continue to speak in external terms. A process called Deconstruction helps moving from a thin to a thick description of the story.[6] This is the process of finding contradictions, gaps and part of the story unintentionally left out while contributing to the problem. In addition, questions are important as they map the history of influence for the problem. It helps trace the history of

2. Morgan, *What is Narrative Therapy?* 2.

3. Mucherera, *Meet Me at the Palaver*, 109–11.

4. Morgan, *What is Narrative Therapy?*

5. Ibid.

6. Monk et al., *Narrative Therapy in Practice.*

the problem and makes a connection of the different parts or "windows" of a person's life and how the problem has affected those parts.[7] During this time of conversations, the counselor is listening for mentions of Unique Outcomes or Sparkling Moments. These are mentions of times or events that are outside the theme of the Dominant or Problematic Story. These are known as "Sparkling Moments" as they shine in contrast to the Dominant or Problematic Story.[8] Externalizing and Deconstructing moves into a co-creation of an Alternate Story, one that is sparked by Unique Outcomes and/or the Miracle Question and then reconstructed including the client's skills, capabilities, and strengths.[9] The client is the co-author of this Alternate Story. Sometimes the counselor will have to help the client see the value of events, and the values of the Unique Outcomes. Time spent adhering to the problem story (the Dominant Story) can cause a person to devalue the times when they overcame the problem or had other storylines involved in their life. The counselor's part in co-authoring is helping the client see the value of these unique/ sparkling moments.[10] While pointing out the value of these moments there is a need to historicize the moments so that each moment builds together "so that they do not hang lifeless and disconnected."[11] Monk further states that the counselor has a need for persistence at this juncture of the process as it can be difficult for the person to give up the old (the problem) take hold of the new (the Alternate Story). In the same vein, creating an Alternate Story is the Re-authoring process. Re-authoring not only looks at the future but also looks at the past abilities and competencies of the person so that they can redefine their identity and their ability to handle the current problem.[12] The counselor helps the client move back and forth in reflecting on actions and identity while considering what these (actions and identity) mean for the Alternate Story. Narrative Therapy is both present and future oriented with the use of the past where applicable to the future.

During Re-authoring and Remembering (memory), Re-membering (membership) also takes place. Remembering is important because one cannot build a story on Unique Outcomes or past abilities and competencies if one cannot have a recollection of his/her past. Narrative Therapy

---

7. Morgan, *What is Narrative Therapy?* 33.

8. Monk et al., *Narrative Therapy in Practice.*

9. Ibid.

10. Ibid.

11. Ibid.

12. Monk et al., *Narrative Therapy in Practice.*

depends on a person being able to use one's memory that is, *remembering* one's life story.

Re-membering is about the members in your social system or circle of concern. "Re-membering Conversations involve people deliberately choosing who they would like to have more present as the members of their club of life, and whose memberships they would prefer to revise or revoke."[13] There are some people in our lives by choice and others we had no choice at all in being involved in our lives. There comes a time when it is beneficial to cognitively take a look back or remember events (memories) and discern the significant people whose position should be elevated and the people whose position should be decreased or disconnected all together. The connecting with new persons (new membership groups) is essentially what Re-membering means.

Re-authoring also involves a process of Definitional Ceremony or Ritual Celebration, which includes outsider witnesses.[14] Outsider witnesses are those significant people who would not be surprised at the client's abilities, capacity, and his or her success stories or Alternate Story. Monk calls it creating an audience, and it definitely includes those significant people who have an elevated position in the person's life.[15] These outsider witnesses can both witness the success of the client as told by the client and they also contribute by telling what they see as the client's strengths and successes. The client can again retell their success/Alternate Story with the incorporation of the contribution by the outsider witnesses. It is a process that cements the Alternate Story. The Alternate Story is hope-filled and creates new life.

This book is about hope through the Narrative Counseling approach. Everyone is unique and individual stories about our lives can never be duplicated by anyone. In a world filled with other humans, we can have others help us re-story our lives despite the fact that we are the experts of our own life stories. Even in the darkest hour of our lives there are "Unique Outcomes," but many a times these exceptions are overshadowed by the problem-saturated events. We can allow ourselves to learn from our past experiences and others' life stories in order to maneuver and re-story our lives for alternate hope-filled life stories, or we can live "non-existent," vanquished, unstoried lives. Some of the authors in this book share personal experiences of how they found hope through Narrative Counseling

13. Morgan, *What is Narrative Therapy?*

14. Ibid.

15. Monk et al., *Narrative Therapy in Practice.*

in the face of sexual abuse, infertility, grief, being a parent to siblings as a child, and surviving colonialism. Other stories are of healing brought about through the Narrative Approach in cases of abortion, childhood fears, adoption, divorce, bullying, and overcoming anger.

In presenting these stories, some of the authors reflect theologically on evil, the meaning of forgiveness, reconciliation, grace, and hope in God and through the process of Narrative Counseling. They explore the questions: How did they find God in the midst of their suffering? How did a sense of community through the lenses of narrative become the "Outsider Witnesses" or a "Cloud of Witness?" In sharing these stories these authors are affirming that it is only through sharing our stories in light of the meta-narrative (scriptures) and experiences of God's daily saving grace that we find hope to continue the journey called *life*.

Chapter 1 presents a personal journey and story of one who was adopted. Adoption is presented positively in Christian scriptures. Paul writes in two different letters, "But when the fullness of the time had come, God sent forth His Son, born of a woman, born under the law, to redeem those who were under the law, that we might receive the adoption as sons (children) (Galatians 4:4–5).[16] Further he writes, "He predestined us to be adopted as his sons (children) through Jesus Christ, in accordance with his pleasure and will—" (Ephesians 1:5).[17] As much as adoption is presented in a positive light in scriptures, it is not always experienced the same way for those who go through the processes of being adopted by non-biological parents. This chapter tells the story of one person who was adopted into a culture other than that of her birth culture. The author considers the impact of adoption upon children who are adopted internationally and raised in cultures where they look different from those around them. She addresses the issues faced by such bi-cultural children as they learn to navigate who they are ethnically and who they are culturally. She further discusses her search for ethnic identity and the challenges she faced, such as internal dissonance and a sense of isolation as she was raised to be someone whom she was not, born Asian but raised in a Caucasian family and society. This chapter considers Narrative Therapy as an appropriate form of therapy for persons struggling with ethnic and cultural identity, as Narrative Therapy gives one the space to tell one's story, verbalize concerns, express confusions, and ask questions that may possibly have never been spoken of before. Persons dealing with issues related to conflicting

16. Cokesbury, *The Holy Bible* (NRSV), 1007.

17. Ibid., 1009.

ethnic and cultural identities may be provided the opportunity to make meaning of their experiences as they re-author their story.

The second chapter presents an outline of the practice of Narrative Counseling as applied to a case of bullying. While there are certain broad traits and characteristics of the use of Narrative Counseling in general, bullying presents the counselor with specific issues that must be considered as the counseling relationship proceeds. Indeed, bullying often manifests itself as an abuse of power by way of the intentional assertion of a negative Dominant Story. As such, counselors will need to be aware of the influence of power in the counseling relationship. This attention to power places Narrative Counseling, with its emphasis on empowering the client, in a unique position to offer healing. Furthermore, while certain problems may present clients and counselors with covert, or even unintentionally negative Dominate Stories, bullying is often an overt, intentional propagation of a negative Dominant Story. Here, again, the practices of Narrative Counseling, with emphasis placed on the Re-authoring of healthy Dominant Stories, are remarkably beneficial. In sum, Narrative Counseling, when practiced properly, is revealed to be a potentially valuable tool in assisting clients who are combating the problems of bullying.

The third chapter addresses how the need for a pastor to please those around them is powerful and very deceiving. Everyone wants to be liked, however, it is often worse when this is pertaining to a pastor. There is the tendency for people to believe that being "liked and therefore people pleasing," is equal to being holy and upright. Unfortunately, a majority of clergy find themselves driven by their own insecurity and lack of self-confidence. There is nothing wrong with being "nice," however, as pastors we are called to be "faithful." This can drive a pastor to unhealthy ministry habits, and an inability to faithfully follow the call to ministry in the fullest sense of the word "call." Narrative Counseling is an effective treatment modality for those who experience the need to please others to an unhealthy degree. This chapter focuses on one person's journey into self-awareness, where not only a people-pleasing nature is discovered but Narrative Counseling unearths the foundational experiences that set this need to please into motion. The end result is more than a healthy ministry; it is wholeness as a follower of Christ, one who is trying to answer the "call" in the most complete way as possible.

Chapter 4 addresses how sexually abused children carry long-term scars, which impact how they adapt to adult life. In many cases sexually abused children are left with fundamental issues of trust, autonomy, guilt resulting in low self-esteem, and the inability to develop healthy long-term relationships. Through the story of an adult survivor of childhood sexual abuse we will illustrate the major conceptual components of Narrative Therapy. Narrative Therapy focuses on the individual Deconstructing the story of sexual abuse and constructing an Alternative and preferred Story. This allows this person to define her role in the relationship and be in control of the outcome. We will see how the focus shifts from the individual to the problem, where the person is not the problem but that the problem is the problem. The result is symptom alleviation, personal growth, and personal competency using the Narrative approach to Counseling.

Chapter 5 presents a case study involving a fourteen-year-old girl named Seana who was adopted when she was five years old. When Seana was first adopted there were some reactive attachment issues. As Seana got older this was eventually resolved. Recently she began having trouble in school, which her teachers brought to the attention of her parents. One night Seana's mother discovered Seana was engaging in self-harming behavior. Seana had cuts all over her body and her mother found bloody razors and tissues hidden away. Seana's parents decided to bring her into therapy. The chapter moves into some snapshots of a couple of sessions with Seana engaged in Narrative Therapy. The healing of Seana is a journey she has to take by "cutting the cutting out of her life."

Chapter 6 focuses on how Narrative Counseling helped empower John, a seven-year-old boy, to stand against the problem that prevented him from sleeping in his own room each night. Children, just as adults, have a story to share and have the capacity to use their strengths to work against difficulties they face. Narrative Counseling with children often requires creative and playful approaches to engage the child. This chapter progresses step-by-step through the Narrative Counseling process with a child and his parents. The hope of defeating a problem in superhero-like ways begins to emerge little by little as the child, parents, and pastor work together through story-sharing, Externalizing, Naming, and Mapping the Problem, as well as finding Unique Outcomes that show John's potential for overcoming the problem. The Bible and its stories are also incorporated into the Narrative Counseling setting in order to allow God's narrative to partner with John's narrative as they Re-story the problem-saturated story in a palaver-type setting. This chapter illustrates the effectiveness of Narrative style Therapy with children when used in appropriate Pastoral Counseling settings.

The focus of chapter 7 is complicated grief. The recognition of complicated grief as a disorder in and of itself is relatively new. Employing the techniques of Narrative Therapy will not only help unravel all the facets of the grief one is experiencing, but will also enlighten the grieving person as to why they have experienced these reactions to their grief. The therapist and client journey together in these discoveries and together they strive toward the new life story that the client desires. In this chapter the author tries to illustrate how those who try to travel the journey of grief alone are stifled by it, but when you share it (grief) in the company of others, it gets better.

Chapter 8 explores current research in regards to domestic violence and how the application of Narrative Approach can help a survivor with the healing process. Though the client is safely out of the marriage, there is one memory in particular that causes her to feel "stuck" and unable to forgive herself. It is the memory of the night her abusive husband became violent with their son. Each of the specific areas in Narrative Counseling will be used to help guide the client through her story and into the healing process.

In chapter 9 an overview of using Narrative Counseling is presented in the healing process after an abortion is performed. The details of the struggle and pain unfold through the Narrative Counseling modality. This chapter is a personal story of the grief and pain of an abortion, followed by the hope and healing given through the process of Narrative Counseling. It is a story of redemption, atonement, and hope. This truth is revealed, "When I could not find hope, Christ and the ones who stayed with me through the journey became my hope and strength."

Chapter 10 addresses how the dissatisfaction with Western hegemonies and values began and continues to spread around the world, which is particularly felt in the areas where western rules and approaches to life formerly dominated indigenous inhabitants and continue to do so. This dissatisfaction is touching almost all areas of knowledge and practice, including psychology, theology, biblical studies, pastoral counseling, etc. The Narrative approach to knowledge has been found to be a very helpful alternative. Following the legacy of Narrative therapists and theologians, this chapter argues for a Narrative approach to using the Bible in Pastoral Care and Counseling in Benin, a former French colony of West Africa called Dahomey. Far from being a mere accommodation to contemporary Narrative Therapy practice, the chapter is grounded in the rich indigenous Narrative approaches to life in Benin. It also seeks to look at biblical texts as narrative literatures calling for a Narrative Approach to appropriating God's caring messages. The narrative natures embedded in the indigenous culture and the Bible provide a basis for adapting Narrative Therapy concepts and practice for use in Benin. A contemporary approach to counseling in Benin reflects both the indigenous stories and God's story in Christ as sources of healing.

In chapter 11 Narrative Counseling, a therapy that rediscovers and reconstructs favored experiences in life so that the client is seen as a courageous victor rather than a victim, is explored. The chapter uses a case study involving Henry, a ten-year-old boy who is referred for counseling by his school counselors due to his continual disruptive behavior. In the initial session, Henry tells his story (a personal myth), through play-acting with puppets, and a dialogue ensues. The puppets allow Henry to move from Internalizing Conversations to Externalizing his Problem. The process continues with "Deconstruction," or listening for what is not said in the dialogue. Once the problem has been "named," the collaborative effort between Henry and his therapist, the Scaffolding process, a Mapping out of the Problem, the Re-authoring of the story, as well as the Re-membering process in which Henry sees himself through the perspectives of others are presented. Henry is able to tell a "new" story where he is free from the problem; Rituals and Celebrations are used to recognize the process of moving away from the problem.

Chapter 12 is based on stories of struggling children left as orphans due to the HIV/AIDS pandemic. No child expects to be parenting their siblings by the age of twelve and fourteen. It is abnormal that children are raising or taking care of other children. These children quickly find themselves in the world of adults and are expected to act as adults. At the same time, when these children try to live into the world of adults, they are also reminded they are still children. Even with these mixed messages, they have to grow up fast, yet there is no place for them to fit in. This is true in many parts of the world today, especially the South Central part of Africa due the HIV/AIDS pandemic. In this chapter the author presents some true stories of few families that are child headed. The children narrate their struggles and the pain and grief of losing parents at a young age. Many report the pain of having to deal with the way the community and extended families treated them—the very people from whom they expected support treated them in an abusive manner or deserted them. In the midst of these grim situations these children find hope, especially given by some church people and individuals who took interest in their daily affairs. Their ultimate hope was found in God, the One who created and sustains them day-in and day-out.

Chapter 13 addresses the issues of loss of identity and identity confusion experienced by people who go through divorce. Divorce can affect the entire family. In a short time the story of their lives can become different from what it was previously thought to be. This can be disconcerting and distressing. The Narrative Therapy process not only helps a person facing divorce identity issues to find relief but also find their strengths, Remember their lives, Re-author their future, and gain support from their Outsider Witnesses. This chapter is a walk through the Narrative Therapy process within the context of a story of divorce identity issues.

The final chapter represents the story of one couple out of the more than 7 million who are directly affected by issues of grief and loss surrounding infertility. Written partially from the author's own experiences, she combines both personal experience and an understanding of Narrative Therapy practices to create a therapeutic model of how one might apply the principles of Narrative Therapy to those suffering from the effects of infertility. Within the chapter she first defines the general problem of infertility along with the grief and loss dynamics that often accompany those experiencing infertility. The therapist and client work to Re-story the problem of infertility, and the author applies basic techniques of Narrative Therapy such as the use of Externalizing Conversations, Naming the Problem, and Deconstruction techniques to Re-author and Re-member the problem of infertility, concluding with the use of Ceremony as a way to acknowledge defeat over the problem of infertility.

1

Identity is in One's Story

Healing Identity Wounds of Adoption through Narrative Therapy

TRISHA L. KRAAL

I WAS BORN IN South Korea and adopted at the age of five months by a family in the United States. My new family was of Dutch heritage and lived in west Michigan. The town was not especially diverse, so it was no small thing for my parents to adopt internationally and bring an Asian child into the all-white, Dutch community in which we lived.

I was adopted into a family of three older boys, all biological children of my adoptive parents. I was raised always knowing that I was Korean and that I was adopted. When I was a child, my mother continuously spoke to me about how special I was because I was adopted. I accepted this at a very young age, but such conversations between my parents and me ceased, as I grew older. I then began to experience a strange, internal dissonance that was, at times, unnerving.

My family seldom spoke of my Korean ethnicity or about Korean culture, traditions, or customs. In my community were a few children who were adopted also from Korea, but our ethnicity was never used as a point of connection. I spoke, acted, and dressed as a white, Dutch girl. My mother curled and permed my hair; she dressed me in traditional, Dutch costumes for annual festivals; and both my grandfathers taught me Dutch vocabulary. My Korean heritage was acknowledged only to the extent that it was necessary for medical forms—the manila envelope and small box in which my mother had placed a few items from my arrival in the U.S. (my adoption papers, the yellow outfit I wore, and my booties). Growing up, I consciously marked that I was 'Asian' on medical forms, school documents, and later on college applications, but whenever I looked into the mirror I saw a white person staring back at me. When I looked at family photos, I did not discern my Asian features as being different from my blonde-haired, blue-eyed parents and brothers. When I was younger, I interpreted this lack of concern for, or consideration of, differences to mean that I had been successfully integrated into an all-white family. Today, I strongly beg to differ.

I now interpret my experience as an adopted child as one that is quite sad, because my Korean heritage was uncelebrated. My family unintentionally ignored the reality that I *was* different—but I *am* different. I am Asian; I am Korean. Yet, I was raised as a white person. Only my physical features were acknowledged as a point of difference between my family and me. Although my mother enjoyed my Asian features that made me a "cute" child, and she told me that being adopted made me "special," I knew that I was expected to be Dutch in every other way. I did not consciously analyze and interpret these experiences when I was young, but I now understand that the message I received while growing up was that I was not supposed to be Korean; I was supposed to be white. The message resulted in an internal dissonance that came from knowing that I was not completely white, but also not knowing what it meant to be Korean. It was a tremendously frightening and almost out-of-body-like experience to look into the mirror and know that I was not white, but I also did not see Asian. Those experiences left me feeling strangely lost and scared. My coping mechanism was to believe that if I worked hard enough it would be possible for me to be like "everyone else."

My experience is perhaps not unlike that of other adoptees, specifically those who have been adopted internationally. According to Lee and Quintana[1], children who are adopted into families that are ethnically different from the adoptee will find the process of identity formation to be more challenging. Let us further consider this issue of ethnic identity and how such a challenge might be addressed using a specific psychotherapeutic approach called Narrative Therapy. I will also examine more closely the theory and techniques of Narrative Therapy and consider the ways

1. Lee and Quintana, *Cultural Diversity*, 130–43.

in which this particular form of counseling can be used to address issues concerning one's ethnic identity.

Ethnic Identity

I am certainly not alone in my struggle to achieve an ethnic identity. In 2006, 20,670 international adoptions took place in the United States.[2] Children are adopted internationally from over 100 countries.[3] Nearly 60 percent of these children come from Asia[4] and nearly 90 percent come from twenty countries, mainly China, Russia, South Korea, and Guatemala.[5] Each of these adopted children will need to decide for themselves if and how they will claim their ethnic identity. Several professional counselors and therapists who have worked with international adoptees have observed that developing a solid ethnic identity can be an especially difficult task for these persons due to "their membership in bi-ethnic families."[6]

Tajfel's (1981) Social Identity Theory proposes that a person's positive social identity contributes to them having a strong concept of self. Bhugra[7] states that if one discerns that his or her ethnicity is negatively perceived or received by others, feelings of shame can become a part of that person's identity. Considering the diversity found among the U.S. population today resulting from international adoptions, interracial marriages and relationships, and immigration, many people seek to find their place in this country, in this world, and in this life.

Narrative Therapy and Ethnic Identity

There are several ways in which a counselor can approach issues such as identity and cultural identification. Narrative Therapy has been acknowledged as a preferable form of therapy for issues related to ethnic identity based upon the assertion that identity is found in each person's life story.[8] Our identity is comprised of the various components of our story. *Ethnic*

---

2. Suter, *Journal of Family Communications*, 126–47.

3. Lee et al., *Journal of Family Psychology*, 571–80.

4. Basow et al., *American Journal of Orthopsychiatry*, 473–80.

5. Lee et al., *Journal of Family Psychology*, 571–80.

6. Basow et al., *American Journal of Orthopsychiatry*, 473–80.

7. Bhugra et al., *International Review of Psychiatry*, 244–49.

8. McAdams, *Review of General Psychology*, 100–22.

identity has been defined as "the degree to which individuals identify as members of an ethnic group."[9] Phinney[10] also defined ethnic identity as a person's relationship to his or her own group and the attitude toward that group.

In a study conducted by Syed & Azmitia,[11] a Narrative approach was used in an attempt to capture a better understanding of the link between the process of ethnic identity formation and the content of ethnic identity. According to Syed & Azmitia,[12] attention has been given to the *process* of forming an ethnic identity, but a closer observation of the *content* of that identity has been neglected. In other words, *what* is it that makes a person's ethnic identity their ethnic identity? What is one's ethnic identity comprised of? Syed and Azmitia[13] were especially interested in exploring the information about "the experiences that prompt adolescents and emerging adults to explore and construct, revisit, or potentially change their ethnic identities."

James Marcia[14] expounded upon the work of Erik Erikson and developed an ethnic identity status model in an effort to better understand the *process* of identity formation.[15] Marcia[16] identified four phases of identity crisis that one experiences later in adolescence: achieved, moratorium, foreclosed, and diffused.[17] However, this particular model was applicable to individuals in late adolescence, perhaps ages fourteen to eighteen years. A new phase of human development has now been identified, known as "emerging adulthood."[18] This period refers to the space between late teens and young adulthood—about eighteen to twenty-five years, often the college years, and is an appropriate phase during which to begin searching for identity. Phinney used Marcia's model to name three ethnic identity statuses that are applicable to persons in the stage of emerging adulthood: achieved status, moratorium status, and unexamined status.[19]

9. Syed and Azmitia, *Developmental Psychology,* 208–19.

10. Phinney, *Psychological Bulletin,* 499–514.

11. Syed and Azmitia, *Developmental Psychology,* 1012–27.

12. Ibid.

13. Ibid.

14. Marcia, *Journal of Personality,* 551–58.

15. Syed and Azmitia, *Developmental Psychology,* 1012–27.

16. Marcia, *Journal of Personalit,* 551–58.

17. Syed and Azmitia, *Developmental Psychology,* 208–19.

18. Arnett, *American Psychologist,* 469–80.

19. Syed and Azmitia, *Developmental Psychology,* 1012–27.

Persons with an *unexamined* ethnic identity status are those who have experienced "minimal explorations of the meaning of their ethnicity along with no clear personal understanding of their ethnicity."[20] Persons with an ethnic identity of *moratorium* status "displayed an increasing awareness of their ethnicity and were actively engaged in the process of exploring its meaning to them, without having made a commitment."[21] Those with an *achieved* status of ethnic identity had explored "what their ethnicity meant to them, together with a sense of acceptance and internalization of their ethnicity and an identity."[22] In Phinney's model, emerging adult transitions from each status, from unexamined to moratorium to achieved status, as they have more experiences and opportunities to make meaning of their ethnicity.[23] Syed and Azmitia investigated the ways in which these experiences coincided with the ethnic identity status that the emerging adult claimed for himself or herself at the time of the experience.

Before issues related to ethnic identity can be understood in the context of Narrative Therapy, one first needs a basic understanding of the principles, goals, techniques, and structure of Narrative Therapy. Narrative Counseling is described by Morgan[24] as a therapeutic approach that allows a client to tell his or her story. It is an approach that views the client and therapist as a team working together to understand and resolve the problem presented by the client. The client is considered to be the expert about himself or herself and is respected by the therapist as such. Narrative Therapy views the problem as being separate from the client—the client is not the problem; the problem is the problem. Therefore, the therapeutic environment is to be free of judgment. Narrative Therapy emphasizes and utilizes the strengths-perspective of clients and their ability to help them. Narrative therapists should possess an optimistic orientation toward all clients, from all backgrounds and circumstances.[25] Therapists must have the ability to identify the potential for healing and growth, which exists in each client, as well as their present strengths and available resources.

According to Morgan,[26] the goals of Narrative Therapy include helping the client to identify the problematic dominant stories in their lives

20. Ibid.
21. Ibid.
22. Ibid.
23. Ibid.
24. Morgan, *What Is Narrative Therapy?*
25. Monk et al., *Narrative Therapy in Practice.*
26. Morgan, *What Is Narrative Therapy?*

and to then replace those stories with more preferred alternative stories. The techniques by which the therapist and client will accomplish these goals include Externalizing the problem, Deconstruction, and identifying Unique Outcomes. I will further explain these techniques in the next section.

Narrative Therapy sessions are not conducted according to a strict structure; the client's storytelling process determines the direction of a session. However, general structure does exist that a Narrative therapist attempts to follow:[27]

1. Name the problem

2. Identify the effects of the problem

3. Evaluate the effects

4. Justify the evaluation

Let us now consider how Narrative Therapy might be implemented and utilized to help persons struggling with issues concerning ethnic identity.

Before the problem can be Named and Externalized a Narrative therapist must first learn from the client what the Internalized Conversations taking place in the client's mind are. Morgan[28] defines *Internalized Conversations* as those conversations that determine the problem to be found within the person—the person sees himself or herself as being the problem. These conversations usually carry negative connotations and portray a negative image of self, highlighting one's imperfections and shortcomings. Furthermore, Internalized Conversations often consist of generalized evidence, meaning that a person recalls instances that place them in a less-than-favorable light and those instances are perceived as the norm for this person's life.[29] A Narrative therapist begins a session by allowing the client, me in this instance, to share my concerns and problems by telling my story:

I realize that my family has unconsciously wanted me to be someone other than who I am. According to my family, I am not supposed to be Korean; I am supposed to be white. The result has been that I work harder at denying my Korean ethnicity and claiming my right to status as a white person. I used to express very little interest in learning about Asian culture or meeting persons from those cultures. I developed and maintained a

27. Ibid.

28. Ibid.

29. Ibid.

worldview that perceived Asians to be an inferior and odd group, and I sepa-
rated "them" from "us." Not all that long ago, I wanted to style my hair like
my female white peers; I wished for skin that was white rather than yellow; I
resented the fact that I could not use the same cosmetics as those used by my
friend because such colors and application did not look "right" on me. My
belief has been that I am not good enough because I am Korean. Sometime I
think that something within me is defective because of my ethnicity and my
adoptive status.

After listening to my story, it could be helpful for a Narrative therapist to offer information that might affirm and normalize my thoughts and
feelings. According to Benson, Sharma, and Roehlkepartain,[30] 20 percent
of transracially adopted children wish that they were of a different race.
Furthermore, Basow[31] asserts that some minority adoptees will cope with
their internal dissonance by assimilating into a majority ethnic group that
is more positively viewed. Such information in addition to that pertaining
to the life phase of the emerging adult verifies that my feelings, thoughts,
and behaviors are normal for circumstances such as mine.

NAMING THE PROBLEM

A Narrative therapist would then move on to find a name for my problem
and help me to shift into a mode of Externalized Conversation. According to Morgan,[32] *Externalized Conversations* are those conversations that
place the problem outside of the person where the person is no longer the
problem—the *problem* is the problem. The advantage of speaking using
Externalized Conversations is that clients no longer accept their problems as components of their identity. Clients can comfortably separate
from their problems, seeing those as entities outside of themselves. This
distance provides space to talk about the problems openly and honestly,
increasing the potential for clients to resolve their problems successfully.

The first step for engaging in an Externalized Conversation is to give
a name to the problem.[33] By naming the problem as a proper noun, it takes
on a personality and life of its own. Again, the separation of the problem
from one's self assists in the creating of space for discussion and resolution
of the problem. For example, clients struggling with ethnic identity might

30. Lee and Quintana, *Cultural Diversity*, 130–43.
31. Basow et al., *American Journal of Orthopsychiatry*, 473–80.
32. Morgan, *What is Narrative Therapy?*
33. Ibid.

benefit from a technique such as Externalization because they are then free to examine their ethnicity and experiences from a perspective that is nonthreatening to their sense of self and which does not invoke upon them any feelings of shame. In this example, after considering my description of the problem, a Narrative therapist and I might agree to name the problem Being Different.

IDENTIFYING AND EVALUATING THE EFFECTS OF THE PROBLEM

As is the case for nearly every counselor and client relationship, the counselor gathers as much information as possible about the problem before launching any intervention or resolution techniques. In Narrative Therapy, this step is referred to as *Scaffolding*. When implementing the Scaffolding technique the counselor asks questions that prompt the client to share pieces of their story. Through the storytelling, the counselor hopes to gather information about when the problem first appeared in the client's life, the ways in which the problem has affected the client, how the problem has progressed in intensity and breadth, who was connected with the problem, etc.[34] The therapist seeks to build an understanding of the client's story in order to be more effective as a helper. A conversation between a Narrative therapist and client to what follows:

When did Being Different first appear in your life?

The first conscious memory that I have is of the time when my mother briefly thought that she was pregnant. I freaked out. I worried that if the baby was a girl, my parents would return me to Korea. I believed that the only reason my mother adopted me was because she desperately wanted a girl and had given birth to boys three consecutive times. Adoption was my mother's Plan B, as she did not want to risk having a fourth boy. My logic as an eight-year-old was that if my mother were pregnant with a girl of her very own, my parents would not need me or want me anymore.

I also recall several experiences of looking in the mirror and having a very strange sense of disconnectedness from my body. It was as if the "real" Trisha was located elsewhere and was watching a stranger live in her body.

34. Ibid.

When I consider these experiences now, I wonder if I somehow intuitively knew that I was living a life that was not authentic to my identity.

Were there other times when Being Different was present and dominant in your life?

I felt alienated from my family when my oldest brother and his wife had their first child, my nephew. I was very excited to become an aunt, but my nephew's birth was an occasion upon which I realized that I could not ignore the differences between my family and me. My nephew looked exactly like other persons in my family, and he definitely looked nothing like me. The exclamation of delight over the similarities of his eyes, nose, and mouth to that of the rest of our family was a conversation in which I could not participate.

My nephew's birth marked the beginning of a journey that has continued for many years. I went away to college shortly after my nephew was born, and I was greatly disturbed to realize that I was a minority at the university where I attended. Raised in an all-white community, I had learned to dislike minorities. "They" were different from "us" and were not warmly welcomed into our town. Until entering college, I had laid my eyes on only a few minorities. When I looked in the mirror, I did not see a minority looking back at me. Thus, when I attended a large university and began to see and meet persons of all different colors and backgrounds, I quickly assessed that I was more like the minority student population and did not belong with the White student population. Such a realization was disturbing and made me angry. I resented looking Asian—I wanted to be White.

In what ways has Being Different affected your daily life?

I often struggle with feelings of worthlessness. I feel unconfident around others, always wondering if they like me. Even if they do, I worry that any mistake I make might cause that person to dislike me. I feel detached, as if I do not belong with everyone else. I feel as if I am an outsider looking into the rest of the group. I am simply not as good of a person as those around me are. I am not worth as much as they are.

I was the brunt of many jokes while growing up, some of which I am ashamed to admit I even made of myself. I often participated in jokes about how I was the 'token Asian' in the group so that our group or organization could achieve the status of being 'diverse.' Sometimes others asked me if I was ever offended by the jokes or ever struggled with being adopted. I honestly was not offended, but I understand better now that this was not due to being unaffected. Rather, I did not take offence to such comments because I did not respect or value my ethnicity enough to be offended. I did not celebrate my diversity; therefore, I did not know that I should have taken offense to such jokes and certainly should not have participated.

DECONSTRUCTION

After gathering the history of the problem and learning what kind of meaning the client has given to the problem, a Narrative therapist will use a technique called *Deconstruction* to help the client examine these meanings from various perspectives and evaluate the accuracy of these perceived meanings. Morgan[35] defines *Deconstruction* as the 'taking apart' of "the beliefs, ideas, and practices of the broader culture in which a person lives that are serving to assist the problem and the problem-story." Morgan[36] believes that the beliefs about a problem that often motivate and sustain its existence are actually lies that have been mistaken for truths. Therapists will ask pointed questions that prompt clients to examine more carefully certain components of their thin story. The client is encouraged to look at these 'truths' from a variety of angles and to consider them against a new background. One approach a Narrative therapist might utilize is to investigate a client's mythologies.

MYTHOLOGIES

Wimberly[37] defines *mythology* as "the beliefs and convictions that people have about them, their relationships with others, their roles in life and their ministry." A *birth mythology* is one's myths about the story of their birth. An aspect of Narrative Therapy is to emphasize the myths or stories that a person has believed about them and their birth and to help clients inspect those themes more closely for accuracy.[38] In my instance, a Narrative therapist may choose to ask about both my birth and adoption mythologies.

35. Ibid., 45.
36. Ibid.
37. Wimberly, *Recalling Our Own Stories*, 4.
38. Ibid.

What do you know about your birth and adoption?

I know that I was born on November 8, 1981 in the province of Kang Wong Do, South Korea. I was born in a maternity home in the city of Won Joo. I remained at the maternity home for only two days before being trans-ferred to a foster home in Seoul, where I remained for a little more than five months. One year ago I would not have been able to provide you with this much information about myself. I knew my birthdate, country, province, and approximate age upon adoption, but my adoptive parents never discussed information beyond this; no one offered to review with me at the documents of my adoption process once I was old enough to understand.

I was told that my biological mother was too poor to care for me. She wanted me to have a life better than that which she could offer me in Korea. Thus, she made the difficult decision to allow me to be adopted by someone with more resources. My adoption papers record that my mother made the decision before I was born. I also learned that she did not give me my name; my foster mother gave me my birth name, which is Kyungsook. My family name was Lee, but I do not know if I received the family name of my birth mother or my foster mother. When I arrived in the U.S. my parents changed my name to Trisha Lee. This is one way that my adoptive mother honored my ethnicity—she let me keep part of my name.

Anyway, I used to believe this story in its entirety about my birth mother's choice. After all, is this not a beautiful story about a mother sacrifi-cially placing the well being of her child before her own desires? As an adult, however, I now question certain aspects of this story as I learn more about Korean culture. My adoption papers state that I was an illegitimate child, and as I learn about the cultural standards for the family system in Korea during that time and the importance of bloodlines and genealogy, I do not believe that my mother would have been well received as a single mother. Yet, my adoptive family and I never talked about any of this.

My adoptive parents' story is that my mother desperately wanted a daughter. She gave birth to three sons in a row, and then she decided to adopt. I knew that they adopted me to meet my mother's need for a daugh-ter. I felt pressure while growing up to be very feminine. My mother dressed me all the time in lace, ribbons, and bows. She did not want me to become a tomboy in any way, so I was not allowed to play sports. My father was very concerned about my appearance when I arrived in the U.S. from Korea, because I was plump with full cheeks and black hair that stood straight up. My father told me that he was relieved when I grew older and he saw that I would be pretty. When my parents were adopting me my dad was also concerned about whether or not I was 100% Korean; he did not want a bi-racial baby.

The study conducted by Basow[39] revealed that persons with higher levels of self-acceptance also had higher levels of ethnic identity. A Narrative therapist might notice that my adoptive parents' standards for accepting me were rather particular. A Narrative therapist might point out that it is difficult for one to improve their acceptance of self when they are consistently not feeling accepted by others. Additionally, this may also be a place for a Narrative therapist to offer some different perspectives of the client's story.

Trisha, it sounds like your situation came about because of the choices of others. Your birth mother decided that she could not provide for you. Your adoptive mother had her own needs to meet. I want to look at this story in a different light. I wonder if your birth mother thought you were too special to have anything less than the best. I wonder if your adoptive mother wanted you, her daughter, badly enough that she was willing to go through the whole adoption process so that she could have a baby girl to love.

A Narrative therapist might also explore my personal mythologies to identify any connections between the themes found in my birth mythology and those found in my personal mythologies. Wimberly[40] describes personal mythologies as "the convictions and beliefs that we hold about ourselves." He explains that these personal mythologies are comprised of a variety of themes, which have been created by memories, relationships, and our experiences.

I guess I have always believed that I am not good enough because I am different. I was regularly teased about my size while growing up, because I was quite short. My brothers teased me about my flat nose and small eyes. Everyone in my family complained about my hair. My hair is thick, long, and coarse so I shed black hair all over the house. I was not able to help this problem, but I sure felt badly about it.

Also, while growing up, I tired of the list of question that was usually directed at me when someone learned of my adoptive status. Was it ever strange to be the only Korean in a Dutch family? Had I ever visited Korea? Did I want to visit Korea? Had I ever considered searching for my birth parents? Did I have any memories of my time in Korea? Did I speak or understand any Korean? I tried to my best to not become irritated, but my honest inner reaction was, "Good heavens, I was five months old! Does anyone

39. Basow et al., *American Journal of Orthopsychiatry*, 473–80.
40. Wimberly, *Recalling Our Own Stories*, 15.

*remember anything from when they were five months old?" I responded with
what I believed were "right" answers—"Yes, I did want to visit Korea one
day and no, I did not want to find my birth parents." I wanted to believe that
being adopted was a good thing, but the fascination expressed by those who
learned that I was adopted seemed to emphasize that there was something
different about me and peculiar about my adoptive status.*

From Thin to Thick Descriptions

Clients lead the way on their journey of storytelling and the Narrative
therapist follows them. The therapist's responsibility is to remain present and curious with the client throughout the telling of the story, asking
questions that prompt the client to think critically. Eventually, the therapist prompts the client to recall any situations in which their problem was
not dominant in their lives. This is called moving from a thin to thick
description of one's story. The foundation of Narrative Therapy is found
in the element of thin to thick descriptions. According to Morgan, "thin
description allows little space for the complexities and contradictions of
life."[41] In other words, *thin descriptions* are the result of tunneled vision. A
person's story consists of a few experiences without fully considering the
bigger picture, and evidence supporting an Alternate Story is not considered. Often, persons are led to such conclusions with the 'help' of others,
especially those who exert any amount of power over the person's life.

These thin descriptions of our stories often comprise our Dominant
Story.[42] A person's *Dominant Story* is the story by which they identify
themselves and see themselves. However, the story is often negative, in-
accurate, and an incomplete descriptions of the individual and their life
journey. The Narrative therapist desires to help the client *thicken* their
story. The thickening of the story occurs through the process of implementing the various techniques mentioned above, enabling a client to
consider their story from other perspectives. The thickening of their story
results in an *Alternate*, healthier, and more preferred Story. The Narrative
therapist understands a client's Alternate or preferred Story to be one that
is told and re-written from a new perspective. The therapist is listening
for alternatives within the client's original telling of the story for a new
storyline, from a perspective that bring positive meaning to the client's life.
In my case, a Narrative therapist works to Deconstruct my myth that I am

41. Morgan, *What is Narrative Therapy?* 12.

42. Ibid.

not good enough or acceptable as myself and begins to build an Alternate Story by inquiring about any experiences in which I did accept myself.

Was there ever a time in your life when Being Different did not bother you?

When I was younger, I was drawn toward diversity. Even though I fought with Being Different, I thought that there was something cool about diversity. When I was a little girl, toy companies had begun to manufacture dolls that were 'ethnically diverse' and I chose the non-white dolls; sometimes they were Asian, and sometimes they were Black. Perhaps I identified with their appearance. When I was older, I chose friends who were also adopted from Asian countries.

Another experience occurred when I lived overseas in the country of Romania for two years after I graduated from college. I was the only Asian living in the city, and the people's exposure to diversity was minimal at best. Romanians constantly mocked me as I walked through the city, and I was the recipient of stares every time I entered a store or boarded public transportation. The stares made me very uncomfortable and I wished that I were invisible, yet I did not wish to be of an ethnicity other than Korean. I was proud of the fact that I was Asian, and I did not wish to be something different— I only wished that Romanians would receive me better and not be so ignorant and insensitive. Furthermore, I realized that I had the opportunity to expose the children and young people whom I was serving to diversity, as well as an experience of being in relationship with a person very different from them, but who loved them deeply and worshiped the same God as they.

Also, when I became a graduate student, I met an international student from Korea. He was very curious about my history and took it upon himself to teach me many things about Korea. One of my most significant experiences was seeing my birth name written in Korean. Suddenly, I felt as if I had been given a piece of my identity.

What was it about those experiences that helped you to ignore Being Different?

When I chose to have a minority baby doll rather than a white baby doll, I think that I honestly thought that they were pretty. I also feared that no one else would choose those dolls, and I did not want the dolls to be left behind, so perhaps I made the choice out of pity. Nevertheless, I think that I perceived the dolls as being pretty.

I refused to think less of myself while I lived in Romania because I knew that I had been faithful and obedient to God's call. I suppose that I gained confidence from God's blessing as I saw relationships begin to flourish between Romanians and me. I realized that they loved me and accepted me as I was. This was positive reinforcement for me and served as a defense against mean comments that others aimed at me.

When I learned how to write my name in Korean, I began to feel equal with others. I had received a part of my birth history and story, and this helped me to feel more complete. I felt as if I finally had a story since Day 1 of my life, just as everyone else has.

Syed and Azmitia[43] would agree that exploration is the key to experiencing change in one's ethnic identity. My exposure to Korean culture through others provided me with prime opportunities to explore a part of myself I had not ever before known. A Narrative therapist emphasizes these experiences to encourage me to continue to expose myself to Korean culture.

MEANING MAKING AND NAMING AN ALTERNATE STORY

Morgan[44] defines *Landscape of Action* questions as those questions that counselors ask in reference to the identified Unique Outcomes. The counselor is interested in any surrounding circumstances that may be connected in anyway to the Unique Outcome. These questions focus on any contributing components leading up to, or immediately following, a Unique Outcome. A Narrative therapist might ask me to consider any occurrences that happened immediately before or following my experiences in Romania or time with my Korean friends that enabled me to not yield to Being Different.

In Romania, I suppose that I knew that God wanted me to be in that city for that particular time. I was confident about this because the Lord orchestrated every event to make the move and experience a possibility. He helped me to raise the money, He put together all of the logistical details of travel, and He prepared a place for me upon my arrival. The entire experience had God's name written all over it; perhaps I saw that He was using me to accomplish His work and I could be proud of who I was. Maybe my logic was that if He was using me, then I must be okay. I tried to see the opposition that I encountered while living there as evidence of Satan working so hard

43. Syed and Azmitia, *Developmental Psychology*, 208–19.
44. Morgan, *What is Narrative Therapy?*

to interfere with God's work. This was confirmation for me that I was doing God's work.

My new Korean friends were excited to meet me. When approached by many Koreans, my initial reaction was to feel completely inadequate because I did not speak Korean. At first, I was afraid to attend a Korean church, yet I also felt strangely drawn to it. The people there were eager to teach me anything I wanted to know about Korean culture. They seemed to understand the importance of me understanding my birth culture, and it was almost as if they were aware that they were bearers of precious information for me. They seemed to take delight in my curiosity and encouraged me to learn and ask more questions. I suppose I inferred that if my Korean friends thought I was worthwhile enough to spend time with, teach, and answer questions for, then perhaps I was good enough after all.

Landscape of Identity questions are intended to prompt an investigation of "what the development means in terms of the person's desires, intentions, preferences, beliefs, hopes, personal qualities, values, strengths, commitments, plans, characteristics, abilities, and purposes."[45] A Narrative therapist would be interested to know how I interpreted my experiences with my Korean friends. What have I determined these experiences to mean about me as a person?

Spending time with my new Korean friends helped me to feel as if I belonged. I belonged with a group of people who looked like me. They have helped me re-write the first few chapters of the story of my life. I know about my roots now—I came from somewhere and do belong to a particular group of people, just as everyone else has. This realization has shaped and strengthened my identity. I might be different from many of those around me, but I am also a person; I am equal.

RE-AUTHORING

In reference to Re-authoring a new story, Wimberly states that such an act "recognizes that change in convictions and beliefs is possible; we are not totally at the mercy of our early childhood experiences, unconscious processes, and cultural conventions."[46] *Re-authoring* involves changing our myths about ourselves. Wimberly contends that it is possible for us to "transform the beliefs and convictions we have long held about our sense

---

45. Ibid.

46. Wimberly, *Recalling Our Own Stories*, 73.

of self."[47] During the Re-authoring process, a Narrative therapist prompts clients to consider questions about the future. The goal of re-writing a person's story is to have a different outcome. Counselors ask clients to consider the ways in which they want their lives to be different. What will that look like? What will the new story be? Narrative therapists might ask a question known as the *Miracle Question*. The Miracle Question asks a version of this question: "If you were to wake up tomorrow morning and the problem was no longer there, what would your life look like?[48]

I believe that people should celebrate ethnic diversity, not ignore it. I want to be proud of my Korean ethnicity, and I want to learn more about my birth culture, its traditions, and the language. I feel more complete as a person because blank pages of my story are not blank anymore. I now know more about Korean culture and ethnic characteristics. I want to continue building relationships with other Koreans. I want to feel thankful and glad that I am Korean. I suppose that if God had wanted me to be Dutch, then He would have created me to be so. For some reason He decided that I needed to be Korean. Perhaps, rather than believe that I am not good enough as a Korean, I can believe that God had a special plan for my life if He brought me all the way over to this side of the world from Korea. Maybe He needs me to teach others some things. So maybe my story is not so much about being different and not good enough; maybe, it is a story of love and acceptance, worth, and value.

A client's response to the Miracle Question offers information to the therapist for guiding the client through the process of making these perceived 'miracles' become possibilities. A client's response gives the therapist insight into what the client hopes for and truly desires.

RE-MEMBERING

Part of the Re-authoring process involves Re-membering. Morgan[49] explains *Re-membering Conversations* as those conversations about who will continue to be a part of the client's intimate circle of support and who will no longer be a member. Narrative Therapy strongly encourages resolution and healing to take place within a community, so a Narrative therapist will focus heavily on helping clients build and gather for themselves a

47. Ibid., 73.

48. Mucherera, personal communication, June 10, 2010.

49. Morgan, *What is Narrative Therapy?*

community of support. In other words, the client chooses who will be a part of their support system and whom they want to remove from that group.

One consideration that may help a client decide who to invite and who to reject is to ask who would be the least surprised about the changes in their life and who would be the most surprised. This could include friends, family members, teachers, etc. In my instance, I may want to consider asking those persons to be a part of my support system who would understand and support my claim to ethnic identity, and I might choose to limit contact with those persons whom I believe would not be supportive. I may surround myself with other Koreans, as well as with other adoptees. I have experienced a significant change in my status of ethnic identity, from unexamined to moratorium to achieve,[50] and as I embark on this new journey I will need to do so in community. In Narrative Therapy the client writes a new story, but there are still many experiences to be had; it will be important for clients to have trusted people supporting them as they seek to live out their new story.

A component of this gathering of support can happen in a *Definitional Ceremony*. Morgan[51] defines Definitional Ceremonies as "processes in which audience members act as witnesses, in very particular ways, to the conversations between the therapist and those coming to therapy." The audience members can be a part of something known as *Outsider Witness groups*, that consist of two more persons who are significant figures in the life of the client.[52] These groups can participate in a Definitional Ceremony that marks the beginning of the client's new story. The members of the Outsider Witness group serve as witnesses to this new phase and express their support of the client.

Conclusion

McAdams[53] contends that the telling of our life stories is what helps us to form our identity. Narrative Therapy embodies this belief, as well as the perspective that life is comprised of experiences. Narrative Therapy reinforces McAdams' assertion that lived experiences are the building blocks of our life stories and are that which enable us to change our ethnic

50. Syed and Azmitia, *Developmental Psychology*, 1012–27.

51. Morgan, *What is Narrative Therapy?* 121.

52. Ibid.

53. McAdams, *Review of General Psychology*, 100–122.

identity. Perhaps the biggest milestone for someone who struggles with ethnic identity is the willingness to tell his or her story—to talk and to share about the shame, disappointments, and questions. My experience has been that the greatest challenge has not been facing the problems; it has been verbally acknowledging that this story is my life. I wanted *my* story to be one of love and acceptance. I remained silent for many years, never daring to vocalize the dissonance and incongruence that had always been present in my life. Yet, the day came when someone asked me to share my story and the Lord prompted me to open the door to this part of my heart. I could not have begun to re-author my story if I had not been willing to tell my original story. It was only then that I could remember my origins and begin the process of Re-membering and Re-authoring.

2

Recovering One's Self-Image from Years of Bullying

A Narrative Approach

BENJAMIN M. LOVELL

A NARRATIVE APPROACH TO BULLYING

The Case Study

MICHAEL IS A FRESHMAN in high school. His teachers, concerned that he is becoming both quiet and withdrawn, have referred him to counseling. Generally speaking, Michael is a good student. His grades are among the highest in the class and all homework is turned in on time and according to expectations. While Michael has never been a very popular kid, none of the teachers can remember a time when other students have overtly injured him in any way. Michael's parents have noticed, however, that he lowers his head when his classmates are around. Typically outgoing and happy, his whole demeanor changes in the presence of other students. There is a general tendency to avoid functions where other students may be present. In conversation with teachers, his parents have voiced concern that things may be happening at school of which they are not aware. Michael does have a close circle of friends that he spends time with on a regular basis; however, they are rarely involved in the more mainstream activities of their peers.

In conversation with his parents and teachers, Michael has made casual statements about how much he dislikes his classmates. When asked, he explains that they are "jerks." His parents are concerned for his well being due to a growing sense of separation that they have noticed. Increasingly, Michael's writing, drawing, and music have become angrier in nature. While he has not shown any signs of aggression, his parents are concerned that this change reflects a hurtful situation of which they are unaware. They suspect that bullying may be at the root of his mood change, but have yet to find a way to get Michael to open up about it. When he was younger, he would often come home from school crying, explaining that his classmates had said hurtful words as a result of lingering, visible effects of a birth defect. His parents had largely written the taunts off as "kids being kids." The hope among all involved is that through Narrative Therapy answers will be discovered as to what has brought about these changes in Michael's demeanor, and solutions will be found that benefit all involved.

INTRODUCTION

This chapter will address the above case study of bullying using the principles of Narrative Therapy. The unique nature of bullying, its impact on individuals and groups, and its particular relationship to the practice of Narrative Therapy will be examined.

An Overview of Narrative Therapy

The practice of Narrative Therapy begins with a particular view of the manner in which human beings experience the world where they live. Specifically, counselors making use of this technique affirm that one's experience of reality is largely subjective, and that one expresses this subjectivity by way of the stories through which reality is defined and described. "Our lives are multistoried. There are many stories occurring at the same time and different stories can be told about the same events."[1] Indeed, if one's experience of reality is largely subjective, then it stands to reason that in a population of people experiencing the same reality subjectively there would be multiple stories by which people would make sense of the world. "The simple idea from which the narrative approach is developed is that people make meaning, meaning is not made for us."[2] This meaning

1. Morgan, *What is Narrative Therapy?* 8.
2. Drewery and Winslade, "The Theoretical Story," 32–33.

is made by the stories that people tell and choose to believe. Taken further, the meaning created by the stories used to define reality can ultimately become a force for the shaping of reality. "Humans create culture, and in turn culture helps construct an individual's identity."[3] Perception of reality, then, actually determines the lens of reality through which others are perceived. Stories beget stories. It is the desire of Narrative Therapy to engage these stories as they relate to the particular circumstances of the client.

Counselors in this field stand in opposition to approaches to therapy that would place the therapist in the position of a trained expert, with sole possession of the skills and knowledge necessary to fix what is believed to be faulty in the client.[4] The subjective view of the counselor is not viewed as more authoritative than the subjective view of the counselee. Additionally, the therapist is not afforded some artificial sense of perceptual neutrality.[5] In fact, the Narrative therapist's tool of choice is to treat "people as experts in their own lives."[6] Rather than telling the client what is wrong with him or her and how to correct it from an artificially authoritative position, the Narrative therapist seeks "a stance of curiosity . . . asking questions to which [he or she] genuinely [does] not know the answers."[7] In taking this approach rather than issuing uninformed proclamations disguised as expertise, Narrative therapists enter into a "journey of coexploration" with the clients as they seek to address the problem as co-laborers in the task.[8] As such, the Narrative approach to therapy takes the form of a conversation, with the therapist in the position of a genuinely inquisitive partner in a quest for a more beneficial and complete story by which the client may give shape to her or his own life.

Indeed, the ultimate purpose of Narrative Therapy is "the transformation of problems through the restorying of problematic stories."[9] These problematic stories are the dominant stories by which the lives of clients have been defined to this point. Dominant stories "are often expressed as a truth about the person who is struggling with the problem and their identity . . . These thin conclusions, drawn from problem-saturated stories, disempower people as they are regularly based in terms of weaknesses,

3. Mucherera, *Meet Me,* 18.
4. McKenzie and Monk, "Learning and Teaching," 84.
5. Besley, "Foucauldian Influences," 73.
6. Winslade et al., "The Therapeutic Relationship," 68.
7. Morgan, *What is Narrative Therapy?* 2.
8. Monk, "How Narrative Therapy Works," 3.
9. Williams and Winslade, "Co-authoring," 64.

disabilities, dysfunctions or inadequacies."[10] In the practice of Narrative Therapy, then, the counselor and client work together to re-write this story. Through a process of conversation and exploration, the details that are left out of the Dominant Story for its own preservation, in a way that oversimplifies the complexity of human life, are discovered and brought to light.[11] With the inclusion of these details, the client can rewrite his or her life as a reflection of the fullness of a new and beneficial story.

Suffice it to say, this is the general roadmap, but detours may occur with some frequency. Narrative therapists are, after all, "working with a bustling, dynamic, living, breathing culture, represented in the counseling setting by individuals, couples, or groups."[12] The process must never take precedence over the needs of the client at any particular moment. As mentioned above, this is a cooperative approach to therapy, with the client situated in the position of control and authority. The therapist is there as a facilitator, not beating a drum that demands a march but playing a duet where, in cooperation, counselor and client dance to the finish line together at a pace that is practical, not mechanical.

BULLYING AND ITS RELATIONSHIP TO NARRATIVE THERAPY

Prior to applying the above principles to Michael's particular case, it is important to first take time to carefully examine the specific nature of bullying and its potential implications for the manner in which therapy may proceed. While therapists should avoid trying to simply categorize clients based on general factors, in light of the complexity of humanity, it is worthwhile to educate oneself concerning the potential issues that may come up in counseling sessions. In particular, bullying carries with it certain implications for interpersonal interaction that may have an impact upon the manner in which a conversational approach is built on a trusting relationship.

Due to the broad number of activities that can fall under the umbrella of bullying, narrowing the term down to a particular meaning can be difficult. Perhaps the most effective definition of bullying is as "a class of intentional and repeated acts that occur through physical, verbal, and relational forms in situations where a power difference is present."[13] It

10. Morgan, *What is Narrative Therapy?* 13.

11. Monk, "How Narrative Therapy Works," 14.

12. Ibid., 3.

13. Bradshaw et al., "Bullying and Peer," 362.

addresses the reality that bullying is more than physical violence among peers, or schoolyard taunts among children. Rather, the practice of bullying has an impact not only upon one's physical well being, but also one's emotional and social well-being. Indeed, the old adage that "sticks and stones may break my bones, but words will never hurt me" may need to be reassessed in light of the above explanation of the scope of bullying. "Although there are no visible scars, [verbal and emotional] bullying can have devastating effects."[14] As such, a preconceived understanding of bullying as a physical assault on one's person has the potential to ignore real abuse that may be happening. This fact is but one illustration of the importance that a therapy practice with an emphasis on listening will play in bringing healing to students like Michael.

One of the more notable traits of bullying as it relates to Narrative Therapy is the role that the perception of power plays. "Bullying and harassment is about power."[15] It is a behavior that finds one person or a group of people making use of a position of power to launch an assault upon the well being of another. Such an abuse of power may rule out the viability of any type of counseling in which the therapist is presented as an authority figure or expert. When someone in a position of power has injured a client, opening up to yet another person in a position of power in a way that would allow healing but leave room for further injury, may seem somewhat daunting. Again, this potential aversion to power differences, or, more specifically, positions of perceived weakness on the part of the client presents both an opportunity and hurdle for the use of Narrative Therapy in cases of bullying. As mentioned above, Narrative Therapy calls for the therapist to enter the conversation by placing the client in the position of power as an expert where the given situation is concerned. "Therapists must always assume that they are participating in domains of power and knowledge and are often involved in questions of social control. Therefore, therapists must work to demystify and unmask the hidden power relations implicated in their techniques and practices."[16] One of the aforementioned goals of Narrative Therapy is for client and counselor to combat the problem together. Therapists must be prepared for some resistance while this relationship is established.

14. Smokowski and Kopasz, "Bullying in School," 102.

15. Dixon et al., "The Dunedin Safer Schools," 5.

16. Besley, "Foucauldian Influences," 77.

Bullying as a Form of Exclusion

One of the barriers to the establishment of this relationship stems from yet another characteristic of bullying: the impact on the place of an individual within a given community. "Humans are shaped by their relationships in their communities of embeddedness."[17] Not only do people find identity in community, but "humanity was created to live in community."[18] As such, the "social exclusion" that is so common in acts of bullying is particularly devastating.[19] "Peer relationship problems are prevalent in schools and significantly influence children's school-based adjustment and increase risk for future negative outcomes."[20] Not only are the identities of victims of bullying being shaped by an environment that is hostile to them, but victims are also being excluded from the very community that should be a source of strength and support in times of need. This compound assault upon individuals may leave victims feeling as though they are "outcasts and failures."[21] Such feelings will only serve to increase the hurt associated with being a victim of bullying while additionally increasing the likelihood of future bullying through further separation from a supportive social structure. As such, "prevention and intervention efforts need to include not only the individual, peer group, family, and school, but also the community."[22] Where Narrative Therapy is concerned, Re-membering Conversations that invite others into the Alternate Story will be key as a new, supportive community from which the client can draw strength is identified.[23] More attention will be given to this topic below as the process of Narrative Therapy is applied to Michael's case.

One aspect of bullying in particular involves the use of story to intentionally manipulate the status of an individual within a community. "[S]tories are used to fashion one's social status in relation to others and also to evaluate the actions of others. Through developing a reputation, the victim of bullying [can be] isolated from social interaction with the rest of the . . . community."[24] While certain dominant stories may be subtle, or even

17. Mucherera, *Meet Me*, 96.

18. Ibid., 81.

19. Butler and Platt, "Bullying," 19.

20. DeRosier, "Building Relationships," 200.

21. Smokowski and Kopasz, "Bullying in School," 104.

22. Espelage and Swearer, "Research on School Bullying," 378.

23. Morgan, *What is Narrative Therapy?* 77.

24. Hamarus and Kaikkonen, "School Bullying," 337.

inadvertent, there are clear instances of individuals identified culturally as bullies intentionally using story to influence the community-at-large, and define the identity of the victim in a negative way. "A bully who defines what is different in the . . . community creates the group of 'us' and 'them' and through the definition gains acceptance for the values represented by 'us.'"[25] While in many instances a therapist and client may face the task of writing a new story in the face of a fairly subtle Dominant Story, bullying presents the potential for a Dominant Story that is aggressive and intentionally resistant to change.

This type of bullying actively seeks to avoid the telling of another story by preventing the voice of the victim from being heard. "When the victim has been made a stranger through public humiliation and having fun, and when the desire for uniformity within the group becomes stronger, the victim is isolated and isolates him/herself from the community."[26] The voice of the victim, then, is silenced through exclusion. As such, the ability of someone in Michael's position to contribute to the authoring of the Dominant Story is severely limited. The bully names the trait that he or she believes warrants the bullying, creates a story that supports that identity, and develops a community around the story.[27] The client and therapist working together to confront such a problem will truly be in for a battle that will only be won through cooperative efforts of a community intent on the telling of a healthier story. Such a battle will be difficult, but not impossible. Together, the counselor and the client need only to draw into focus the excluded input and tell the new story that is seen in the fullness discovered. With that task firmly in sight it is now time to turn to Michael's case as a practical example of what has thus far been discussed in theory.

Narrative Therapy in Practice: Internalization

Narrative Therapy generally starts from a position of Internalization. "When people seek the assistance of a therapist, they often speak about the problem in ways that assume that it is somehow part of them, or within them. . . . These internalizing conversations (conversations that locate problems inwardly) usually have negative effects on people's lives."[28]

25. Ibid., 342.
26. Ibid., 339.
27. Hamarus and Kaikkonen, "School Bullying," 342.
28. Morgan, *What is Narrative Therapy?* 17–18.

This tendency is particularly strong where victims of bullying are concerned. As they hear the repetition of a Dominant Story that describes them "as outcasts and failures" they may come to believe this about themselves and internalize the story in a way that allows it to become their identity.[29] From this perspective, neither bullying nor the negative attitudes and actions of peers are viewed as the issue, but the victim sees himself or herself as the source of the negativity by which the Dominant Story is defined. The client, in short, identifies herself or himself as the problem.

"When individuals view themselves or their relationship as the problem, it hinders their ability to solve the problem."[30] Understandably, if the problem is viewed as being within an individual, any attempt to alleviate or remove the problem will first have to overcome personal barriers without making the client feel rejected once more. Internalizing statements "locate whatever problem the person has been experiencing deep in some unchanging aspect of the individual's nature and therefore make it hard to change."[31] An approach to counseling that operates solely in this first stage runs the risk of "inadvertently reinforc[ing] dominant ideas that may be supporting the problem."[32] Internalizing conversations, though a starting point for the therapy process that should not be rushed or excluded, as it will most likely be the emotional starting point of the client, should not remain as the end point of a counseling relationship. It is a step that must be taken, but must also be left behind in favor of more productive conversations and understanding. Ultimately, one of the first goals of Narrative Therapy is to aid the client in discovering a view of the problem that separates it from him or herself. This process will be addressed below.

An Example of Internalization in Michael's Case:

Counselor: Hello Michael. Thank you so much for agreeing to meet with me.

Michael: No problem. Mom and Dad thought it might be a good idea. They think something's wrong with me.

Counselor: What do you think about that?

29. Smokowski and Kopasz, "Bullying in School," 104–5.

30. Butler and Platt, "Bullying," 22.

31. Winslade and Smith, "Countering," 164.

32. Morgan, *What is Narrative Therapy?* 22.

Michael: I don't know. If everyone else thinks something's wrong with me, then doesn't that mean something's wrong with me? People wouldn't be bugging me so much if I didn't give them something to make fun of.

Counselor: Can you tell me more about that? What do you mean by giving them something to make fun of?

Michael: Well, I'm kind of the loser at my school. I always have been. As far back as I can remember I've been called "Chicken Legs" or something like that because I was born with clubbed feet. You can't tell when my legs are covered up because I can walk normally and stuff, but when I wear shorts you can see the scars and tell that my legs are scrawny. I'm not normal. I can't run well. I'm not good at sports because I was in the hospital for so long. I'm different. I'm just . . . a loser.

Counselor: Is that what they tell you?

Michael: That's how they treat me. I live it daily and that's what I have become. I just feel like there's something wrong with me. Everyone else gets along, but they all gang up on me. Why can't I just blend in?

Morgan says, "One of the first things that a Narrative therapist is interested in doing is to separate the person's identity from the problem for which they seek assistance."[33] This is where the process of Externalization comes into play. "[E]xternalizing conversations allow for explorations of the relationship between the person and the problem."[34] Whereas Internalization creates an environment within which the problem cannot be confronted without confronting the client himself or herself. Externalization identifies the problem as something outside and apart from the client. In doing so, room is given to move "away from self-attack, recrimination, blame, and judgment—attitudes that work against productive and positive outcomes in counseling."[35] Externalization positions the counselor as one who is not seeking to "fix" the client, but to work with the client to address an external problem that is at issue.[36] This step, beyond simply identifying the problem as something outside of the individual, fosters a view of the problem that makes it less daunting. Rather than being some inseparable aspect of the identity of the client, the problem is approached as something external that is either changeable or avoidable altogether.[37] While both the client and the counselor will likely come to the conversation with

33. Ibid., 17.

34. Ibid., 28.

35. Monk, "How Narrative Therapy Works," 6.

36. Ibid., 12.

37. Morgan. *What is Narrative Therapy?* 24.

an understanding that something is wrong and needs to be corrected, Externalization creates a scenario whereby the thing that needs to be corrected is viewed by all involved as something other than the client.

A vital step, and perhaps the pivotal step, in the process of Externalization is that of giving a name to the problem. In Naming the Problem, it is "immediately [situated] away from the person."[38] The problem becomes something that has its own identity and role in the story. As such, it is now something with which the client can interact, and beyond which the client can move. Of great importance in the naming process, however, is the clear delineation of the respective roles of the client and the counselor. Given the history of bullying, and the general consensus among most involved that bullying is the root of the issue, the counselor could be tempted to name the problem "Bullying" without much input from the client. This would be a mistake. It is vital that "the language and name for the problem comes from the person consulting the therapist and is selected by them. . . . The therapist does not want in any way to impose a name on them."[39] This issue is particularly sensitive in light of the role of power in bullying relationships. "When people have the knowledge and power to name something, they have the power and some control over the thing."[40] While the counselor is free to suggest names through leading questions, the decision must ultimately be left to the client. If the therapist truly believes that the client is the expert of her or his own life, then it must be left up to the one seeking therapy to name the enemy.

An Externalization Conversation in Michael's Case Is as Follows:

Counselor: How has not blending in been an issue in your life?

Michael: It's the reason for everything. I got made fun of because my legs were different. I got made fun of because I couldn't do the same things that others did. I got made fun of because I had to get braces and glasses over the same summer. Everyone always picks on me because I'm different!

Counselor: It sounds like the comments have been very difficult over the years.

Michael: Yeah. They tease me all the time. They're always picking on me. It's like a mosquito that's always buzzing around, and you can't get away from it.

38. Ibid., 19.

39. Ibid., 20.

40. Mucherera, *Meet Me*, 39.

Counselor: For the purpose of our time together, is it okay if we call the problem "Teasing"?

Michael: The teasing is a big part of it, but I think it's more that there's nowhere to get away from it. Could we call it "The Mosquito" instead?

Counselor: I think that's a good name. We'll start referring to the problem as the Mosquito.

Narrative Therapy in Practice: Scaffolding and Deconstruction

Once the problem has been identified and the counselor and Michael have agreed upon a name, the task turns to gaining a greater understanding of the nature of the problem in the life of the client. This process is characterized by two approaches working in tandem: Scaffolding and Deconstruction. Scaffolding is a process whereby the history of the problem is explored through a series of questions that yield greater insights at each stage, ultimately leading to an examination of the problem's impact in the life of the client at present.[41] The desired effect is that both the counselor and the client will gain a better understanding of the problem through discussing the manner in which the Dominant Story has functioned in the life of the client to this point. In short, the effort is akin to seeking to know one's enemy. Scaffolding, however, is not the only tool in this endeavor. It moves into, and works alongside, the process of Deconstruction. Deconstruction is "[t]he pulling apart and examining of 'taken-for-granted' truths" that facilitate the Dominant Story within which the problem operates.[42] "This helps to reveal the unstated cultural assumptions that contributed to the original construction of the problem."[43] Deconstruction is a methodical dissection whereby the client and counselor work through the story, taking it apart and looking for weak spots.

As the client recounts the story of the problem, "the narrative therapist looks for hidden meanings, spaces or gaps, and evidence of conflicting stories."[44] This is a technique called "double listening" as it "involves hearing the conflict story but at the same time keeping an ear out for openings to an alternative story."[45] Among these weak spots that are being sought

41. Morgan, *What is Narrative Therapy?* 33.

42. Ibid.

43. Monk, "How Narrative Therapy Works," 8.

44. Drewery and Winslade, "The Theoretical Story," 43.

45. Williams and Winslade, "Co-Authoring," 67.

out are Unique Outcomes. "A unique outcome can be anything that the problem would not be like, anything that does not 'fit' with the Dominant Story. They are instances/events that would be difficult to achieve in the light of the problem."[46] The purpose is to examine the role of the problem in the life of the client in an effort to discover occasions when the client has overcome the problem, perhaps without even realizing it. The goal, then, is to emphasize the victories that have already been experienced up to this point as a means of undermining the dominance of the Dominant Story. Once these exceptions to the Dominant Story, the story that exists in support of the problem have been identified, the stage is set for the next step, the construction of an alternative story that makes room for the Unique Outcomes that had previously been excluded or ignored.

An Example of Scaffolding and Deconstruction in Michael's Case Is as Follows:

Counselor: Would you mind telling me a little bit about times when the Mosquito has shown up?

Michael: It's usually after I've had a bad day. Sometimes I've done something kind of goofy, and other times they bring up something that happened a long time ago. Then there are other times when I don't do anything at all. When I get home, I can still hear the Mosquito telling me that I'm not worth anything. I usually try to do something to get my mind off of it.

Counselor: What does the Mosquito sound like?

Michael: It's just voices in my head telling me the same things I've heard all along from everybody else. Sometimes I feel like I'm always hearing echoes of what the kids have said at school; like the Mosquito just keeps whispering them in my ear to make sure I don't forget that I'm not good enough. It doesn't let me get any time away from being made fun of. When the other kids aren't there saying it to my face, the Mosquito is whispering it in my head.

Counselor: When was the first time you heard the Mosquito?

Michael: I don't know. I guess it started in grade school when other kids started to notice my legs were different and that I couldn't do things they could do. In preschool and kindergarten it didn't really matter. We were all just kids that got along, but in grade school people that used to be my friends stopped talking to me or only talked to me to make fun of me. It made me

46. Morgan, *What is Narrative Therapy?* 52.

self-conscious all the time. That's when the Mosquito first jumped in. It told me the other kids were right. There was something wrong with me.

Counselor: How did hearing the Mosquito affect you?

Michael: I started to shut down around the other kids. I wouldn't be myself. Even when I was happy, I would always be watching myself to make sure that I didn't give them anything to make fun of. Everything I did was affected by wanting to not do anything that would make the Mosquito louder.

Counselor: You mentioned that you do things to take your mind off of the Mosquito. I'd like to go back to that comment if that's okay.

Michael: Sure.

Counselor: What kind of stuff do you do to get your mind off of the Mosquito?

Michael: Usually I'll play video games or something. Lately, I've been learning to play guitar and I've found that it really helps me to clear my head.

Counselor: Do you think much about the Mosquito when you're playing the guitar?

Michael: At first yes, but the longer I play though, the less I care about what people said to me. I just want to get better at playing music.

Counselor: That's interesting. It's sounds like you've found a pretty good tool in music to help you overcome the effects of the Mosquito.

Michael: Yeah. I mean, when I'm playing guitar I just don't think about that stuff. It gives me room to just be me.

A great deal of the importance of Unique Outcomes is found in the fact that they "can be doorways to alternative stories" that are more favorable and healthy for the life of the client.[47] As with the above exploration of the role of the problem in the life of the client, it is important for the practitioner of Narrative Therapy to ask questions that help to "trace the history of the unique outcomes, firmly ground them, make them more visible, and link them in some way with an emerging new story."[48] The idea is that the counselor and client will work to flesh out the narratives that involve and enable the Unique Outcomes. Just as the problem is not made manifest in a vacuum, there are particular circumstances that set the stage for Unique Outcomes that exist apart from the problem. It is to these circumstances that the therapist must steer the conversation.

In addressing the history of Unique Outcomes in the life of the client, Narrative therapists speak in terms of Landscape of Action and Landscape of Identity/Consciousness. "Landscape-of-action questions focus on past

47. Ibid., 55.
48. Ibid., 59.

events featuring favored unstoried experiences" with the intent of discerning more clearly the environment within which the Unique Outcomes came about.[49] Essentially, the Landscape of Action is the situation within which the client was able to step outside of the story of the problem. Additionally, "landscape-of-consciousness questions encourage clients to evaluate and reflect on how they produce the kinds of experiences mapped out in the landscape of action."[50] Here the focus is on what the presence of particular Unique Outcomes says about the client as a person. Emphasis is placed on what is said about "the person's desires, intentions, preferences, beliefs, hopes, personal qualities, values, strengths, commitments, plans, characteristics, abilities, and purposes."[51] Together, questions focused on the Landscape of Action and the Landscape of Identity serve to place flesh on the skeleton that is built by the Unique Outcomes. The client begins to see a story that exists apart from the Dominant Story, a story that is the home of successes rather than failures.

The name given to this process is Re-authoring or Re-Storying, and it is the ultimate pursuit of Narrative Therapy.[52] "To be an author is to have the authority to speak—especially to speak in one's own terms and on one's own behalf."[53] The goal is to help the client to find the voice with which to write this new story. There is an Alternate Story already at work in the life of the client, and through a series of questions and discussions, the client and counselor work together to break the bonds of the harmful Dominant Story so that the client can define his or her identity in a healthy and meaningful way. Re-authoring "assumes that we are not powerless, not without agency in shaping the myths that inform our lives."[54] Together, the client and counselor work to help the client find that place of power; to help the client find his or her voice among the countless other voices. It is in these Alternate Stories that hope is discovered and preserved.[55]

As was mentioned above, however, the old story did not exist in a vacuum. It has the support of a community that agreed upon its validity. Similarly, a community of its own must support the new story. "Conflict stories do not exist only in the experience worlds of the major protagonists

49. McKenzie and Monk, "Learning and Teaching," 109.

50. Ibid., 109.

51. Morgan, *What is Narrative Therapy?* 61.

52. Mucherera, *Meet Me*, 113.

53. Winslade et al., "The Therapeutic Relationship," 55.

54. Wimberly, *Recalling Our Own Stories*, 73.

55. Mucherera, *Meet Me*, 3.

but are woven into the webs of relationship and discourse communities of which they are a part. So too must an alternative story. . . . be woven into these same relationship webs and discourse communities."[56] This is accomplished through a process of Re-membering, whereby clients "deliberately [choose] who they would like to have more present as members of their club of life."[57] In selecting people with healthy mindsets who will help in the crafting of a healthy story to be a part of his or her life, the client lends strength to the Alternative Story that can only be found in community. These will be people who will both participate in and echo the new story in the life of the client.

An Example of Re-Authoring in Michael's Case May Be as Follows:

Counselor: You mentioned that you like to play guitar; that the Mosquito isn't there quite so much. What do you think it is about that time that quiets the Mosquito?

Michael: I think it's a thing that I know I'm getting good at. It's a place for me to let out emotion without other people making fun of me. I can write songs and put my thoughts out there.

Counselor: So you've written songs? Have you shared them with anyone?

Michael: I played them for some of my friends and they really liked them. I may try to make a CD on my computer.

Counselor: What if you woke up tomorrow and the Mosquito was gone? What if that voice wasn't whispering in your ear anymore? What do you think you'd do with your music then?

Michael: I don't know. I mean, my friends say the songs are pretty good. Maybe I could start playing my songs other places. If I wasn't worried at all about what people thought, I might put on a concert or something. I'd love to play music more often. My parents have always loved hearing me sing.

Counselor: Does "Michael the Musician" sound like a story that you'd like to be a part of?

Michael: (laughs) More like "Michael the Rock Star".

Counselor: Who do you think would support you in that?

Michael: I think my friends may help me out. Jeremy and Levi have been talking about playing together sometime. Maybe we could start a band!

56. Williams and Winslade, "Co-Authoring," 72.

57. Morgan, *What is Narrative Therapy?* 77.

My parents and teachers are always asking me to play and sing for them now that I'm getting better. I'm sure they'd be happy to help us out.

Conclusion

This has been but a brief overview of how Narrative Therapy might apply in a case of bullying such as Michael's. In actuality, the conversations would have been much more drawn out, and the progression through the phases would have occurred over the course of many sessions, and, most likely, in a less linear fashion. It is a practice that calls for an attitude of humility on the part of the counselor so as to welcome the telling of the client's story. In developing a genuine and cooperative relationship, therapists utilizing this method have the potential to help their clients discover power within themselves that has been long ignored by a limited and limiting Dominant Story. The role of Narrative Therapy in giving a voice to the voiceless makes it uniquely powerful in the pursuit of healing in cases of bullying such as Michael's fictional scenario above. While this is not the only application with such a remarkable fit, it is definitely worth noting and exploring further.

3

A New Life Story after Death to "People Pleasing"

JIM BERLAU

MATTHEW IS A THIRTY-SEVEN-YEAR-OLD man with a wife, Rose, and two young children, James and Lee. Matthew is currently serving as the Director of Student Ministries at a local church, but within the past three years has begun the process of exploring candidacy and acquiring official certification as a candidate for ordained elder status within the denomination. Matthew has arrived at the therapist's office due to a deepening feeling of depression, burnout, fatigue, and unhappiness within his marriage. Matthew has been wrestling with these issues for five years, and has now decided to seek help outside his normal sphere of influence. Matthew has a generally nice and easy-going demeanor, but from the outset is visibly uncomfortable with the idea of speaking with a therapist about his innermost feelings and his past. Matthew was raised in a typical suburban neighborhood, just outside of Baltimore, Maryland by his two parents, Henry and Virginia. Matthew has one older brother, Henry Jr. who was adopted at the age of 3 months old. Matthew grew up in the same house for his entire adolescence, and upon graduation from college, married Rose and moved to Atlanta, Georgia. Rose and Matthew began their life in Atlanta, away from all family and friends, developing their career tracks and lifestyle together. Upon Matthew's entrance into church work as Director of Student Ministries, Rose became pregnant with their first child James. Also at this time, Matthew's mother was diagnosed with a terminal brain tumor. Within one year, Matthew had shifted career paths, moved into a new house, became a father, and buried his mother. Signs of depression began to emerge at this point, and then ongoing and increasing work habits through the last eight years have led to the feelings of burnout and fatigue. Three years ago as Matthew began to feel the call into ordained ministry, tension between he and his wife sharply increased. As Matthew went further into the journey of exploring his call, his wife, while vocally supportive, became increasingly at odds with this path through her actions. Matthew feels the problem is a misunderstanding of what the pastor's life will mean for Rose.

When a client enters into the Narrative therapist's office, they bring with them volumes of stories from their past that have laid the foundation for the client's understanding of who they are and what the main plot of their life story is. Narrative Therapy exists to peel back the multiple layers of a client's many different life stories and assess the meaning that has been derived and internalized through them. The therapist works to discover the root problem that has now become at odds with the client's dominant life story, and separate that problem by having the client name it, and use language that speaks of the problem as being outside and removed from the client. The therapist, using persistent questioning and Mapping of the client's history, begins to search for alternative stories that may exist within the annals of the life of the client. Once discovered, the therapist and the client begin to work together to re-author an alternative storyline, one that re-imagines the client in an existence of positivity, victorious over the named problem, and having hope. Alice Morgan, in her book "What is Narrative Therapy" explains the use of this type of therapy as "a respectful, non-blaming approach to counseling and community work, which centers people as the experts in their own lives. It views problems as separate from people and assumes people have many skills, competencies, beliefs, values, commitments and abilities that will assist them to reduce the influence of the problems in their lives."[1]

With Matthew it was important for us to begin our time with sharing his feelings over what had brought him to the place of needed professional help. For Matthew, his tendency to speak of his life in terms of a story was already present, and so to approach his therapy from the narrative perspective was a natural place to start. As we started, Matthew began by explaining his desire to continue to explore the call to ministry, despite the unwillingness displayed through his wife's actions. Initially, this lead

1. Morgan, *What is Narrative Therapy?* 2.

us into what Alice Morgan would call an Internalized Conversation where the problem is located internally.[2] The danger in keeping the conversation focused inwardly is that the client begins to see him or herself as the problem. This can result in a "negative effect on people's lives and result in thin conclusions."[3] Thin conclusions overpower a client, leaving them to feel weak or overburdened. Our goal is to separate the client from the problem, allowing the client to view the problem from an external perspective, disassociated from him or herself, and to offer hope in a more positive outcome.

Therapist: Does your wife support this decision to stay in ministry?

Matthew: She says she does. She is constantly telling me how there is no doubt in her mind that I should be a pastor, and that it seems like the right path for me.

Therapist: Then why do you say her actions say otherwise?

Matthew: Because she continually shares her fear of being the stereotypical 'Pastor's Wife.' And through the past few years, she has begun to drink alcohol more and more, she has grown distant from me intimately, and we have had a few times where she has acted out in public through embarrassing me or being disrespectful to me.

Therapist: I see...ok...

Before I could begin to question what 'embarrassing' or 'disrespectful' may mean to Matthew, he interrupted.

Matthew: But I know why she is acting out. It's because for years I have put my job as Youth Director over my family. I am a workaholic; I've become obsessed with my job. I have spent way too much time focusing on the ministry instead of the needs of Rose or my kids. Here I am, feeling the call to enter into ordained ministry, and my wife wants nothing to do with the lifestyle that I have created over the past eight years.

At this point, one might see the marital issues as paramount, feeling the need to press Matthew on the reality of the unhealthy state of his marriage. But often, when clients begin to explain their problem, they see themselves as the problem. What Matthew has done has been to over-identify with the problem to the point that the problem has become an 'intimate enemy' to him. By 'intimate enemy' I mean the problem that has become such a strong part of one's Dominant Story that she/he no longer feels you can live without it. Matthew had positioned himself as the problem, and could not see how a future in ordained ministry could exist,

2. Ibid., 18.

3. Ibid.

or his marriage for that matter, without this problem. This is what Alice Morgan would call a 'thin description' of the problem, a meaning that has been created over Matthew's entire life, defining his Dominant Story. "Often, thin descriptions of people's actions/identities are created by others—those with the power of definition in particular circumstances. They often have significant circumstances."[4] This is why, instead of jumping directly into the issue of Matthew's marriage, in order to begin the process of finding hope for Matthew I began by helping him see the problem as something outside of himself and not of his own doing.

The attempt to move the problem outside of the client is called an Externalizing Conversation. Monk describes the purpose of this important step on behalf of the client as being "to open up the possibilities for interacting with the problem without being paralyzed by the effects of self-blame and self-judgment."[5] It becomes one of the primary tasks of the therapist to begin to use Externalizing language in the earliest interaction with the client in order to relieve the client from any self-responsibility or burden. Part of this language would be to 'Name' the identified root problem. Once a client's problem has been Externalized, the therapist must work with the client to decide how the problem will be referred to from this point forward. The act of giving the identified problem a title, or a name, is best done by the client and not the therapist. To empower the client by giving them the privilege of having 'naming rights,' the therapist is able "to make the client the expert in their own lives."[6] Instead of trying to impose upon the client a collegiate or medically driven term that may over-generalize the client's situation, giving the client naming rights validates the role of the client and further separates them from the problem.

Therapist: You say you are a workaholic. Talk to me about that.

Matthew: Through the years, I have found myself taking on way too much in my work. And it stinks, because I usually end up letting down the very people I'm trying to help. I'll be unable to make a follow-up phone call; I won't be able to find time to meet with someone. I'll forget an appointment I made. And I also can't seem to allow myself to settle on a project. I'm always pushing myself to get the teaching time perfect. To find the perfect song for worship, or the exact right questions to ask in a small group time. I just feel like I can never say, "No."

4. Ibid., 13.

5. Monk, et al., *Narrative Therapy*, 99.

6. Ibid., 68.

Therapist: And how does this make you feel when you can't accomplish this perfection?

Matthew: I'm exhausted. I feel like I'm a hamster on one of those wheels, and it just keeps spinning and spinning, but I'm not getting anywhere.

Therapist: Do you feel this way because you love to work, or is there something more?

Matthew: No, I'm actually kind of lazy. But I just don't want to let anyone down. I feel like I owe it to the church to work 110 percent because they gave me this opportunity when I didn't know what I was going to do with my life. I don't want to fail them.

Therapist: What an oxymoron — "a lazy workaholic." So, the problem sounds more like a need to please those around you instead of working too much. What would you call that problem?

Matthew: I don't know . . . I guess something in the line of "People Pleasing"?

Therapist: So what if you yourself weren't the problem? What if the problem was more an entity that existed in your life? If you had to give this imposing entity that exists in your life a name, what would you call it?

Matthew: Umm, I guess I would call it "The People Pleaser."

Therapist: Great. So from now on, when we talk about that entity in your life, we're going to call it "The People Pleaser", sounds good?

Through the Externalizing of Matthew's thin description of himself, we were able to separate Matthew from his problem, and give the Problem the Name, "The People Pleaser." The fact that Matthew had dealt with this was of no surprise to me, since most people entering into the ministerial profession have struggled with this very same thing. Harriet Braiker, in her book "The Disease to Please" defines those dealing with people pleasing as those "who are ensnared in burdensome and self-defeating mindsets that perpetuate their Disease to Please problems. If you are in this group, your people pleasing is driven by a fixed thought that you need and must strive for everyone to like you. You measure your self esteem and define your identity by how much you do for others whose needs, you insist, must come before your own."[7] Often, being nice is thought of as a good trait, however in the life of a people pleaser, the character trait of 'being nice' usually exists as a protective character flaw, existing only to keep the person from experiencing rejection. Carter writes, "While, of course, it is good to be a pleasing person, it is always possible to carry a good trait too far. Kindness, servitude, helpfulness . . . these are qualities

---

7. Braiker, *The Disease to Please*, 5.

that are common to people who have an uncanny knack for inadvertently contributing to unbalanced relational patterns. Unhealthy people pleasing can be defined as the tendency to cater to others' preferences to the detriment of personal well-being. It is a pattern of living that allows others to be manipulative or, at the very least, insensitive."[8]

From a pastoral standpoint, ministers find themselves filling the role of caregiver to others not because of a need to walk alongside the poor and the sick as inspired by God, but rather out of their own need for validation and approval. When this begins to take place, problems arise. Wimberly writes, "We face role conflicts, when, as willing caregivers, we spend more time in the roles that are demanded of us than in the ones we would prefer. And we face our own unresolved family-of-origin issues, as they are aggravated by the expectations of those who receive our care."[9] Matthew had been falling into the same trap as so many before him, and yet The People Pleaser did not show up upon his initial acceptance of the role of Director of Student Ministries, nor did it appear when he first sensed the call to ordained ministry. In fact, Matthew had been wrestling with The People Pleaser since the day he was born.

Now there was a need to begin to genuinely dig deeper into the history of The People Pleaser, and to ask with sincere curiosity about Matthew's history in living with this. This portion of Narrative Therapy focuses on tracing the history of the client in an attempt to thicken the client's story and description of the problem. Alice Morgan calls this element of Narrative Therapy 'Deconstruction', or more specifically, "the pulling apart and examining of taken-for-granted truths."[10] Deconstruction allows the therapist to take time going through the history of a client in an effort to gain a broader picture of the Dominant Story of the client and how the problem has affected that story, as well as the other less dominant stories. Our natural inclination to apply meaning to our lives is lived out through the information we take in from the day we are born, the social context in which we were raised, and the community of people we were surrounded. Drewery writes, "Thus, we make sense of our lives in the context of our social history, shaping stories about the groups we belong to and about how we came to be who, how, and where we are."[11]

---

8. Carter, "Learning About People Pleasers," June 2010.

9. Wimberly, Recalling Our Own Stories, 14.

10. Morgan, What is Narrative Therapy? 46.

11. Monk, et al., Narrative Therapy, 34.

Therapist: So when do you feel like you first began to wrestle with The People Pleaser?

Matthew: I think from the day I was born. You see, my brother was adopted when he was three months old because my parents had tried for years to have a baby, but couldn't. The doctors could not figure out why. After having my brother for three years, and continuing to try, my mom became pregnant with me.

Therapist: And so has The People Pleaser led you to feel like you single handedly came into this world as the answer to your mother and father's predicament?

Matthew: I guess so. I've always been told that when I was born, I wasn't crying or anything in the nursery, and as my father looked at me through the window, he told those around him, "Wow, this baby has no personality."

Therapist: What has The People Pleaser said to you when you have heard this story being told?

Matthew: I'm not worthy. That I have to earn my father's approval and love by being who he wants me to be. My father and I have not had a good relationship through the years.

Therapist: How has The People Pleaser affected your relationship with your dad when you were a child?

Matthew: It made me feel like I could never make him happy. He had me involved in Soccer throughout my childhood, and I didn't always want to play in the winter or spring leagues. But The People Pleaser told me I had to so my dad would be proud.

Therapist: Did he ever tell you he was proud of you during this time?
Matthew: No.

Therapist: What effect has The People Pleaser had on you as a father?

Matthew: I tell my kids I love them and am proud of them every chance I get.

As we began tracing The People Pleaser's history, we found that Matthew's relationship with his father had been deeply affected by The People Pleaser through the years, beginning with the 'birth mythology', which is a formative story shared through the life of the client that contributes to the meaning attached to their identity.[12] Matthew's birth myth had laid the foundation for a struggle with people pleasing that would not be exclusive to pastoral ministry. This formative story of Matthew in the nursery of the hospital as a newborn would be told at birthday parties and special occasions for years to come. Matthew would be reminded of his inability to

12. Ibid., 23.

please his father throughout his years of education. He would find that this need to make his father happy would affect every part of his life from his other relationships with male figures in his life to his spirituality and faith.

From there I felt it was necessary to continue to map out some more of Matthew's history, and the interactions he had with his family. Wimberly writes in his book, "Self-identity develops based on the quality of internalizations we take in from the significant others in the environment of our early lives. If these internalizations are positive and accepting, then we have internalized an enduring source of self-identity that can nourish and sustain us throughout our lives. Conversely, if our internalizations are punitive and frustrating, we have taken into ourselves sources for undermining and sabotaging our self-development. Such internalizations become continuous sources of shame."[13] Through persistent questioning, we discovered together that Matthew had felt the need to be the child his parents had always wanted but didn't have in his older brother. Because of Henry Jr.'s own emotional and personal issues he had been diagnosed with ADHD, and his behavior was continually disruptive at home and at school. The People Pleaser had convinced Matthew that it was up to him not to fail, and to fill the role of "the good son" as he grew up.

I dug deeper into the social context in which Matthew was raised and we came to discover that one of Matthew's father's most important social views was to always put others before yourself. The insistence of this 'others first' hospitality was even further perpetuated in the religious upbringing Matthew experienced. His family faithfully attended their local Methodist Church, and as Leon Seltzer quotes Jay Earley in his web article, "The "training to become compliant and agreeable (in a word, "pleasing") may come not just from a person's family but from their culture as well. People-Pleasers may have learned, in general, 'to put other people first . . . that it is [their] job to make them happy,' and that their own "feelings and needs don't count."[14] This training may come from school, peers, and indeed, from society at large. Moreover, the "lesson" of compliance may also derive from being poor, female, from a minority group, or of a religious group."[15]

We dug further, discovering that upon any accomplishment Matthew would experience, his father would always say, "I'm happy for you, but I don't want you to get a big head." The People Pleaser would force Matthew

13. Ibid., 61.

14. Seltzer, "From Parent-Pleasing to People Pleasing."

15. Ibid.

to downplay his achievements, causing him to never experience the joy of being proud of oneself. Matthew experienced ridicule and bullying as a part of growing up, being beaten up on the way home from elementary school and having his entire soccer team in middle school ostracize him due to a mistake he made in a game. All of these social and community contexts had contributed to the stranglehold that The People Pleaser has had on Matthew's life. Mucherera writes "To have life is to have one's story unfold in the midst of community. Individuals understand the fullness of their individual story through interpersonal relationships within their community of embeddedness."[16] Over time, Matthew had become convinced by The People Pleaser that he was not worthy, that he should never be too proud of himself, and that above all else he should put others needs over his own.

What Matthew and I had done at that point was to begin to elevate ourselves to a position of being able to overlook Matthew's entire life, and then begin to trace the effects of The People Pleaser along the different plot lines running through his life, and to see the strength The People Pleaser has had over him at times, but also highlight the times when The People Pleaser had a weaker hold over Matthew. Alice Morgan describes the 'Deconstruction' aspect of an Externalizing Conversation as one that further shifts the internalized focus to an externalized focus, "on ideas and beliefs, the histories of these ideas and beliefs, their effects and different possibilities. As a result of these conversations people often feel freer from the influence of the ideas supporting the problem and this in itself alters their relationship to the problem and the problem story."[17]

Drewery writes, "Narrative theory suggests that we do not have complete control over the possibilities for our lives: we can only ever speak ourselves into existence within the terms or stories available to us."[18] In Matthew's case, due to our Deconstruction, he began to see that The People Pleaser had been created not as a wrongdoing through him, but as a byproduct of the society and family within which he was raised. Because of this, Matthew had no other reality to compare his existence to, and through the years, Matthew had come to normalize what was truly abnormal internal choices by placing one's own happiness in the background in order to find acceptance and love from others by placing their needs first. As Drewery goes on to explain, it is the job of the therapist

16. Mucherera, *Meet Me*, 1.

17. Morgan, *What is Narrative Therapy?* 50.

18. Monk, et al., *Narrative Therapy in Practice*, 42.

to join Matthew in beginning to look deeper into those times where The People Pleaser did not have such a strong hold, and to join Matthew in beginning to discover alternative story lines that exist in his life, whether he was aware of it or not. Drewery writes, "The narrative counselor listens for alternatives to the "problem" story that the client is telling. Although we believe people struggle to give coherent accounts of their lives, no account is so consistent that we cannot find elements that contradict the problematic story."[19]

Therapist: So has there been a time in your life where The People Pleaser could have gotten in your way, but it didn't?

Matthew: Well, actually one time last year, it was my day off, and I had been in the car driving to pick up lunch for my family. I got a call from one of the student's parents, asking if I could come up to let them into the church for something, because the church was locked. That night our church was going to be having worship, and deep inside I found myself beginning to calculate how much time it would take for me to change directions, stop by the church, let him in, and then proceed on to getting lunch. But I decided against it, and said, "Sorry, I can't. But why don't you come back later when the church will be open for worship."

Therapist: That's a great victory. Tell me, what was going on inside you as you made that decision? What did you say to The People Pleaser?

Matthew: I was thinking about my kids and my wife back at home. We had been having a great day together, and I didn't want anything to get in the way of that. So I told The People Pleaser, "Not this time. This time I win."

Therapist: That's great. What does it mean to you that The People Pleaser did not win at this point?

Matthew: That I could overcome that need to take care of that person's problem.

Therapist: Did this person get mad, or ask that you be fired from the church or did they tell you that you were a failure?

Matthew: No, not at all. I felt really great when I got home with lunch.

At this point, we had identified what Narrative Therapy calls a 'Unique Outcome,' a moment of victory over the identified issue, where there is an alternate outcome that is at odds with and contradicts the Dominant Story line. This is more than just 'pointing out the positive,' for the most important aspect of finding a 'Unique Outcome' is that the client views it as such, and sees this as a significant circumstance. Matthew came to the realization that he had overcome The People Pleaser, he had

19. Ibid., 42.

done it on his own, and there had been zero negative consequences. From this point, a therapist wants to take this Unique Outcome and explore the meaning of it in an attempt to link it to an emerging new story that may be written. This activity would be called 'Landscape of Action,' where, as Morgan writes, "Landscape of Action questions involve inquiries not only into the details of the particular Unique Outcome but also into any other actions and events that may be linked to the Unique Outcome."[20]

From surveying the Landscape of Actions the therapist can then also include surveying the Landscape of Identity, giving the client the opportunity to see firsthand their truest desires and values. Through the action that Matthew took, I could then help him identify that there was a deep-seeded desire to care for and protect his family. He was able to discover how good of a husband he truly was, and to not have to lean on the need for that validation from his wife. Matthew was able to see that his choice in keeping someone else's unfair expectation from getting in the way of his focus on caring for his family did not result in a loss of respect or support from the parent. Through the work of Landscape of Identity, fresh discoveries and new understandings of oneself will likely, "cement the Unique Outcome into a foundation of other events across time" for the client.[21]

What was determined through this broader vantage point for Matthew was that when he returned home and relayed the story to his wife, there was a short time period of euphoric victory. Matthew described his inner emotions as pride, peace, and joy. He felt similar emotions coming from his wife as they enjoyed the rest of the day together. We spent some time examining the events of the day leading up to that point, the choice to designate a day as being "off from work," the choice to spend that time family focused, and how inner strength may have been garnered from creating that boundary from other's supposed expectations. At this point, we began to consider the alternative story we had begun to write. Through this action of rewriting the client's Dominant Story, a therapist can ask what is known as the 'Miracle Question.' This would be a solution-focused question that begins to draw out a more rich description of an alternative story or plot line for the client. To ask questions, such as "What would be different if. . .", or "What does this look like . . ." creates a valuable resource for the client to draw on. As Alice Morgan writes, "If the Dominant

20. Ibid., 61.
21. Ibid.

Story attempts a comeback, these resources will assist" in overcoming the problem.[22]

Therapist: So what would be different about the exploration of your calling if most days were more like this day?

Matthew: Well for one, I think my wife would be much more emotionally supportive. I think the love we once had for each other would reemerge. I think my home would be released from a lot of the tension that exists there now.

Therapist: What else would be happening if you woke up tomorrow, and a miracle had happened over night, and The People Pleaser no longer existed for you?

Matthew: I would be a better pastor. I think I would be more in control of the work that I do. I would be more at peace inside, and have a better ability to share that peace with those I minister to. I would be way more present for my kids, and especially my wife. I would be able to be the husband for her that I want to be.

Therapist: What does a husband who is not a people pleaser look like?

Matthew: One, who looks after their wife, takes care of her the way she deserves to be taken care of. One who listens to her sincerely, but is also up front and honest when she does things that make him unhappy. That love that used to be there would return.

Therapist: How do you think your wife would respond to this kind of husband? What would she do differently?

Matthew: I think she would be ecstatic. She would be more open to me, and allow herself to more fully love me. I think she would allow herself to let me in a bit more, and to open up to being more emotionally engaged with me.

In this stage of the therapy, I had begun to shift the language towards what is known as 'Re-authoring.' 'Re-authoring' is the process of taking a Unique Outcome, and beginning to create a new or alternative, non-problematic storyline for the client. Wimberly describes it as recognizing, "that change in convictions and beliefs is possible; we are not totally at the mercy of our early childhood experiences, unconscious processes, and cultural conventions. While altering our myths is a slow process with much struggle and resistance, Re-authoring moves forward as our resolve grows that we are neither totally passive in creating and formulating myths nor acquiescent in living out the stories that myths entail."[23] This is

---

22. Ibid., 68.

23. Wimberly, *Recalling Our Own Stories*, 73.

an important point of Narrative Therapy, because at this point despair and hopelessness are erased, giving way to optimism, opportunities, and hope. This would be important for Matthew's future as an ordained minister.

Matthew would need to have skills in church leadership, and maintain his sense of self-pride and confidence, in order to make decisions, and effectively lead a congregation. The danger in people pleasing as a minister is the inability to listen to a person in need without focusing on how this will impact him/her. Nouwen writes, "We no longer listen to what he is saying but to what we can do with what he is saying. Then the fulfillment of our unrecognized need for sympathy, friendship, popularity, success, understanding, money or a career becomes our concern, and instead of paying attention to the other person we impose ourselves upon him with intrusive curiosity."[24] True, as Nouwen writes, "The beginning and the end of all Christian leadership are to give your life for others."[25] However, is this idea of martyrdom what a minister is ultimately called to?

The minister, as well as therapist, is called to a greater sense of walking alongside those in pain, and directing them to the hope found in Jesus Christ. Nouwen later writes, "This hope stretches far beyond the limitations of one's own psychological strength, for it is anchored not just in the soul of the individual but in God's self-disclosure in history. Leadership, therefore, is not called Christian because it is permeated with optimism against all the odds of life, but because it is grounded in the historic Christ-event, which is understood as a definitive breach in the deterministic chain of human trial and error, and as a dramatic affirmation that there is light on the other side of darkness."[26] This is the intention behind the 'Re-authoring' of a client's Alternative Story, to use this Narrative Therapy to point the client to hope. This is also the role of the minister, a role that Matthew was going to need to embrace as having been gifted to fill, despite The People Pleaser's voice telling him he was not worthy or to not allow him the ability to affirm these gifts.

Wimberly best explains this ownership over the 'power' of a minister. "In ministering, it is essential to claim power. We learn to feel confident in our ministerial identity, functioning and affirming our gifts for ministry. "Affirming our power" does not mean power over anyone or the power to dominate; it means being empowered to do what God has called us to do. If we are to be effective in ministry we need to learn to claim the power

24. Nouwen, *The Wounded Healer*, 90.

25. Ibid., 72.

26. Ibid., 76.

that we have."[27] This was essential for Matthew, and our breakthrough came as Matthew began to consider the many spiritual gifts he had been given.

Matthew: Preaching, teaching, leadership. I guess discernment would be another one. Listening, counseling.

Therapist: How does it feel to list these gifts as your own?

Matthew: Good, I can see that God has gifted me for this. I just never was able to believe it in myself.

Therapist: But now you see it, and it's OK, right? It's OK to say you have these gifts?

Matthew: Yes. I guess this is God's grace.

Therapist: Right. It's OK to be proud of yourself, and to say you do a good job in certain things.

From here, we began to try and thicken the description of Matthew's new story by considering those in his life who would play an important role in the continued authoring of this new story. This process is called 'Re-membering', and is described by Alice Morgan as conversations that, "involve people deliberately choosing who they would like to have more present as the members of their club of life, and whose membership they would prefer to revise or revoke." Re-membering Conversations are powerful ways of identifying and linking specific people that can become partners with the client in the clients continued journey of Re-authoring their story.

Therapist: Who would be the least surprised to hear you make these claims about your gifts?

Matthew: My wife, my friend Edward, my mentor Robert.

Therapist: If I were to ask any of them what gifts they see in you, would they say anything different?

Matthew: Probably not.

Therapist: What would they say if I asked them to tell me about a time that the People Pleaser got the best of you?

Matthew: My wife would go on for hours about how the family has been forgotten in the face of my ministry. My friend Edward would probably complain about how I don't keep in touch enough. My mentor would mention times that I have been late to meetings, or forgotten them altogether.

Therapist: But where are they now in your life?

Matthew: They are still there, wanting the best for me.

---

27. Wimberly, *Recalling Our Own Stories*, 19.

Therapist: What do they see in you that gives them reason to stay in your life?

Matthew: That I'm a husband, good person, a good friend, with potential. They see that I have worth.

From this point, we began to discuss the potential of their joining Matthew on this journey of 'Re-authoring' where they would become members of the Matthew Support Team. We began by writing letters to each one of them, inviting them to come and spend some time with me so I could better get to know them, and they could understand the goals that Matthew and I were laying out for him. From there, Matthew and I drew up a declaration of his freedom from the oppression of The People Pleaser. This document was copied, and included in the letter so everyone could see and celebrate in the progress Matthew had already begun to make. From there, I asked Matthew to consider beginning a small Director of Student Ministries support group that he could lead, in order to assist anyone else who may be struggling with this same thing. Morgan writes, "Finding ways to link together people who have experienced similar difficulties, and creating processes through which these people can share and build upon each others' skills of living is a significant part of the work of therapists engaged with Narrative practices."[28]

There were many future sessions with Matthew as together we walked through the journey towards healing and wholeness. Matthew's marriage was in need of restoration, as well as his relationship with his father. But until The People Pleaser had been written out of the story, Matthew would find no success in his other areas. The story would continue to be written, only this story would eventually become free of the people-pleasing problem, hope would be found in the resolution, and as a result of the Narrative Therapy light would be found on the other side of darkness.

28. Morgan, *What is Narrative Therapy?* 118–19.

4

An Adult Survivor of Childhood Abuse

Healing the Scars Inside and Out

DEBBIE DALEY-SALINGER

PAMELA'S STORY

Meet Pamela, a forty-year-old female sex abuse survivor, who views her life as one of ruin and powerlessness crippled by fear. Pamela migrated to the United States at age thirteen to live with her aunt and uncle. Pamela describes her experiences with a story that began at age fourteen when her uncle Joe sexually abused her. Joe had been Pamela's favorite uncle and they had developed a close and loving relationship. Her uncle even took care of her when she was sick. For example, he would pick mint leaves from the back yard and make her tea and rub her tummy during severe menstrual cramps.

Pamela was a very attractive girl, physically mature for her age. Over time her uncle's affection began to be expressed more physically. This came at a time when she was feeling awkward and uncomfortable with her developing body and the attention she was getting from the boys in school. Joe showered her with encouragement and appreciation. When he asked her to satisfy him sexually he did so in a context where her refusal could only be interpreted as ungrateful and unloving. Because she loved her uncle, Pamela submitted to his request, not just once, but repeatedly for almost six years. Pamela came to therapy complaining about the effects depression, alienation, and sexual repulsion was having on her life. She was unable to keep a job and moved frequently. At the time she presented herself for therapy, Pamela was living in a boarding house. Her story will serve to illustrate the major conceptual components of Narrative Therapy.

Long-term Effects of Sexual Abuse

Often sexually abused children cling to the hope that growing up will bring escape and freedom from the entrapment of their abuse. Unfortunately, the personality formed in such a controlled environment is not well adapted to adult life. "The adult is left with fundamental problems in basic trust, autonomy, and initiative."[1] Pamela's childhood environment was an entrapment where she had to face the tasks of adaptation: "find ways to preserve a sense of trust in people who are untrustworthy, safety in a situation that is unsafe, control in a situation that is terrifyingly unpredictable, power in a situation of helplessness."[2]

Regardless of the underlying causes, the impact of sexual abuse and the problems created are very real for the victims and their families. It is important for professionals to appreciate both the incomplete state of knowledge about the consequences of sexual abuse and the variability in effects. Such information can be helpful in recognizing the wide variation in symptoms of sexual abuse victims and can prevent excessive optimism or pessimism in predicting their impact. The meaning survivors and others attribute to the abusive events and resulting symptoms can make a difference in determining the ways therapists invite clients to talk about their problems.

John Briere suggests four helpful categorizations of the long-term effects of sexual abuse: Posttraumatic Stress, Cognitive Effects, Emotional Effects, and Interpersonal Effects.[3]

Posttraumatic Stress is the primary and, many times, most pervasive long-term effect of sexual abuse. The child is traumatized by their experience of fear, helplessness, horror and physical discomfort and/or pain. White & Epston explains that the "consequence for anyone of such an insult to the body and mind is called Post Traumatic Stress Disorder . . . although the suffering is over, the suffering does not stop . . . they suffer in

1. Herman, *Trauma and Recovery,* 110.
2. Ibid., 97.
3. Briere, *Therapy for Adults Molested,* 5–34.

their minds, especially at night when the suffering is relived in nightmares, and by day as they feel full of terror and an overriding sense of fear . . . and in their mind as they are being beaten and raped over and over again."[4]

The perpetrator is more powerful than the child and uses his power to accomplish his abusive acts. The force he uses may be psychological or physical. As a result of the imposition of the perpetrator's power upon the child, the child is forced to make a new meaning of their world, a meaning contextualized by fear and helplessness. Common symptoms of Post Traumatic Stress as described in the Diagnostic and Statistical Manual of Mental Disorders, Fourth Edition (DSM4) include flashbacks, nightmares, hyper vigilance, feelings of detachment or estrangement from others, restricted range of affect, and exaggerated startle response, etc.[5]

Sex abuse alters the world in which the child exists. It is not only "the mechanics of the act (i.e., who did what to whom) but also . . . the matrix of other injurious events that coexist with or follow from sexual victimization."[6] Not only is the child's body violated in sexual abuse, but also the world, as they know it, is transformed. New realities are made of "trust," "safety," and "love."

The event of child abuse quickly introduces concepts and emotions that are intense, difficult, and in conflict with the child's understanding and expectations of the world. A perpetrator, in order to accomplish and continue his activities with the child, must help the child make meaning of their encounter, or ongoing encounters. This permits the perpetrator to accomplish or continue his abusive acts regardless of the child's feelings. The child will take this meaning and try to integrate it into her own experience. Symptomatic meanings that results from abuse include "(a) negative self-evaluation and guilt, (b) perceived helplessness and hopelessness, and (c) distrust of others."[7]

Frequently perpetrators convince their victim that they are responsible for what is happening or has happened, that the perpetrator has or had no choice but to be attracted to or to punish the victim. Unclear about how they have "asked" or "deserve" this abuse; the victim will often cooperate with the perpetrator's efforts to keep the events shrouded in shame and secrecy. Unable to make any other meaning of the events, the victim believes there is something "wrong" with them and feels guilty if they try

4. White and Epston, *Narrative Means*, 106.

5. American Psychiatric Association, 1994.

6. Briere, *Therapy for Adults Molested*, 22.

7. Ibid., 14.

to "blame" the perpetrator. Later in life, even if the survivor is able to hold the perpetrator responsible for the abuse rather than themselves, it is often difficult to deconstruct the belief that "I got what I deserved" because of the survivor's desire for a "just world." That is, as Lerner notes, "people want to and have to believe [that] they live in a just world so they can go about their daily lives with a sense of trust, hope and confidence in their future."[8]

Emotional Effects Resulting from Childhood Sexual Abuse Include Anxiety and Depression

Briere explained that the "the cognitive aspects of abuse anxiety seems to involve (a) hyper vigilance to danger in the environment, (b) pre-occupation with control, and (c) misinterpretation of neutral or positive interpersonal stimuli (e.g. intimacy and relatedness) as evidence of threat or danger. This definition also suggests that 'anxiety is to be differentiated from fear . . . [which is] a reaction to a real or threatened danger, while anxiety is more typically a reaction to an unreal or imagined danger.'[9] Given the conditions in which child sex abuse occurs, it makes sense that a survivor would suffer from feelings of anxiety. If the survivor has no power to control what happens to their life and has been overcome by very painful events, they may feel anxious about what will happen next, when it will happen, how it will happen, and how they will deal with it.

"Because child abuse occurs, by definition, within the context of some sort of relationship, however brief or destructive, sexual abuse survivors often experience problems in the interpersonal domain."[10] Briere goes on to say, "Sexual abuse may be relatively unique among forms of interpersonal aggression in that it combines exploitation and invasion with, in some instances, what might otherwise be evidence of love or caring" (e.g., physical contact, cuddling, praise, perhaps some positive physical sensations).[11] Given the confusion that can result, it makes sense that survivors may be ambivalent about intimate relationships, especially sexual or romantic ones. Survivors may have difficulty being in relationship with others if there is an inability to trust others.

8. Ibid., 15.

9. Ibid.

10. Ibid., 23.

11. Ibid.

TREATMENT OF SEXUAL ABUSE

One of the foremost needs of survivors of sexual abuse is to regain a sense of control over their lives. Control was taken from them when they were abused. The symptoms they suffer continue to take away their control. Briere writes:

> By definition, sexual abuse occurs in a context of powerlessness, intrusion, and authoritarianism. Because therapy for sexual abuse trauma is intended to remedy the effects of such dynamics, it is important that the treatment process not recapitulate them. Experience suggests, in fact, that authoritarian, power-laden interventions are likely to result in a variety of "negative" survivor behaviors, such as manipulation, rage, or "acting out."[12]

NARRATIVE THERAPY—INTERPRETATION: THE MAKING OF MEANING

Narrative Therapy is based on a theory of interpretation. The observer recognizes that there is meaningful data in their life. This meaningful data is considered to be information, which can be ordered and influenced by time; the observer orders this information into a text, that has "readers" and "writers."[13] Readers are those who read the text and find the data. Writers are those who write or create the text. White goes on to explain the word "text" suggests a neutral orientation to the ordered data and "observer" suggests a neutral data collector. Because interest and power are involved in the reading and writing of text, there is neither a neutral text nor observer. Every observer is both a reader and writer of text, but where they locate themselves in relation to particular data determines whether they perceive themselves to be more a reader or a writer. If the observer feels they have power in relation to particular data, they will feel that they are a writer. If the observer feels powerless in relation to particular data, then they will feel they are a reader. Narrative Therapy helps a survivor recognize their own power, the power to read and write their own story.

---

12. Ibid., 81.

13. White and Epston, *Narrative Means*.

Dominant Story

Gerald Monk defined Dominant Story as "the 'normal' way of construing a situation, or the set of assumptions about an issue that has become so ingrained or widely accepted within a culture that it appears to represent 'reality.'"[14] Each person is born in a place and time. The place is the basis of their culture; the time creates their history. It is from our culture and history a person attaches meaning of the information they observe. They are raised to notice certain aspects of their environment, to ignore others, and to interpret data in a particular manner. Responding to the power disparity of their story, a survivor of childhood sexual abuse will attempt to write a personal story within the context of the Dominant Story or socially constructed context. It is when their personal story conflicts with that Dominate Story they seek therapy. In therapy the abused hope to realign themselves with the Dominant Story by learning ways they can re-write their personal and preferred story within the confines of the Dominant Story.

As with Pamela's case, people typically bring their stories to a therapist when they begin to experience difficulties or problems in their lives. Pamela had constructed a preferred social reality as she interacted with her family and the people around her and consequently 'constructed' this preferred meaning of her life. Pamela presented her story explaining the events, that led to her problems. She presented a "thin description" narrative, which provided minimal space for any contradiction and allowed little space for one to derive their own meaning from a particular action and the context within which things happened.[15] In other words, because Pamela had already reached the conclusion(s) or meaning(s) for why she is experiencing problem, it limits the exploration of possible outcomes or alternate stories and consequences. An added 'danger' of thin descriptions/conclusions is that it leads people to seek supportive evidence for the Dominant problem-induced Stories.[16]

The Narrative therapist's goal is to engage in conversations, that establish stories of identity and will aid the client "to break from the influence of the problem they are facing."[17] The Dominant Story as reported by Pamela included facts substantiated by a variety of the following influences:

14. Monk et al., *Narrative Therapy in Practice*, 303.
15. Morgan, *What is Narrative Therapy?* 12.
16. Ibid., 14.
17. Ibid.

Facts from the Culture of Family Included:

- Children should respect their elders
- Children should love their family
- Children should be seen and not heard

Facts from the Culture of Love Included:

- If you love someone, you will do anything for him or her.
- If you really love someone, you will not just satisfy them, but you will feel satisfied by your actions as well.

Facts from Pamela's Perpetrator Included:

- You are so beautiful and sensitive and caring, I cannot help but be attracted to you.
- You want this as much as I do. It's an expression of our love.
- Because you want it as much as I do, if you deny me, you are a tease and you know no one likes a tease.
- If you do not do this for me, this is evidence that you are an unlikeable person.
- If you feel anything contrary to what I want you to feel, there will be hell to pay, either by my continued harassment of you, or because I will intentionally or unintentionally confirm your fears that you are unloving and unlovable.

It is in this context that Pamela was compelled to comply with her uncle's wishes. She could not resist the overwhelming force of objective reality that dictated the kind of person she was and what she was capable of doing. In her Dominant Story she considered her only choice to be either an unloving or a loving niece. She preferred the role of the loving niece so she always complied with her uncle's sexual advances.

Externalizing the Problem

Morgan states that one of the initial focuses of a Narrative therapist should be in separating the person from the problem.[18] White states that "the Externalization of the problem-saturated story should be encouraged and then Mapping of the problem's influence in the person's life and relationship should externalize the problem."[19] This is where the Narrative therapist would shift into what is called Externalizing Conversations. Michael White writes:

> "Externalizing" is an approach to therapy that encourages persons to objectify and, at times, to personify the problem that they experience as oppressive. It is in this process, the problem becomes separate entity and thus external to the person or relationship that was ascribed as the problem. Those problems that are to be inherent, as was as those relatively fixed qualities that are attributed to persons and to relationships, are rendered less fixed and less restricting.[20]

In expanding on White's statement, objectifying people is an act of control and perpetration. It denies the objectified person's subjective reality (Dominant Story) and denies that the objectified person is indeed a person.

In Narrative Therapy the person is not the problem; the problem is the problem. A survivor seeking therapy with feelings of depression (a common survivor symptom) has, in the language of Narrative Therapy, "come to be under the influence of depression." That is, the survivor is not depressed (herein objectified) nor is she making herself depressed in response to the problem, but rather, depression is inviting her to think, feel and do certain things. White says, "I have found the externalization of the problem to be helpful to persons in their struggle with problems."[21]

Pamela concluded that it was her fault for her predicament in life. On occasion she could appreciate Joe's self-serving manipulation of the facts and his responsibility for their sex, but she found little relief in these thoughts and feelings. In her view, Joe had come and gone from her life

18. Ibid., 17.

19. White and Epston, *Narrative Means*, 16.

20. Ibid., 38.

21. Ibid., 39–40.

and she remained the on-going source of all that was wrong. Even after self-examination, Joe had seemed very congruent in his expressions of love for her. She was the one that did not like the sex, not him. It wasn't Joe who had become a grotesque character. The one consistent factor in the misery in her life was Pamela. She was a bright woman and had been in therapy previously. She had learned that she could not hold others responsible for her life. She had learned to accept responsibility for herself. When she had tried to learn ways to live her life differently and failed, she was convinced she was unable to change her life. Her failures were further evidence that she was inadequate and ineffectual. When Pamela tried to confront the Dominant Story of her life and failed, she attempted suicide.

The purpose of Deconstructing the Dominant Story of Pamela's life is an invitation to consider what story she would prefer to live and to initiate conversations in therapy that facilitate her discovering how she might go about living that story. In a world where reality is socially constructed, Pamela's preferred story will contain elements authored by her and others. The insidiousness of Joe's initial authorship of Pamela's story is that he cited authorities other than his own. Joe's facts were actually intertwined with those of their culture and of Pamela's. Over time, Pamela was unable to distinguish between her story and Joe's. Though she was burdened by their sexual encounters in such a way that resonated throughout the rest of her life, Pamela loved her uncle and wanted him to love her. In this context, it was not helpful for Pamela to vilify her perpetrator or to pursue questions of personal responsibility. Deconstructing and diffusing the Dominant Story allowed room for additional story elements to be introduced by Pamela.

In considering the exceptions Pamela had described earlier, the qualities of her character came into question. Given that there was evidence (produced by and meaningful to Pamela) that suggested she was indeed a loving person, what was it that made her vulnerable to the stories as presented by Joe?

Fear had invaded Pamela's life when her body began to change from girlhood to young womanhood. Fear had convinced Pamela that the changes in her body made her deformed. It told her she would stand out in a crowd and be the object of derision, especially from boys. Fear told her that "all an ugly girl had going for her was her willingness to comply with the wishes of others" and she would never be a leader, only a desperate follower. Pamela had to sacrifice herself for the interest of others because that's what ugly girls do. When Joe made his request for sex, he had enlisted the aid of fear to convince Pamela that if she did not comply, she would be alone and lonely in the world, an ugly deformed freak. In reassuring and appreciating Pamela, the relief he offered was self-serving and dependent upon the on-going influence of fear. Had fear not plagued Pamela, would she have been as vulnerable to the facts as fear presented them? Pamela believed she might have been able to resist his sex. Was she not still under the influence of fear, she believed her life might be quite different.

At first, Pamela felt responsible for having surrendered to fear. However, Pamela began to consider that she was not to blame for having been vulnerable to fear and instead considered her struggle to be a common one. Pamela began to think of herself as "normal" and no longer an unloving person doomed to a life of misery. Instead, she was a woman plagued by the powerful and seemingly irresistible fear. Relieved of the responsibility for her problem, the subject of her character was now open for discussion. In this context, Pamela could determine for herself whether she wanted to be in charge of her life or let fear continue to run her life for her.

Re-Naming the Problem

Combs points out that Naming the plot or the problematic story is a useful aide to Externalizing the problem.[22] Both the plot and the problem can have the same name or they may be different. In Pamela's story the problem was named "Fear" and the plot was "unloving person."

Technical medical language can emphasizes pathological processes and deficits and often makes it difficult for clients to accept more preferred or desirable stories about themselves.[23] Narrative therapists encourage the use of client rather than medical descriptions of the problem. When Pamela created a personalized "working label" for her problem, she in turn gained power and control.

Deconstructing the Dominant Story

Freedman & Combs writes:

22. Freedman, *Narrative Therapy*, 63.
23. Monk et al., *Narrative Therapy in Practice*, 158–92.

We believe that listening with an externalizing attitude has a powerful deconstructive effect. It biases us to interact differently with people than we would if we saw them as intrinsically problematic. It creates a different "receiving context" for people's stories, one in which we can work to understand their problems without seeing them as problematic or pathological.[24]

In Deconstructing the Dominant Story, Pamela deconstructs their prepackaged meaning and makes new, more personally relevant, meanings from the components. Deconstructed, the parts of the Dominant Story are not as compelling as when thematically united and when their sources are exposed and the authorities that created or perpetuated the facts come into question. In questioning these authorities, Pamela begins to find her own authorship abilities. Though she may not yet be prepared to author an Alternative or preferred Story, she is considering questions that begin to create a context where she has increasing authority.

The overarching goal of Narrative Therapy is to help the client replace the problem-saturated story by constructing a preferred story. The building blocks for this new story are found in the discovery of hopeful moments, thoughts, or events that do not fit with the problem-story.

White borrowed Erving Goffman's term 'Unique Outcome' to describe "an aspect of lived experiences that lies outside of, or contradiction to, the problem story."[25] These exceptions are helpful in asserting the value and legitimacy of her authorship authority against the objective reality of the Dominant Story. White explains, "When Unique Outcomes are identified, persons can be invited to ascribe meaning to them" and that "success in the ascription of meaning requires that the Unique Outcomes be plotted into an Alternative Story."[26] Questions that served to Deconstruct the Dominant Story of Pamela's life included:

- When she was young, whom else did she love?

- What were some of the ways she demonstrated her love?

- Did the people she loved feel satisfied by the ways of her loving?

- If she had been able to discuss her situation with these loving people, would they have supported his interests or hers?

- What difference would it have made in her life if her interests had been supported?

24. Freedman, *Narrative Therapy*, 51.

25. White and Epston, *Narrative Means*, 15.

26. Ibid., 16.

- Who does she love in her life now?

- How does she demonstrate her love to those she loves?

- Do these people love her?

- Given that, in the past, she was unable to discuss her situation with others, what effect is it having on her life talking about it now?

- What does being able to talk about her life suggest about the kind of person she is?

- Does she think of herself as courageous, talking about her life and her longings?

In answering such questions, the Dominant Story broadens sufficiently to become diffused and, eventually, a different story emerges. When the story is sufficiently different, it is no longer a question of the lovingness of Pamela, but rather, given that Pamela is a loving person, how does she express her love?

Alternative and Preferred Stories

Monk defined Alternative Story as "The story that develops in therapy in contradiction to the Dominant Story in which the problem holds stay."[27] Conflict occurs when the preferred story is more compelling than the Dominant Story. The Narrative therapist is interested in finding ways to richly describe or thicken the Alternate Stories and to have these co-authored stories interwoven with the stories of others. The therapist is asking "How can we assist people to break from thin conclusions and to re-author new and preferred stories for their lives and relationships?"[28]

Pamela's Alternative Stories would be any story that places her in roles other than an unloving or loving niece, stories that provide a broader definition of her character and contain possibilities for other, or multiple, plot-lines. Her preferred story would be one in which the facts of the story were subject to negotiation and personalization, where she had some say in defining her role and determining the plot-line of, not just the story in which she was involved, but one she was co-authoring. Pamela and her therapist need to engage in coauthoring conversations where both the client and counselor work to mutually create meanings and Alternative Stories from the Dominant Story presented. It would be understood that

27. Monk, *Narrative Therapy in Practice*, 301.
28. Morgan, *What is Narrative Therapy*, 14.

Pamela is the senior partner, the expert in the particular problem. At the completion of this process Pamela gained "expert" status, that replaces that of a helpless and fearful person.[29] Pamela's preferred story is one where she could be a loving niece and yet refuse her uncle's sexual advances.

RELATIVE INFLUENCE OF THE PROBLEM

Not only is the person not the problem, but also there is more to the person and her life than the problem. It is important also to trace the history of the problem because it provides opportunities for other stories regarding the problem to come to light. This in turn gives the therapist more insight as to where some of the meaning (thin description) about the problem originates. Here the client is invited to "re-tell her story in such a way allowing access to experiences of their own resourcefulness in the face of the problem."[30] Here the conversation focuses on exploring and Mapping the effects of the problem on the person's life. Exploring in details this history not only aids the therapist in better understanding the impact of the dominant problem but also "leads to the discovery of Unique Outcomes—times in the life of the person when the problem has been present but has not been influential."[31] The therapist may use what is being called Landscape of Action questions to explore the details s of a Unique Outcome and to explore the meaning of the Unique Outcome Landscape of Identity questions are used. "From a narrative perspective, problems only survive and strive when supported and backed by ideas, beliefs and principles."[32] Therefore, therapists become "interested in discovering, acknowledging, and 'taking apart' (Deconstructing) these beliefs, ideas and practices in order to make them more available for questioning and challenge. In Mapping out the details and the effects of the Dominant Story, the therapist might ask, "What influence has Fear had on your life? On your relationship with other people?'" . . . and to Map out the 'Unique Outcome,' occasions where she experienced some influence over the problem despite the power of the Dominant Story."[33]

Pamela began to notice ways that she might be able to stand up to Fear. She, based on her experience and knowledge of the ways that Fear

---

29. Monk, *Narrative Therapy in Practice*, 27.

30. White and Denborough, *Introducing Narrative Therapy*, 63.

31. Morgan, *What is Narrative Therapy?* 41.

32. Ibid., 45.

33. White and Denborough, *Introducing Narrative Therapy*, 53.

specifically plagued her, developed these ways. When asked about times when she was able to have influence over Fear, (i.e. resisting Fear, reducing its impact on her, etc.) Pamela provided information about these exceptions that revealed to her ways she might further resist Fear. In creating meaning around these exceptions, Pamela began vigorously authoring her preferred story.

Pamela remembered her father instilling in her as a child that when she is afraid she is to jump into whatever she thinks it is, not to run from it. During the sessions she discovered that she had made a subconscious decision to say, "No" as she got older and began to fight back. It was not easy, but trying gave her more and more power over Fear. She had also made intentional efforts not to be "available" for Joe as she tried to trust other relationships. Pamela had been angry with God for a very long time—angry that He had allowed this ugliness to happen. However, in her quest to resist Fear Pamela allowed God back in her life. This further opened up Pamela to see the wrong in Joe's action despite Joe's effort to convince her otherwise. It was not surprising that Pamela turned to her beliefs to find information about exceptions. She had made a conscious decision, long ago, on how she wanted to live her life without Fear and is now continuing to work towards that life with her therapist. Alice Morgan sums, "By the time a person consults a therapist, they will have already made many attempts to reduce the influence of the problem in their lives and relationships."[34]

Re-Authoring a New Story

Monk defined Re-authoring as "the process of developing an Alternative Story in therapy. When a Narrative approach is used, this project is jointly undertaken by the counselor and the client."[35] Re-authoring the story can begin when the survivor discovers an exception and recognizes their ability to resist the problem. In her conversations about exceptions, Pamela begins telling a new story, one of a bright, energetic and loving young woman who came under the debilitating influence of fear. Though she tried her best to live a good life, to live up to the standards of her parents, of her culture and of herself, she failed. Fear stood in the way of her being able to express herself and succeed in life.

34. Morgan, *What is Narrative Therapy?* 129.
35. Monk et al., *Narrative Therapy in Practice*, 305.

In this new story, Pamela saw Fear not as her friend and protector, but as the self-serving and irresponsible wrecker of her life. Fear had made a mess of Pamela's life, not Pamela. When Pamela was given a choice about how to live her life, she decided that she was better qualified to be in charge than Fear. She decided that the story she would author would be a happier, more productive one.

THERAPEUTIC DOCUMENTATION

Although Narrative Therapy relies primarily on questioning and listening in the search for preferred meanings, it also uses other techniques such as therapeutic documentation, that includes note taking, letter writing, and recognition. Note taking stresses the incorporation of exact patient language and a willingness to share these observations with the client. Letter writing from therapist to client is a powerful technique to summarize key points of a session and, with the advent of e-mail, not excessively time consuming.[36] Documents, such as declarations, certificates, awards, and diplomas specifically created to commemorate significant client developments are also meaningful.[37] All these approaches take advantage of the power of ritual in solidifying and memorializing significant life changes.

What once seemed to Pamela to be only wishful thinking came to be substantiated as fact as more people began to know her as a loving person. Her preferred identity became publicly known first in her conversations with her therapist; he was the one other person who shared her belief that she was a loving person. Letters he wrote to her as a part of their on-going therapy provided evidence outside of his office that she was not alone in her beliefs.

Pamela found that it became easier to talk about her life with others. No longer trying to hide the unspeakable truth about herself, she celebrated her loving self with new friends, acquaintances, and lovers. Though Fear still had influence in Pamela's life, she had taken charge. No longer submitting to the story authored by Joe and Fear, she was authoring her own beautiful and inspirational story, a story truly of her choosing.

---

36. White and Epston, *Narrative Means*, 157.
37. Morgan, *What is Narrative Therapy*, 85.

Glimmers of Hope

Generating Support

One of the most effective ways of strengthening the new, developing story is by creating a receptive audience who serve as "witnesses." The therapist is an important member of this potential audience, but it is useful to have patients identify other audience members as well. A key aspect of a successful audience is that it be comprised of people who are supportive of and optimistic about the patient. Members of Pamela's audience included her boyfriend, her mother, and (symbolically) a deceased aunt.

Summary

Narrative Therapy offers a context wherein a survivor, Pamela, has the opportunity to not only free herself of the constraints of the story authored by others, but to appreciate ways she can free herself of constraints in other contexts as well. Narrative Therapy can be helpful not only in the pursuit of symptom alleviation, but of personal growth. It invites clients and therapists to notice who they are, who they want to be, what they want to do, and the context in which each and all of these considerations occurs. It focuses on personal competency and authorship rights. It is expansive and appreciates the lived experience of clients, preferring their stories and their evaluations of their stories even in the context of the Dominant Story and objective reality.

5

Healing through Cutting the "Cutting"

A Story of an Adolescent's Journey

Adena Bowen

One has to learn how to "cut the cutting" out of one's life in order to live without bleeding from inside out.

Scenario: Meet Seana

Seana is a fourteen-year-old girl who was brought to see me by her adoptive parents. Jocelyn and Andrew adopted Seana when she was five years old. Although she seemed to have a fairly easy time adjusting to life with her new family she did always seem quiet and detached. She would occasionally cuddle with Jocelyn. However, this was rare and she had to be invited to do it. She had recently been having more trouble than usual at school with paying attention and getting her work done. Her teachers had mentioned to her parents that Seana seemed isolated from her peers and, a majority of the time, along with the aforementioned issues, she showed a lack of attention in class and exhibited poor grades. There had been several parent teacher conferences due to the teachers' concerns for Seana. Her parents had tried talking to her on multiple occasions to see what was going on but she was not very forthcoming and often got unduly defensive when confronted. Then one night when Seana's mother,

Jocelyn, was in her room gathering up her bed sheets to do laundry she found some bloody tissues stuffed under the mattress. Jocelyn talked with her husband and they agreed it would be best if Jocelyn alone confronted Seana. The next day Jocelyn confronted Seana about what she found. Seana explained she'd hurt herself one night fumbling around in the dark and grabbed some tissues from her bedside table and didn't feel like getting out of bed to throw them in the garbage. Not being completely satisfied with that answer Jocelyn resigned to let the matter go for that moment. A couple of weeks later Jocelyn was in the bathroom that Seana shares with her two sisters cleaning out the medicine cabinet and found in it, behind some old bottles, a bag with several disposable shaving razors in it. Curious about this she asks the two younger sisters, Alexandria (Alex) and Corinne, about what she found. Neither of the two seemed to know why they were there. Jocelyn then confronts Seana about these razors. Seana says she has no idea why they were in a bag in the medicine cabinet. Jocelyn was still not satisfied with the answers the girls were giving her. A week following this confrontation Jocelyn is again in Seana's room picking up sheets and clothes for laundry and catches Seana coming into the room with just a towel on after having just taken a shower. Seana was not expecting anyone to be in her room and was caught off guard by her mom being there. Jocelyn then sees hundreds of cuts on Seana's arms. Seana is no longer able to deny it anymore and confesses that she has been cutting. In light of this, her parents feel it is for Seana's own safety that they bring her in for counseling.

INTRODUCTION

"For them, the greatest pain in this world emanates from being lonely, rejected, invisible, ignored . . ." More and more adolescents, especially girls struggle with self-harm, which is usually coupled with other issues such as depression. Before going into how Narrative Counseling can be used in Seana's case, a few terms need to be defined and explained. The first is the term "self-harm." Penner defines self-harm as "an attempt to alter one's emotional state by inflicting physical harm on one's own body without the intention of committing suicide."[1] Another definition of self-harm is that "self-injury is intentional in that it is a willful act and not the result of accidental or an ambiguous act that may be unconsciously driven. It is

---

1. Penner, *Hope and Healing*, 32.

a deliberately chosen act used by the self-injurer, often in a repetitive way. The behavior is self-inflicted in that it can be enacted individually or with the help of others."[2] Several definitions need to be given because there are differing perspectives on this topic, yet there are several themes that the majority of therapists agree upon. One is that this behavior is very deliberate and is in an attempt to alter the mood state of the person self-harming. This can be to the end of alleviating troubling internalized feelings such as anger, hurt, pain, sadness, etc. It can also be to the end of eliciting emotion because the person feels so numb that they just desire to feel something, even if it is physical pain. The scary truth, as Penner points out, is that, "most self-injurers will tell you it works. Whether this strategy is being used to create feelings that don't exist or to numb feelings that are overwhelming, it can be a pretty effective one—for a moment. The problem, however, as every self-injurer knows, is that the relief is short-lived at best and often creates an intense need for more frequent and usually more severe episodes."[3] This is the dilemma that counselors working with those who self-injure must deal with. Many clients struggling with cutting feel that it is effective and feel it is too scary to imagine a life without it. The counselor must be willing to work with the client to unravel the story that is behind this behavior and help the client rewrite that new story and thus find that they have the strength and power to deal with life without the aid of cutting. Furthermore, the counselor needs to be aware that the cutting is just a symptom, an outward expression, of something deeper that is going on.

In Seana's case she was also dealing with depression and identity issues stemming from having been adopted. Starting a new school and the pressure she felt to make new friends and to fit in intensified these feelings. As her counselor, I did not come to the conclusion that Seana was dealing with depression lightly. I knew I needed to hear information from many different sources regarding Seana's behavior before I came to that conclusion. As I began talking with the family I got a sense of how much the parents cared for Seana and were genuinely concerned for her well being. Once I finished with them I felt it was best that just Seana and I meet for the next several sessions and then suggested that towards the end of the process I would bring them all back in again to discuss the progress they felt had been made.

2. D'Onofrio, *Adolescent Self-Injury*, 20.

3. Penner, *Hope and Healing*, 32.

In first listening to Seana's story it was determined that Narrative Therapy would be a good avenue to take. Narrative Therapy can be described in this way: "Narrative approach to counseling invites clients to begin a journey of co-exploration in search of talents and abilities that are hidden or veiled by a life problem. Unlike the passive soil that is excavated by the archaeologist's tools, the client is engaged as an active collaborator in the reconstruction of something of substance and value."[4] Narrative Therapy seeks to invite the client to explore their own stories and to begin the process of rewriting a new story based on their exploration. This rewriting requires the participation of both the client and the counselor who work together as co-collaborators. In Narrative Therapy the counselor is not considered the expert. It is the client who is considered the expert on his/her own life; the counselor is seen as a guide and facilitator.

The Process

Internalized Dialogue-Getting the Story

In Seana's case, understanding the story behind the cutting was the first step in walking with her through this struggle. Part of hearing her story was knowing that she would need to be given space to tell her story how and when she wanted to. She in no way needed to feel hurried. She also needed to know that she was really being heard and her story understood. This would be accomplished through the attending skills used as well as the specific language used with her. The questions asked Seana were also very important in accomplishing these things.

During the first couple of sessions I spent time allowing Seana to tell her story and building a trusting rapport with her. Part of the process during this stage involves understanding the Internalized dialogue or Conversation that is going on in the client's head. Narrative therapists define internalized dialogue as "a way of speaking that locates problem issues firmly in the personality of the person suffering under them."[5] As the Internalized Conversation is being uncovered and discussed it is vital that the therapist remain curious and engaged. They must remember that the client knows their own story best. This curiosity can be demonstrated through the questions asked. In Seana's case the questions I asked revolved

4. Crocket et. al, 3.

5. Ibid., 303.

around three main issues that had already been brought to awareness: cutting, depression, and adoption. Some of these questions include:

"Seana, your mom has already told me a little bit about what is going on but I would like to hear from you about what has been going on?"

"When did you first begin cutting?"

"What does it feel like for you when you do cut?"

It was also important to ask about how things were going at school. This could involve asking questions such as,

"Seana I understand that your teachers and parents have been concerned that you might be isolating yourself from your classmates and that you are having trouble paying attention—are they understanding your situation at school correctly?"

"Do you feel you are having a hard time paying attention in class and making friends?"

As these questions were asked it was discovered that Seana was indeed having a hard time paying attention in class. Seana and I determined this to be a result of her believing she was having a hard time making friends since starting high school. She went on to mention that several of the friends she had in middle school had moved away. In being asked how this made her feel she said it made her feel "alone."

One important concept in Narrative Therapy that is vital throughout the entire process is the idea of an audience. Crocket describes this idea of audience, especially as it relates to the initial stages of the process, in this manner, "Through the counseling conversation, what may have been a quite private experience for the client is brought into a more public world of discourse. However, this world is constrained (there may be only one other person serving as audience), and it has boundaries, like the professional ethic of confidentiality, that seek to establish some safety for the public telling."[6]

In continuing to discuss her friendships at school, Seana did mention two girls she had become very close to. I then asked if her friends knew about her cutting and she said they did. With hesitation she then went on to reveal that her friends cut as well.

After discussing the cutting and "sadness" over the first several sessions I deemed it necessary to then begin discussing how being adopted had affected her life. Adoption, no matter how "smooth" the transition, has a profound effect on the new family. Brodzinsky and Palacios bring up this point by stating, "Many adopted children enter their new families

6. Ibid., 66.

after experiences of maltreatment or neglect and a subsequent period in public care in which they may move through a succession of foster placements. These experiences can have a major impact in their relationships and development within their new families."[7] In understanding that the adoption had a huge impact on Seana, I knew this was something she needed to talk about. I was also just genuinely curious as to what her experience had been like. Here are a few of the questions I asked her concerning her adoption:

"You were adopted when you were about 5 correct?"

"Can you tell me about what lead you to being adopted?"

"What was life like before you were adopted; I know you were very young when this happened but what can you remember?"

"What has life been like since your adoption?"

From asking these questions I discovered that Seana's parents died when she was four and there was no extended family willing to take care of her. She then spent some time in a children's home where she was finally adopted. She also explained that she loved her parents, yet doesn't remember too much about them. She did have some memories of the time she got to spend with them and recounted those to me. I asked how it felt telling me these stories and she said that she enjoyed it but it did make her miss them. In response to my question about what life has been like with her adoptive family she said that things are good and for the most part she loves her family but the fact that they aren't her biological family makes her wonder if she really belongs to anyone. I then asked her if she was angry with her parents being taken from her and she said she was. She remembers wondering at times what she did to deserve having them taken away from her. After discussing all of this I wanted to discover how her story had affected how she saw herself. I couldn't help but imagine this story had done a lot to affect how she saw herself and I also imagined it had affected it in a negative way. As we discussed this she revealed to me that every day she is reminded that *she is an orphan.* Along with that she also revealed to me that she feels unloved by her biological family. She was adamant in telling me that she knew her parents loved her but she felt the rest of her biological family didn't love her or want her. She did mention that she felt loved by her adoptive family. Identity was another issue that she brought up as we talked about how being adopted made her feel. She felt that she didn't know who she was because she didn't know her biological family.

7. Brodzinsky and Palacios, *Psychological Issues*, 93.

NAMING THE STORY

The next step in working with Seana was helping her come up with a name for the problem she was struggling with. Naming the story is considered a very big step in helping the client externalize the problem. Naming involves giving the problem-story a one word or one phrase name, which can help the person concisely define the problem. From this point on the problem is called by this Name. As Seana names the problem, it will allow her to separate herself from the problem and help her to understand that she is not the problem, the problem is the problem. This process of Naming the Problem should be given great consideration and should only be undertaken when the problem-story has been fully explored. Language is a huge concept to keep in mind when using Narrative Therapy. The philosophy of Narrative Therapy is based on the suggestion that language determines our perception of things and that in order to change our perceptions we need to change our language.[8] Therefore, the name given the problem is very important.

In working with Seana I felt it very important that she come up with the name herself. I wanted to be there for her as a guide and supporter, but I felt it would benefit her the most if she came up with the name herself. So as we continued talking I asked her, "Seana from listening to your story I wonder if there is a name that can be given to your problem story?" She took some time to think and finally replied, "I have never thought about giving it a name before." I then stated, "What do you think about calling it 'lost and abandoned'?" She was silent for a while after that as she was taking this name in and then said, "Yeah that is a good description of how I feel a lot of the time."

EXTERNALIZING "LOST AND ABANDONED"

Now that the problem had been Named I began to work with Seana to externalize the problem. Before I go into how I helped Seana do this it is important to define the phrase "Externalizing Conversation." Crocket defines this as, "a way of speaking in which space is introduced between the person and the problem issue. The problem may be spoken of as if it were a distinct entity or even a personality in its own right rather than part of the person. This creates an opportunity for the relationship between the

---

8. Crocket et. al, *Narrative Therapy in Practice*, 1997.

person and the problem to be articulated."[9] I could now begin asking her questions about "lost and abandoned." Although Seana had been fairly open thus far I hoped giving the problem a name, which would allow her to separate herself from it, would allow her to be even more open and willing to explore how this problem has affected her life. This process of determining the history of the problem itself and how it is linked to the present situation is called tracing the history or Scaffolding.[10]

I first began by asking her how much "lost and abandoned" had taken hold of her life on a scale of one to ten; one being very little of her life and ten being all of her life. This is an example of a scaling question and helped me understand the intensity of the problem.[11] She responded that it would be an eight on the scale. Here is a little excerpt from the rest of the conversation.

Counselor: "Seana, can you tell me when you first noticed 'lost and abandoned?'"

Seana: "I don't know. . .I guess I first started noticing it after my parents died and I began living with my first foster family."

Counselor "So it seems like 'lost and abandoned' has been around for most of your life."

Seana: "Yeah. . .It has. . .and I'm ready for it to be gone."

Counselor: "Well I am here for you. . .to help you work through 'lost and abandoned' and hopefully we will witness it slowly disappear over time. This is going to be a process that will require you taking many hard, yet important, steps along the way."

Seana: "I don't know how I feel about that. I want it to be over now."

Counselor: "I know you do, and again that is why I am here, you don't have to do this by yourself."

Seana: "I wanna do what it takes, although I know it's going to be hard."

Counselor: "Alright then we'll keep going. Seana, can you tell me how 'lost and abandoned' tricks you?"

Seana: "Hahaha, that's a strange question. What do you mean?"

Counselor "Haha, I know it is. Ok what does 'lost and abandoned' tell you that you think is a lie?"

Seana: "Well I guess it tells me that I have no one in my life. Yeah and it also tells you that you are going to keep having people taken away.

Counselor: "Ok"

9. Ibid., 303.

10. Morgan, *What is Narrative Therapy?* 33.

11. Crocket et. al, *Narrative Therapy in Practice*, 1997.

Seana: "People don't want to be around you and that you have no control over your relationships. You should be furious that your parents and then your friends abandoned you. It tells me that your adoptive family will never love you as much as one of their biological children"

As Seana shared this with me I could tell it was very hard for her to think about these things and I could see that she had been greatly impacted by them.

I knew I needed to help her understand that these thoughts were lies. I also began to get an idea of the pattern of myths that she had begun believing about herself. Wimberley describes several common, personal, familial and ministerial myths to which we can fall prey. In discussing the origins of these myths in our lives, he states, "A personal mythology is made up of the convictions and beliefs that we hold about ourselves. It is made up of specific themes including early memories, whether or not we feel welcomed or wanted . . . gender . . . peer and sibling relationships."[12] Three personal myths that Wimberley describes that I feel Seana had begun believing about herself are the myths of the loner, powerlessness, and the myth of unlovability.

Wimberley describes the myth of the loner as the belief that they have to do it by themselves because they cannot trust people. People who believe this myth often find it very hard to get close to others because of the distrust they feel. Also, they question whether people would want to get close to them because they are too imperfect and flawed.[13] I feel Seana believes this about herself due to her history of detachment with both her adoptive parents and her classmates and in knowing about her struggle with cutting. Wimberley goes on to describe the myth of powerlessness as the belief that you have no power to affect change in your own life or in the lives of others. Those who believe this myth often feel they have no control over the things that happen to them.[14] Again I feel this is a myth Seana has begun believing about herself because of her past of losing both her parents and her middle school best friends. I got the sense that she feels these things happened to her without her having any control over it. Lastly, Wimberley describes the myth of unlovability as the belief that we have to earn others' love and attention by sacrificing ourselves or by not showing others who we truly are. Those who believe this often feel they could never show people their ugly side. This often results in a loss of self

12. Wimberly, *Recalling Our Stories*, 15.

13. Ibid., 21.

14. Ibid., 18.

or voice.[15] Again, I got the sense that this is a myth Seana believes about herself. In hearing about her struggle at school with making friends and in hearing from Jocelyn that Seana had a hard time connecting and bonding with her, I got the sense that Seana was having a hard time accepting that this new family really could love her as one of their own.

I thought it would be wise to then ask her about these myths she had begun believing about herself. I hoped that as we discussed this, Seana would become more aware of the impact "lost and abandoned" had on her. I also hoped that it would begin to help her clarify how "lost and abandoned" had affected her. After explaining these myths to her and asking if she felt she did believe this about herself, I gave her room to respond. She explained that she did feel she believed these things about herself. I then wanted to explore more how "lost and abandoned" affected her behavior, so I asked her, "Is it 'lost and abandoned' that gets you to cut?" She took some time to think about this and she said that it was "lost and abandoned" that got her to cut. I went on to ask her how "lost and abandoned" got her to cut. She explained that she needed some way to deal with the sadness and after her two friends told her that they cut she began hearing "lost and abandoned" say that she should try it because it will help her to feel better. She also explained that now she has to do it to handle her emotions. She described the cutting as being an addiction. In doing research on cutting I discovered that this sense of cutting being addictive is common among those who engage in self-harm. Penner discusses this addictive nature of self-harm in this way, "Unfortunately the reprieve kids get from the self-injurious behavior quickly becomes susceptible to what's known as the 'law of diminishing returns.' What worked yesterday doesn't work as well today. That little cut doesn't do it anymore—or if it does the good feelings don't last as long as they once did."[16] In knowing this I asked her how many times she was cutting a week and she said between ten and fifteen times. I then asked what usually triggered her cutting. She responded by saying that she didn't really know she just did it. I was then curious as to how "lost and abandoned" made her feel after she cut so I asked her about it. She said it makes her feel guilty for doing it and that if anyone found out they wouldn't want to be around her anymore. I suggested that she keep a diary of her cutting episodes and to write about the circumstances and emotions surrounding her cutting. I went on to explain that as she gains more awareness of how "lost and abandoned" specifically gets her to cut,

15. Ibid.

16. Penner, *Hope and Healing*, 103.

she will be able to gain victory over it. Furthermore, in doing research on this issue I found that keeping a diary is a great way to help clients gain insight and awareness. Cohn, Levitt, and Sansone explain the benefits of diary keeping by stating, "To retrieve the potentially relent situational features of [the client's] self-harming behaviors as well as the guiding cognitive and affective process of these behaviors, we resorted to the preceding assessment findings as well as her diary notes, in which she identified situations, cognitions and affects that instigated her self-injurious acts."[17] After discussing this she agreed to begin keeping this type of diary.

After seeing the stronghold "lost and abandoned" had on Seana's life I knew we needed to do a lot of work rewriting this Dominant Story into a more acceptable alternative story. This "Re-authoring" needed to begin with deconstructing the Dominant Story. Re-authoring is defined as, "The process of developing an Alternative Story in therapy."[18] Now for the purposes of the rest of this chapter, the term Alternative Story also needs to be defined. Crocket defines Alternative Story as, "The story that develops in therapy in contradiction to the Dominant Story in which the problem holds sway."[19] To begin developing this story I began by asking what in Narrative Therapy is called a Miracle Question, which is a question that allows the client to paint an ideal picture of how they would like their lives to be.[20] I asked, "What would life be like without 'lost and abandoned?" She responded that it would be a life without cutting or depression. She would feel more loved by her adoptive family and would have more friends. I then asked her if she thought there could be a time in the future where there would be no more "lost and abandoned." She said there are times when she doesn't think so and times when she does. I encouraged her that I thought there could definitely be a time when 'lost and abandoned" no longer had a hold on her life. I then asked her if she could think of any ways that we could work towards loosening "lost and abandonee's" grip over her life. She said she couldn't think of anything new but that continuing to come to counseling and keeping the diary would hopefully help.

Over the next several sessions, as we continued to talk, I began to look for "Sparkling Moments" throughout her story. Sparkling Moments are moments "in any problem-saturated story when the client demonstrates a surprising achievement in defeating or limiting the influence

17. Cohn et al., *Self-Harm Behavior and Eating Disorders*, 139.

18. Crocket et. al., *Narrative Therapy in Practice*, 305.

19. Ibid., 301.

20. Ibid.

of the problem in her life. Such moments, which are often isolated and neglected, are the shining stars in a sky darkened by the dominance of the problem."[21] Here is an excerpt of a conversation that dealt with discovering these Sparkling Moments, that helped Seana begin to write her Alternative Story.

Counselor: "So what are some of your fondest memories of your adoptive family?"

Seana: "Well there was this one time when we all went to Disney World when I was like, thirteen."

Counselor: "What made that trip so memorable?"

Seana: "I remember feeling very happy, like I was a real part of the family, completely included. They asked me what rides I wanted to go on and I was able to tell them. We laughed and talked and took turns riding rides with each other. We took lots of pictures together and shared food and drinks. Also it helped that it was my first time to Disney World and I had always wanted to go there, hahaha."

Counselor: "I can see from your face and eyes that this is such a happy memory for you. Describe for me what you are feeling as you are telling me about this.

Seana: "It makes me feel happy like I want to go back and relive that over and over again. I also feel content I guess."

Counselor: "Do you think you had a part in making that vacation such a happy one?"

Seana: "Huhhh, I had never thought about that before but yeah I guess maybe I did. I mean I didn't give my adoptive parents any trouble and I was able to laugh and joke with them and I helped out by carrying stuff and giving input as to what we should do next, you know, stuff like that."

Counselor: "So it sounds like you cared about your adoptive family even back then. And it certainly sounds like they cared about you too."

Seana: "Yeah I think so, I mean I didn't want to leave. I wanted to have a family that I could call my own again so I didn't want to screw anything up. And even then I realized that they were good people and that they did care about me."

Counselor: "Now had you already begun cutting at that point?"

Seana: "Yeah I had"

Counselor: "Did you cut while you were on this particular vacation?"

Seana: "No I didn't actually. I didn't have any razors and there was hardly any privacy, or time for that matter. We were constantly doing stuff."

---

21. Ibid., 306.

Counselor: "Humm, that maybe true, but maybe that was also one time when you didn't need to cut to cope with the stress and negative emotions. Why do you think that is?"

Seana: "Well I could relax and I didn't have to worry about school and kids annoying me. Also, I think that realizing I was a part of the family during that trip also helped."

Counselor: "Maybe this is one time that 'lost and abandoned' didn't have much of a hold on you."

This is an example of a powerful way that people can begin to look at the story of their lives in a new light and begin to rewrite it in a way that is more substantive and truthful.

After we had come to discover several "Sparkling Moments" and suggesting that this could become an alternative story, I asked her about her name. It seems like a random question but I realized that the meaning of the names given by parents actually tends to be lived out by the child. Plus, Seana is a very interesting name and I was curious. She said that she wasn't sure what her name meant so I asked if maybe that would be something we could do some research on. Here is an excerpt from that session where we discussed our findings.

Counselor: "So were you able to look up what 'Seana' means?"

Seana: "I was and it means 'gift from God' which is pretty cool."[22]

Counselor: "That's the meaning I found as well. I think that name has powerful implications for your life and for how you can begin to see yourself. What do you think some of those implications are? What can you say about yourself from the meaning of your name?"

Seana: "Well, I don't know. I guess it could mean that I have value and importance just like a gift does. It could also mean that I am wanted."

Counselor: "May I suggest that the 'from God' part is really important as well. How do you think that bit could be important?"

Seana: "I'm. . .I'm not sure about that."

Counselor: "Well that could be something you think about in the days ahead. Now what do you think that name suggests about how your adoptive family might see you?"

Seana: "They could see me as an actual gift from God I guess."

Counselor: "How does that make you feel to say that and to actually consider that thought?"

Seana: "It makes me feel. Uhmm. . . . I can't really describe it. It makes me feel loved and very thankful I guess. You know cause it reminds me that I

22. Baby Name Meanings, 2006.

*am wanted and loved by them. I guess I am beginning to see that I am actu-
ally very blessed to have been put with another family that loves me since I
don't have my parents around anymore. God I guess really cares about me."*

Counselor: *"Does it help you see how important you are to you adoptive family?"*

Seana: *"Yeah, it does"*

Counselor: *"I think this could be a very big part of your alternative
story."*

Seana: *"Yeah."*

Counselor: *"In considering the elements of your alternative story so far,
what name do you think we could give?"*

Seana: *"Uhmm. . .I think 'accepted and free."*

Counselor: *"That's a beautiful name. What drew you to that name?"*

Seana: *"I've realized how much my adoptive family loves, wants, and
accepts me. And I think I want freedom from this problem I see happening."*

Counselor; *"That's really good. So you think your family would agree
with this new story we are creating?"*

Seana: *"Yeah, I definitely think so."*

Counselor: *"Yeah, I think so, too. Is there anyone who you think
wouldn't agree or like this new story too much."*

Seana: *"Uhmmm. . .yeah I think my friends who got me started cutting in the first place wouldn't like it too much. I think maybe they might be
jealous of it."*

Counselor: *"That is definitely a possibility. They might be jealous of
the change you are going through. I would encourage you to consider that
maybe these are two friends that might need to be stayed away from. We all
need to surround ourselves with people who will encourage us to be the best
person we can be. That decision is up to you though. I also encourage you
to continue to lean on Jessica and your family as you continue this process."*

This idea of removing certain people from one's life and adding new
people is known as Re-membering or creating an audience.[23]

I have come to realize that, "any success we find ourselves experiencing in life must be celebrated with community, and any downfall pains
both the individual and the community."[24] As I knew therapy was coming
to an end and I had seen that Seana had made tremendous progress I decided to ask Seana if we could bring in her family and Jessica to honor the
progress made with what is called a Definitional Ceremony, a time where

23. Crocket et. al, *Narrative Therapy in Practice*, 21.

24. Mucherera, *Meet Me*, 81.

the counselor and witnesses can help the client solidify this new story and the new image this story helped create.

After we had all gathered, each person went around and described the positive change they had seen in Seana since beginning therapy. They mentioned her increased confidence and joy. They also commented that they felt closer to her because she was more open to letting them in. I personally mentioned that I felt honored to have been given access to her story and to have been allowed to help her rewrite it in a way that was so meaningful to her. This was a beautiful end to a wonderful journey of healing and restoration.

6

Fear of Sleeping Alone

A Boy's Story of Overcoming Nights of Fear

KARI ROMERO

JOHN IS A SEVEN-YEAR-OLD boy who is having trouble sleeping in his own room at night. John is the oldest child with a sibling six years younger than he is. John had been allowed to sleep with his parents since infancy. He is a strong-willed child who is creative and imaginative.

John's parents have tried purchasing a set of bunk beds as an incentive to sleeping alone, which worked for a few weeks until they moved to a new house where John promptly returned to their bedroom. His parents have also tried lying down with him in his bed until he falls asleep at night. John, however, seems to have an internal clock that wakes him up around 1 a.m. to return to his parents' bed.

John's parents' frustration has increased to the point that he now has to sleep in a sleeping bag on their floor if he wakes up in the night and comes to their room. His younger brother sleeps in a toddler bed, but has begun moving to the parents' bed in the middle of the night as well. The parents would very much like to see John sleeping independently in his own room. They are not sure if the problem lies with John's strong-willed nature or fear of the dark. After establishing that abuse was not a factor, Pastor Sims began working with John in a Narrative Counseling style to help him move beyond the fear of sleeping alone.

"Narrative therapists are interested in joining with people to explore the stories they have about their lives and relationships, their effects, their meanings and the context in which they have been formed and authored."[1] This story-sharing process is crucial to Narrative Counseling. By allowing John to share his story, he is granted expert status in his own life. The counselor, then, is simply partnering with John and his parents to overcome a particular problem. Listening to the story will allow the counselor to hear the presenting problem and look for deeper underlying issues.

In dealing with children in counseling situations, using playful approaches is often helpful in establishing a good comfort level for the child. A counselor may also want to get to know the child apart from the problem before proceeding. This allows the counselor to look for abilities that may help the child work against the problem.[2] Some playful opportunities to look for might include knowing that a child likes superheroes (this can lead to a superhero versus bad-guy problem battle) or that a girl is a good mommy to her dolls (this might lead to teaching the problem to obey her as she teaches her dolls). Once the counselor knows the child, he or she should begin looking toward the problem.

As the problem-story is told the family will typically present stories that focus only around the problem, which has become a large part of the child's identity. The child's story will often locate the problem inwardly, which is called an Internalizing Conversation and will create a thin description of who the child really is.[3] The counselor will work to separate that problem from the child's identity by Externalizing it and creating an Alternative Story with rich, or thick, descriptions that include the child's strengths that may help overcome the problem.[4] John, in the first session for example, showed that his sleeping problem was internalized when he said, "I just can't sleep in my bed. I don't like it. I am scared to sleep in my room. I just don't want to sleep there. I'm just a big scared baby. I never sleep in my own bed." The inability to sleep on his own is very much a part of his identity and he considers himself fearful and unable to overcome the problem. His parents may add to this internalization by saying things such as, "John is stubborn and afraid. He doesn't listen when we tell him there's nothing to be afraid of. It seems like he manipulates to get his way

1. Morgan. *What Is Narrative Therapy?* 10.
2. Freeman et al., *Playful Approaches.*
3. Morgan *What Is Narrative Therapy?*
4. Ibid.

at bedtime." They are naming John as the problem, which adds tension to the situation and further discourages John.

A strong-willed child can be defined as one who "occasionally or continually expresses a high degree of willfulness—the power or self-determination to direct, to persist, to resist, and to prevail."[5] In dealing with problems in parenting a strong-willed child, the counselor should remember that parents of strong-willed children often develop excessively negative attitudes toward the child. This can be damaging to the child in multiple ways including creating a vicious cycle of negativity between parent and child.[6] "It discourages the child from making efforts to self-correct, because there is nothing positive to work for in the relationship."[7] The child also comes to see him or herself in the way the parents describe. The counselor needs to look for opportunities to change this mentality and help the parents realize that "being strong-willed has a strong positive side, and parents need to see that, appreciate that, and nurture that so their willful child learns to do the same."[8] Doing this will help John or any strong-willed child more easily overcome his problem.

The narrative counselor should recognize the parents' and child's internalization of the problem and begin to separate the problem from the identity of the child. A main concept of Narrative Therapy is the belief that "the problem is the problem, as opposed to the person being seen as the problem."[9] In order to help separate the problem from the person, the counselor will use a subtle shift in language. This may include putting the word "the" in front of the problem, for example, in John's case Pastor Sims begins saying, "the waking up problem" rather than "John's problem." The counselor must not rush ahead of the client, though, and try to solve or normalize the problem too quickly. Doing this can cause the family "to feel that we have not appreciated the depth or quality of their struggle."[10]

Listening to the problem-story and asking genuinely curious questions will help lead to ideas for separating the problem from the child's identity and overcoming the problem. This type of dialogue is called Externalizing Conversation.[11] Putting distance between the person and

5. Pickhardt, *The Everything Parent's Guide*, 1.

6. Ibid.

7. Ibid., 87.

8. Ibid., 24.

9. Morgan. *What Is Narrative Therapy?* 17.

10. Freeman et al., *Playful Approaches*, 48.

11. Morgan. *What Is Narrative Therapy?*

the problem is the main goal of externalization. "Narrative therapists will listen to the description of the person's experience, hoping to hear a word or phrase that describes what might be getting in the way of the person's life."[12] For example, Pastor Sims asks John to explain what happens at night when he is trying to sleep. John's response includes many descriptive details about the problem when he says, "I can't sleep alone because I am scared. When the lights are out I see pictures that scare me like stuff I see on TV or what I imagine. Sometimes I see things like a man with a chainsaw or a bad guy coming after me."

Pastor Sims is then able to ask John if there might be a good name for the problem, and John promptly names the problem Chainsaw Man. If John had not decided on a name, Pastor Sims would have suggested names such as scary pictures or dark room. The counselor is careful, though, not to impose a name on the problem. The client should have the right to Name the Problem with the counselor in a supporting role, which strengthens the counselor-client relationship.[13] So, Pastor Sims' question might be worded, "John, I was wondering what you might call a problem like this if you gave it a name. Is scary picture or dark room a good name or is there a name that you think describes the problem better?"

Once the problem is named the Externalizing Conversation continues. "The immediate value of Externalizing Conversations is that the subtle change in the counselor's language promotes a separation between the person and the problem."[14] This helps the client move away from blaming self or others. The counselor asks questions about the problem and its effects on the person.[15] Pastor Sims' externalizing questions include, "John, I noticed earlier that you said you can't sleep in your room at all. Does "Chainsaw Man" make you feel that way? What exactly happens when "Chainsaw Man" does this type of thing?" John says that "Chainsaw Man" scares him into thinking he cannot sleep alone by putting scary pictures in his mind. This subtle use of externalizing language is already creating distance between John and the problem.

Pastor Sims next shifts her attention to Mapping the problem which includes examining the Landscape of Action by looking for when and how often the problem shows up, what the problem does while it is there, when it goes away (if ever), and what causes it to go away, among other things.

12. Ibid., 18.

13. Monk et al., *Narrative Therapy*.

14. Ibid., 26.

15. Ibid.

The Landscape of Action is the "realm of human experience in which events occur and out of which we fashion the stories with which we make sense of our lives."[16] Tracing the problem's history in this way also creates distance between the person and the problem by putting it in a longer-term context.[17] Pastor Sims may ask John to name how much influence "Chainsaw Man" has had in his life on a scale of one to ten, with ten being complete control of his life. John's response of five (because "Chainsaw Man" mostly bothers him at night) shows John that he does have some control over "Chainsaw Man." This gives a view of John's life and the problem's life as well as John's potential power over the problem.[18] Both Pastor Sims and John are now able to explore where that power comes from since they have discovered power over Chainsaw Man is, in fact, in John's story.

Another aspect of tracing the history is to explore the effects of the problem on the client's life. John says he feels bad when he comes in his parents' room at night. He says he knows he should stay in his bed, but Chainsaw Man scares him into going to his parents' room. This is an opportunity for Pastor Sims to create further distance between John and the problem by identifying the injustice of the problem's influence on his life. Once a problem is externalized children often imagine themselves as the protagonist or a heroic figure fighting against the injustice of the problem, that is now a sort of antagonist.[19] Pastor Sims, seeing an opportunity to create distance, asks, "John, do you think it is fair for Chainsaw Man to keep you awake and make you feel bad for going to your parents' room?" John responds excitedly that it is not fair at all. "Not surprisingly, the child, seeing an injustice, is highly motivated to test his mettle and challenge this relationship with the problem."[20] The effect of the problem has opened the door to Deconstruct the story and find Unique Outcomes, as defined below, in John's experience with the problem.

While still using Externalizing language, the counselor now tries to Deconstruct the problem by listening for "hidden meanings, spaces or gaps, and evidence of conflicting stories."[21] In John's story, Pastor Sims finds a gap by asking John if there are any times when he has not slept in his parents' bed. John responds, "Only when I spend the night with my

16. Ibid., 303.

17. Morgan. *What Is Narrative Therapy?* 33.

18. Ibid.

19. Freeman et al., *Playful Approaches*.

20. Ibid., 51.

21. Monk et al., *Narrative Therapy*, 43.

friends, but that is because I have friends there so Chainsaw Man doesn't come around much." Pastor Sims identifies this as a Unique Outcome in the story of John and Chainsaw Man and further explores this behavior.

A Unique Outcome is "anything that does not 'fit' with the Dominant Story" of the problem.[22] John is able to sleep away from his parents at someone else's house, which does not fit with the Dominant Story at all. This new information opens the window to creating an Alternative Story of John's life in which the problem has less power than he currently thinks it does. The Alternative Story is the "story that develops in therapy in contradiction to the Dominant Story in which the problem holds sway."[23] Unique Outcomes do not exist in isolation. Narrative therapists "assume that problems are never 100 percent successful and that, therefore, there will be other events across time that can be traced and linked with the Unique Outcome that has been discovered."[24] Clustering Unique Outcomes together will create an Alternative Story, so the counselor must not only look for Unique Outcomes, but also thicken the stories of any Unique Outcomes mentioned. This will move the client's understanding of who he or she is from a thin description that focuses solely on the problem to a thick description of who he or she really is.[25]

Pastor Sims wants to thicken the story around John sleeping all night away from his parents at his friends' houses. She begins by asking Landscape of Action questions that will bring clarity to the events surrounding the outcome. The dialogue opens with, *"John, last time you stayed at your friend's house, where did you sleep?"*

"In my sleeping bag," John replies.

"Did you miss your parents when you slept alone in your sleeping bag?"

"No, but I had my friend there so I wasn't alone."

"Did Chainsaw Man try to bother you that night?"

"No, not really."

"Why do you think that is?"

"Because my friend and me are funny and we laughed so much that I had fun until I fell asleep."

"So, how do you think Chainsaw Man feels about fun and laughing?'

"He must not like it."

"Are you usually a funny guy?"

22. Morgan, *What Is Narrative Therapy?* 52.

23. Monk et al., *Narrative Therapy in Practice*, 301.

24. Morgan. *What Is Narrative Therapy?* 55.

25. Ibid.

"Yes, I make people laugh all the time. It's one of my favorite things to do."

"Do you think if you used laughter and fun against Chainsaw Man, he might stay away more?"

"I think so . . . maybe I could try reading funny books before bed or watch my favorite funny cartoons."

Identifying what caused the Unique Outcome in this way empowers the child to find more opportunities to stand against the problem. Once an Alternative Story begins to emerge, John is able to begin to imagine a life in which he is in control of the problem. Children are imaginative beings and sometimes their strengths, or special abilities, may seem weird or strange to others, especially adults. "Special abilities exist in the realms of intuition, imagination, or wizardry. They may also lie in the child's specific talents, such as playing music, practicing magic tricks, or juggling."[26] One of John's special abilities is to make people laugh. Identifying and putting this special ability to use can often be helpful in creating an alternative story. One way to do this would be to create a superpower around John's gift of wit and humor. John may title himself Captain Silly and have the power to laugh problems away when they sneak up on him.

In Pastoral Counseling settings, the use of Scripture can also help contribute to thickening the Alternative Story. "Biblical stories often contain an invitation to the reader to adopt the perspective, feelings, and attitudes of the characters as a way to influence the life of the reader and hearer."[27] Pastor Sims asks John if he can think of anything besides laughter and fun that he could add to his weapons against Chainsaw Man. John suggests that he could be like David in the Bible when he fought Goliath. Pastor Sims explores this further by asking John which part of the story is like his life. John tells her that David was brave because he knew that God would always fight with him and John thinks that God will probably fight with him, too. The pastor's role is to draw attention to the fact that something is at work deep in the client's heart through the power of God's Word.[28] Pastor Sims says she wonders what God might think about this problem with Chainsaw Man and why John thinks he thought of that story in the Bible.

John says that God helped David defeat Goliath so God can help him, too, and he remembered the story because his Sunday school teacher tells

26. Freeman et al., *Playful Approaches*, 183.

27. Wimberly. *Using Scripture in Pastoral Counseling*, 25.

28. Ibid.

it a lot, so God must think it's important for kids. According to Wimberly, "Identification with Bible stories frequently stimulates the expectation that the Bible reader will be treated in a manner similar to that of the Bible characters."[29] Using biblical narrative helps the child (or adult client) to feel as if the problem is manageable, the child (or adult client) is not alone and that there are new options for the future in regard to the problem.[30] John is at an age when his understanding of God is maturing and becoming a belief that will grow and mature with him or eventually be discarded. Rizzuto believes that whether or not an adult believes in God "depends on whether or not a conscious 'identity of experience' can be established between the God-representation of a given developmental moment and the object and the self-representations needed to maintain a sense of self, which provides at least a minimum of relatedness and hope."[31] From a pastoral counseling perspective the affirmation of relatedness and hope that God provides in a child's, such as John's, struggle is important to the longevity of the child's faith.

Pastor Sims affirms that she agrees with him that David is a good example of how God loves and helps young people. John says that he also has a scripture that helps him not feel so afraid: "Greater is He that is in me than He that is in the world."[32] John thinks he could try saying this to Chainsaw Man and see if it helps. Pastor Sims agrees that this could be helpful and John's parents agree as well.

Having worked through the Externalization of the problem and identification of Unique Outcomes that have helped an Alternative Story to start to emerge, attention can now be shifted to Re-authoring and Re-storying. Re-authoring is the collaborative process between client and counselor (and in this case parents as well) to develop an Alternative Story in therapy.[33] Pastor Sims will work together with John and his parents to create a plan to Re-author the problem story as a supportive and concerned community. This method could be referred to as a palaver. A palaver is a gathering of a community, whether family or the broader community, "to resolve a problem, crisis or conflict and to make other time for educational purposes or just simply for fellowship."[34] Parents can play a

29. Ibid., 93.
30. Ibid.
31. Rizzuto. *The Birth of the Living God*, 202.
32. First John 4:4, KJV.
33. Monk et al., *Narrative Therapy in Practice*.
34. Mucherera. *Meet Me*, 108–9.

large role in helping a child Re-author their story. Parents can brainstorm, join the child in opposing the problem, act as a team with the child, and form an audience to the child's Re-storying, among other possibilities.[35] Because problems do not occur in isolation, but are results of the broad context of our lives including social influences, family influences and cultural influences, working to solve the problems with the help of a caring community is beneficial.[36]

The Re-authoring process should be determined together with John. The counselor should not simply provide solutions that she thinks are appropriate, but should work with John and his parents to help him identify what may work for him. One way to determine what to work toward is to ask a Miracle Question, such as, "If you were to wake up tomorrow and the Chainsaw Man problem were completely gone, what would that be like?" John's response to this question will help identify what he sees as the solution to the problem and what he is working toward in his own mind.[37] Pastor Sims has already identified some options of fun and laughter and relationship with God. She now needs to help put a regular plan in action to help John set and reach goals. Common sleep problems for children John's age include "resisting at bedtime, frequently getting up during the night, and having nightmares," and two of these have been identified as difficulties for John.[38] Pastor Sims begins by looking for ideas to help with the problem of resisting bedtime.

Bedtime rituals that are consistent, calming, and loving are the best method to help prevent bedtime wars between parents and children. "Going to bed is a transition for children. Transitions can be difficult for strong-willed children."[39] Because of this, Forehand and Long suggest telling the child a few minutes before bedtime that bedtime is coming. Creating a bedtime ritual with several steps will also mentally prepare the child for the transition to bed. They suggest "activities that are quiet and soothing, such as a bath, a snack, a bedtime story, goodnight kisses for everyone in the family, and arranging soft animals in his bed."[40] Parents must

35. Freeman et al., *Playful Approaches.*

36. Morgan. *What Is Narrative Therapy?*

37. Freeman et al., *Playful Approaches.*

38. Forehand and Long. *Parenting the Strong-willed Child*, 237.

39. Ibid., 239.

40. Ibid.

be firm with enforcing bedtime and keeping the child in bed, but also affirming when the child complies and loving in putting the child to bed.[41]

Pastor Sims begins the Re-authoring process by asking John if he has any ideas about what he and his family could do each night to team up against Chainsaw Man. John suggests that his parents could check to make sure his room is safe when he is getting ready for bed each night and they could also talk about funny things after reading his Bible story so that he has happy thoughts as he is falling asleep. He also requested sleeping with the lights on and allowing a funny movie to play on his TV or read a funny book as he falls asleep. Pastor Sims then asks if it might be okay with John if his parents turn his light off after he falls asleep and John agreed that this would be okay. Pastor Sims also invites John to name this Alternative Story as well. John decides to call it "project stay asleep."

The next issue to Re-author is the trouble with waking up in the night and moving to his parents' room. Most children who cannot go back to sleep after waking during the night simply have not learned to how to fall asleep on their own. It is important that when a child wakes up in the night, the parent puts the child back to bed while he or she is awake rather than helping him or her fall asleep.[42] After returning the child to bed the parent should firmly say that he or she needs to stay in his or her room. This should be done repeatedly until the waking stops.[43] While this can be very tiring, "this technique works for a majority of parents within the first week."[44]

When John and his parents return to counseling after three weeks of implementing their new bedtime ritual, Pastor Sims asks John how he might defeat Chainsaw Man in the middle of the night when he wakes up. John responds, "Well, I am not waking up as much anymore but I still do sometimes and get in my parents' bed even though I don't want to. But I think it would help if I could turn on some music—maybe some songs from church that remind me that God is helping me like He helped David." Within this statement are signs of Re-storying. John is creating a story that it not dominated by the problem. John's parents contribute to this process by teaming up with him against Chainsaw Man by enforcing the rule of staying in his room at night. They agree to John's suggestions and to put them into practice.

41. Ibid.
42. Ibid.
43. Ibid.
44. Ibid., 244.

Pastor Sims wants to encourage John's progress by thickening the Alternative Story through a process of Re-membering. "Re-membering conversations involve people deliberately choosing who they would like to have more present as the members of their club of life, and whose memberships they would prefer to revise or revoke."[45] This can be explored through questions such as: who else knows about Chainsaw Man and who else would know that you are such a funny and brave boy? The counselor continues to explore what these positive influences would say about John's progress in defeating Chainsaw Man. This creates a community that affirms a positive account of John in relation to the problem. Pastor Sims will also identify negative influences and help John revoke those memberships from his life. John identifies his grandmothers and grandfather as people who would be very proud of his accomplishments. He cannot think of anyone who is discouraging him from getting rid of Chainsaw Man but he does think it would help to remove any movies that scare him.

Having worked through a long process of fighting Chainsaw Man, John and his family are back for their final session with Pastor Sims. Assessing the problem's influence on John's life is important in determining how successful their attempts have been in defeating Chainsaw Man. Pastor Sims asks John again on a scale of one to ten how much the problem bothers John's life. John's previous answer had been five, but now he says it is only a one because Chainsaw Man tries to trick him into going to his parents' room, but he never goes.

Narrative Counseling celebrates the accomplishments of the client's ability to regain power over the problem. This is done through what is called a Definitional Ceremony or Ritual. "Rituals and Celebrations mark . . . significant steps in the journey away from a problem story to a new and preferred version of life."[46] There are many ways to celebrate progress including letters, declarations, and a ceremony with supportive friends and family, and making certificates of accomplishment.[47] In therapy with children, methods such as creating a club for kids who have overcome similar problems or a handbook of overcoming this problem for other children to use later can be a helpful way to celebrate the child's accomplishment.[48] Because John is creative and imaginative, he chose to author a book called "No Monsters" that narrated his battle against Chainsaw Man.

45. Morgan. *What Is Narrative Therapy?* 77.

46. Ibid., 111.

47. Ibid.

48. Freeman et al., *Playful Approaches.*

He then invited his grandparents to come to a special reading of his book to celebrate with him. "Families and children enjoy such rituals at the end of therapy."[49] Being surrounded with a community of supportive people who celebrate with the child enforces the newfound strength.

In conclusion, Narrative Therapy can work well in a Christian counseling setting because it makes the person the expert on his or her own life and allows the pastor to serve as a partner in overcoming the problem, rather than an expert with a quick solution. Externalizing the problem is also complementary to Christian thinking because Jesus often externalized problems in the lives of the people he helped. He saw the person as God's precious creation and the problem as the problem. Pastors who use a Narrative method when appropriate will benefit from counseling by seeing the person as God's creation and the problem as the problem because the focus will be on the person as someone loved by God.

49. Ibid., 140.

7

A Personal Journey
through Complicated Grief

CAROL L. VODVARKA

FIVE DAYS BEFORE MY oldest son Eric's wedding, my youngest son, Kevin, was killed in a car accident. A friend came upon the accident right after it had happened and called us. We arrived at the scene even before the ambulance. We watched them cut him out of the car and perform CPR. We watched as the helicopter flew him to Shock Trauma. The next time we saw him was five hours later after he'd died on the operating table. He was to be Eric's best man. Eric's rehearsal dinner ended up being the "after funeral" meal. Our pastor performed Kevin's funeral in the morning, Eric's rehearsal in the evening and the wedding on the next day. Six weeks later my stepfather passed away. He had been ill and it was the only form of healing left for him. We received the call while on our way to Florida to take our daughter to Chiropractic College. Three months after that my mother died. Even she hadn't realized the toll taking care of Lu had on her. She was admitted to the hospital just before Thanksgiving and died four days after Christmas. Two years after that, five days after our 30th anniversary, one day after we returned from a cruise and hours after our Thanksgiving meal, my husband had a sudden heart attack and died right before my eyes.

Four months prior to my husband's death, we'd built our retirement house. We thought that maybe if we got away from the house we'd lived in for twenty-seven years, in the town my husband and I had lived in for most of our lives, we'd have a fresh start without so many reminders of

Kevin's death. Our home was now so quiet, no longer were there any noisy young people coming in and out, staying for dinner, having bon fires. In six weeks our home had gone from three children to no children.

I have chosen to examine my own journey through complicated grief from a Narrative Counseling approach. Although I benefited greatly from traditional grief counseling, I feel as though I am no longer making progress, and in danger of regressing. I have turned to Narrative Counseling to re-visit and continue my journey toward healing.

Everyone has their own unique compilation of events, experiences, and people, all of which interact and grow into their own personal story. Factors that affect how they and others might interpret this story include biological makeup, culture, events, beliefs, and family. This then forms what we consider to be our life story. The people in our lives, as well as ourselves, may view a part of our story as a problem. In order to support the perception that this area is a problem, the focus is placed upon occurrences, that reinforce this perception and dismissing those, which do not. Should this problem begin to interfere with the processes of daily life, some sort of help should be sought. The use of Narrative Therapy endeavors to discover and focus upon positive areas that may have been overshadowed by the problem in an attempt to come up with a more functional story. The therapist and the client, working together as equal partners in the journey, build an Alternative Story. The client determines the direction the therapy will take and eventually is the one to decide upon a more preferable interpretation of their life story.[1]

When someone important in a person's life dies, grief is a natural reaction. The normal symptoms of grief may include excessive crying, vivid dreams, not recognizing the loved one as truly deceased, self blame, anger, ruminating about the deceased, and depression.[2] The grief journey is unique to each person in symptoms and duration, but at some point the intensity of the symptoms begins to weaken and the person is able to come to terms with their loss and move on with their life. Should these symptoms not dissipate within a reasonable amount of time (Schwartz says most religions determine this to be one year) and cripple the person's ability to function, complicated grief should be suspected and psychotherapy is recommended.

Therapists in a variety of ways have referred to complicated grief as abnormal grief, pathological grief, exaggerated grief, unresolved grief,

1. Morgan, *What is Narrative Therapy?* 4.
2. Schwartz, *Complicated Grief.*

chronic grief, or delayed grief. The symptoms of complicated grief at first mimic those of "normal" grief but then do not follow the usual healing pattern.[3] In the case of complicated grief, the symptoms do not gradually disappear and may even become worse. The griever becomes "stuck" and is not able to proceed with the grieving process. The symptoms dominate every aspect of one's life. These symptoms are also frequently mistaken as symptoms of severe depression. This condition has only recently been recognized by health professionals as separate from normal grief or depression and is now referred to as Complicated Grief or Prolonged Grief Disorder.[4] They have compiled detailed criteria to be used by grief and bereavement specialists known as the *Consensus Criteria for Prolonged Grief Disorder*. If one suffers from three or more symptoms of separation distress, five of the nine cognitive, emotional and behavioral symptoms, and has felt this way for six months or more, one may be suffering from Prolonged Grief and should seek help.[5]

According to The Mayo Clinic the following are signs and symptoms of complicated grief: Extreme focus on the loss and reminders of the loved one, intense longing or pining for the deceased, problems accepting the death, numbness or detachment, preoccupation with sorrow, bitterness about the loss, inability to enjoy life, depression or deep sadness, difficulty moving on with life, trouble carrying out normal routines, withdrawing from social activities, feeling that life holds no meaning or purpose, irritability or agitation, and lack of trust in others.[6]

Many factors in a person's life and/or those surrounding the death can lead to complicated grief. Although there is no specific cause, the interaction of heredity, personality, and the environment have a direct relationship upon the propensity to suffer from complicated grief.[7] There are many risk factors that may indicate the likelihood of developing complicated grief. The Mayo Clinic lists the followings circumstances:

- An unexpected or violent death

- Suicide of a loved one

- Lack of a support system or friendships

- Traumatic childhood experiences, such as abuse or neglect

---

3. Ibid.

4. Grief-Healing-Support.com, *Complicated Grief/Prolonged Grief Disorder.*

5. Ibid.

6. Mayo Clinic, *Complicated Grief.*

7. Ibid.

- Childhood separation anxiety
- Close or dependent relationship to the deceased person
- Being unprepared for the death
- In the case of a child's death, the number of remaining children
- Lack of resilience or adaptability to life change (www.mayoclinic. com)

Allen Schwartz listed the following as other factors involved:

- People who tend to be depressed have a greater vulnerability to complicated grief.

- Parental loss of a child is always deeply traumatizing, leaving the family in a state of shock and in which parents are vulnerable to depression.

- The more complicated the relationship to the dead person was, the more difficult the mourning process. In other words, parents who were abusive, angry, intrusive and difficult can result in the surviving children having a hard time working out their feelings of loss.

- When death is violent and unexpected the surviving relatives may experience Post Traumatic Stress Disorder.[8]

Very rarely is there just one risk factor indicating the likelihood of developing symptoms of complicated grief. The death of a child is an exception to that generality. Experiencing the death of a child is considered complicated grief in and of itself, with no other symptoms or circumstances necessary. "For parents, the agony of losing a child is unparalleled. When their child dies, the parents die; a vital part of them has been severed. Parents grieve the lost child for the rest of their lives, never to be whole again. A parent's grief is forever. Only memories remain."[9] There were a myriad of other issues stemming from my experiences and the complicated grief that followed. Contained within the list prepared by the Mayo Clinic of the symptoms of complicated grief, the only ones I was not experiencing were the bitterness about the loss and irritability and agitation. In fact, I was quite the opposite of those. Any type of negative emotion was directed toward me. In regard to the risk factors listed above, the most devastating was the loss of my son unexpectedly and violently. The death of my husband two years later was also unexpected. Given their ages and their

8. Schwartz, June 23, 2010.
9. Arnold and Gemma, *A Child Dies.*

good state of health, needless to say I was unprepared for their deaths. The deaths of my stepfather and mother were not unexpected but occurred within six weeks and four months respectively after the death of my son. I also have a family history of depression. Needless to say I fit the description of someone suffering from Complicated Grief.

As with most therapies, the client relating the reasons begins the process for which they are seeking help. What separates Narrative Therapy from traditional therapy is the role of the therapist. The therapist is not the expert; the client is.[10] The client knows more about what their life experiences have been, how they feel, what they are thinking and what actions they have taken in which circumstances. The therapist works alongside the client in an effort to come up with a better way of looking at and handling their problem. There is no diagnosis or problem solving on the part of the therapist. Instead, there is a new way of looking at oneself through the development of a new storyline. Burrell Dinkins describes his view of the client-therapist relationship as more akin to friends having a conversation.[11] All parties to the conversation are on equal footing. The therapist leaves behind his overt technical training and enters into the other person's story, providing support, and working as a co-narrator.

The first step in the use of Narrative Therapy is the client's description of the problem. This is known as Internalized Conversation and is described as "a way of speaking that locates a problem of issues firmly in the personality of the person suffering under them."[12] Such conversation can be identified by "I" statements such as "I am sad," "I'm depressed," "I can't read well." They may feel or have been told they have acted improperly, that something is wrong with them, or they have been labeled or diagnosed as "having something." The internalized story I presented is known as a *thin description*. Others or ourselves ascribe meaning to events we've encountered that lead to what has become a problem. We come to identify or be identified as that problem. Subsequent events supporting this perception of who we are tend to be the only ones retained. Events that do not support it are cast aside. This leaves no room for any other interpretations. Without the addition of all the other parts of our life, this narrow view becomes a thin description of who we are.[13] My thin description was that I had done something wrong resulting in my being punished

10. Morgan, *What is Narrative Therapy?* 2.

11. Dinkins, *Narrative Pastoral Counseling.*

12. Monk et al., *Narrative Therapy in Practice*, 164–66.

13. Morgan, *What is Narrative Therapy?* 12.

by God. When my son was killed, I looked at it through the lens of what God was trying to teach me. When my stepfather died six weeks later and my mother within three months after that, then my husband two years later, I again felt somehow these deaths were my fault. What was I being so thickheaded about that this had to keep happening? How many more times was this going to happen before I finally corrected whatever it was God was punishing me for? What was wrong with me?

When presented with more than one problem the therapist and client must discern if they would like to attempt to deal with them all at the same time since they are inter-related. Given the number of issues I was dealing with, unless the therapist could provide compelling evidence to the contrary, I chose to tackle each incident separately beginning with the death of my son. His death and the circumstances surrounding it were by far the most distressing. If I could move on from that, everything else appeared easy.

Once the Internalized Story has been presented, instead of simply listening to what the person feels is wrong with them; the therapist listens for a common theme or repetitive thought. This leads to the naming of the problem and the Externalized Conversation. Since I felt all of these deaths had been my fault this would indicate feelings of guilt. Even if I hadn't actually used the word guilt, it was a common theme in the story I had related. Once the therapist picked up on the theme, he or she would ask the client to try to come up with a name describing these feelings. "Guilt" was definitely a proper name to give my problem. At this point, the process of Externalization has begun. It is where the therapist begins to separate the person from the problem. Morgan says Externalization is the foundation to most Narrative Conversations. She explains that the person and the problem need to be separated into two different entities. The person is the person and the problem is the problem.[14] It is accomplished by a shift in the use of language by referring to it not as a part of the person as in the "I am" statements but to changing its status to being that of an independent entity. This can be accomplished by simply placing "the" in front of the feeling or changing an adjective or a verb into a noun. She cautions however that this cannot simply be a learned technique or skill but must be "an attitude and orientation in conversations." To the client, the problem presented is a part of their identity. The therapist's role is to show them they have an identity outside of the problem. The problem does not define who you are. It has an influence over your life but it does not define

14. Ibid., 17.

who you are. Attaching the name to the problem gives it an identity of its own. As such, the client can begin to assert control over the problem. I was not the guilty person; I was a person plagued by "guilt." I would not be in a battle with myself but with something else.

In order to better understand the nature of the issue at hand, the Externalizing Conversation is expanded to investigate the history or story of the problem. The conversation can focus on tracing the person's history with the problem.[15] In my case, the history was fairly recent. I had suffered the deaths of several close family members in a short period of time and had suffered severe trauma by what I had witnessed. As stated before, the absolute worst of these experiences was with my son's accident. My reaction to these experiences left me barely able to function.

Given the relatively short history of the problem, we would begin to unravel perceptions concerning areas such as the beliefs and expectations of myself, my family, and my culture in order to discover why I reacted the way I did and why I felt these events were my fault. This is the process of Deconstruction. The personal beliefs and expectations could have been a process set in motion before I was even born. Wimberly uses the concept of personal myths as one way of tracing a problem's history. He defines a myth as being made up of "the convictions and beliefs that we hold about ourselves."[16]

These myths are the groundwork for how we feel about ourselves, how we relate to others, and how we behave in general. They have their origins in our childhood experiences. There are specific personal themes including early memories, whether or not we feel welcomed and wanted, our birth order in relationship to other siblings, gender, name and nickname, peer and sibling relationships, roles we played (or still play) in family of origin, parental discipline in family of origin and in school, how our parents related to each other, and the stories with which we identify.[17]

A personality trait that consistently appears in any type of testing or assessment about me is that of perfectionism. This is a myth Wimberly specifically addresses and feels that all other myths are connected to. He feels that perfectionists actually feel they are unacceptable. We seek to please others perfectly in order to win favor or love. A myth that grows out of the myth of perfectionism that I identify with is that of the loner.[18]

15. Ibid., 33.
16. Wimberly, *Recalling Our Own Stories*, 4.
17. Ibid., 92–95.
18. Ibid., 21.

It is characterized by distrusting the world. You want closeness but are afraid of intimacy. Privacy is coveted and, therefore, there is a desire to work alone. Avoiding close relationships stems from believing we are imperfect and helps us deal with the sense of imperfection. We receive our self-worth through our perfectionism and therefore cannot afford to have a close relationship impede that goal. The myth of sole responsibility is due to taking on adult responsibilities at an early age.

My parents were older than normal to be having a baby as set by the standards reflective of our socio-economic status. My siblings were ten and seven years older than I was. Given the atmosphere of our home, I was expected to act much older than my chronological age. When I did act age appropriately, I was scolded by my parents and ridiculed by my brother. No matter what I did, I could not perform at the level they expected of me. My sister was the only one who embraced me as a child. As such, I strove to reach perfection in order to gain their approval. I was distraught if I didn't make straight 'A's.' While in the third grade, I received a 'C' in Social Studies one marking period. I remember being admonished for this and told that a C was totally unacceptable. It did not matter I had gotten 'A's' in everything else. In the seventh grade I received an end of the year award in all of my classes. In my mind this wasn't good enough. I should have worked harder to receive the top award in at least one of my classes. When I played softball in high school, my coach pointed out whenever I made a mistake and I immediately looked at my father. In early adulthood I could not bear to admit I'd made a mistake. I would attempt to either out-argue or twist the story to prove I hadn't made a mistake. Once married, these myths influenced my perception of what a family, a wife, and mother should be. I tried to mold my husband and children to fit my image of a perfect marriage and a perfect family. If it was not perfect, it was my fault and my responsibility to "fix" it.

Focusing mainly on my son's death, as a mother, there is a natural instinct to protect one's children. I could not protect him nor ease his suffering. I could not fulfill my role as a mother. A mother is to teach her children how to behave. Had I been a better mother he would not have decided to be speeding. He also would not have endangered the lives of his friends. I was the "strong one," the "glue that holds them all together." I felt as though I failed my family because I just couldn't handle my responsibility to them. Our society is one of individualism; I should have been able to handle this on my own. Society also expects a quick rebound. I was given three days off from work. This is the typical amount of time allotted for bereavement. As more was uncovered about the history of the problem I was experiencing, new characteristics came to light. It became apparent that a new problem had emerged. My "guilt" was being fueled by my need for perfectionism. I was supposed to be able to take care of everything for everyone in every circumstance. It was time to Re-name my Problem "wonder woman."

Another form of mythologies is biblical mythologies. These occur when there is a Bible story, verse, or character you relate strongly to. The first instance of this was when my son was killed. I related to the story of David.[19] He had lost a son and went through the grieving process. The difference in this case was that his son had been ill and he had been fore-warned of his death. He grieved before his son died. I found this story to be very condemning. David had taken the wife of another man, had him killed so he could marry her and this child was the result of their union. I had never done anything close to what David had done and I had lost my son, too. Why was I punished in the same manner? Once I had suffered the four deaths and several other major life stressors, I related to the story of Job. I could take some solace in that he lost many more family members than I had and suffered from severe physical ailments that I did not. The fact that his family and possessions were restored to an even greater state did not comfort me. I wanted my original family members back. The premise of the story also caused me great disappointment in God. Why did God feel he had to prove himself to Satan by wagering a bet with Job at the center of that bet?

During the Deconstruction of my story, my Dominant Story emerged along with probable influences from my past determining why I had formed that story. My story was—had I been a better mother and stronger person the events would not have happened and I would not be crumbling. I had let everyone down. Examining the development of my belief systems would help the therapist achieve the goal of guiding the client to expand upon her story; to give more details, more insight as to how and why she thinks and acts as she does; to thicken her story. The movement from the *thin description to the thick description* exposes discourses in the story; those thoughts that help form our ideas of how we feel we should act or react to situations or how we feel we are expected to act or react. Morgan states that this movement toward the thick description is accomplished by what she refers to as developing a "rich" description of the clients' life. The therapist must find a way to encourage her client to

19. Second Samuel 12:14–31.

reveal the details of her life.[20] The therapist is looking for inconsistencies in these discourses such as times the client did not react in the same manner. They are also looking for gaps of time unaccounted for which may indicate other experiences that do not support these ideas or beliefs. These events may not have been mentioned simply because the client did not consider them important. An abrupt change in the direction of the story may indicate areas of pain the client may not want to discuss. When there is an inconsistency, gap, abrupt change, or any other indication of a weakness in the Dominant Story, however minor it may seem, the therapist should explore it extensively. This in-depth exploration is an attempt to develop a "Landscape of Action" accomplished by what Morgan refers to as discovering "an event, thought, belief, idea, dream or hope that does not fit with the Dominant Story."[21] The therapist needs to ask the proper questions to elicit as many details as possible. I was focusing on everything I could think of that I had done to indicate I was a bad mother and responsible for the accident. The therapist would inquire more about my comment that I could not protect my son. We would focus on how it was unreasonable to expect a mother to be able to protect her child no matter what age and no matter what circumstances. My reference to "his decision" to speed would be investigated. It would point out that the accident was a result of his decision and not the result of anything I had failed to teach him. Of course, I had taught him not to take chances and explained what the outcome of those decisions might be. The therapist would grasp that and try to point out it was his decision that caused the accident, not my being a bad mother.

The insights gleaned through the Landscape of Action leads to the discovery of a Unique Outcome. This is an incident wherein the person did not follow the actions the Dominant Story would have dictated. It is preferable to discover as many of these Unique Outcomes as possible.[22] Each one is indicative of the Landscape of Identity, which helps with how to interpret the areas the Landscape of Action has highlighted. The Landscape of Identity supports the concept of the Unique Outcome. Situations describing how hard I had tried to protect him, sometimes with success, sometimes with failure, would indicate I was not a bad mother. I did my best to be a good mother and some things are just out of my hands. Had we gone the route of my deficiency in teaching him properly, we would

20. Morgan, *What is Narrative Therapy?* 15.

21. Ibid., 60.

22. Monk, et al., *Narrative Therapy*, 108–9.

have highlighted the things I had taught him, how he had listened to them and how he benefitted from them. Those would be contrasted to the times he did not listen and the consequences he incurred. I had taught him well, but had no control over whether he would heed my words. Even though it is usually only the bad decisions you hear about due to the repercussions, there have been instances where his choices made me proud of him (and quite relieved!). As an example, when he was on the high school baseball team, one of his teammates egos had turned the other players against him. At Kevin's funeral this young man was exceptionally upset. He said that when everyone else hated him, Kevin was the only one who would talk to him. There was also the incident when some of the boys in his class, as a senior prank, decided to carry an outhouse into the high school lobby. Thankfully and wisely, he had chosen not to participate. These are specific instances, but I think it was the feedback from his friends, their parents, his teachers, coaches, and employers about what a great kid he was that made the biggest impact upon me. The absolutely most comforting decision he ever made, and which is the one I cling to the most, occurred when upon returning from a Youth Rally he told me he had accepted Jesus Christ as his Lord and Savior.

Using these Unique Outcomes leads to the ability to Re-author or Re-story an Alternative to the Dominant Story. Working together, the therapist and I would have endeavored to discover and solidify a different view of my life story. It is still the story of my life but it is a more complete story. It is not focused on the instances that upheld the Dominant Story but also reintroduced many other facets of my personal identity, strengths, talents and abilities that had become hidden underneath the Dominant Story. The influence of the problem is diminished and new possibilities, ones the client would like to live, are brought to the surface. It would have been up to me to decide who I want to have in my life, who I don't want in my life, and what relationships I would like to change. I also would have chosen people, dead or alive, who I feel would be or would have been supportive of my new story; who could give credence to the possibility of my success.

I agree with Wimberly when he says, "The goal of Re-authoring personal myths is to revise the story that runs through our personal behavior, to heal wounds and transform them into sources of strength in service to others."[23] I continue to make strides in my grief journey, but when I look back on the memories of him I would like to smile and not tear up all

23. Wimberly, *Recalling Our Own*, 80.

the time. I am hopeful that some day I will have the peace of not having to worry about when the next time of grief will ambush me. I want to continue my journey into the future without the fear that at any moment grief will win and my goals will end. I am hanging on to hope, which gives me the energy to face a new day.

8

The Promise was a Marriage Full of Life, But Ours Died at His Hands

Spousal Abuse

KRIS ANDREWS BONDARENKO

NARRATIVE APPROACH TO HEALING FROM DOMESTIC VIOLENCE

Domestic violence is all too common and, though an under reported crime, it is still considered a leading cause of injury to women. Research indicates that domestic violence is responsible for the harm of women between the ages of fifteen and forty-four in the United States, more than car accidents, muggings, and rapes combined.[1] That is a staggering statistic. Even more staggering, is the reality Al Miles points out—that this phenomenon exists in Christian and non-Christian homes alike. In fact, Christian doctrine, Scripture, and church tradition are often used to perpetuate this abuse against women—not only by batterers, but by church leaders and congregants as well.[2]

Lundy Bancroft, a leading expert in the field, defines domestic violence as "a pattern of coercive control that may be primarily made up of psychological abuse, sexual coercion, or economic abuse, that is

1. Committee on the Judiciary. "Violence Against Women, 3.

2. Miles, *Violence in Families*, 52.

punctuated by one or more acts of frightening physical violence, credible threat of physical harm, or sexual assault."[3] This is a comprehensive definition because it does not simply focus on the violence alone. In fact, Bancroft continues by saying, "It is common for batterers to be highly physically frightening and psychologically cruel with few incidents of actual physical assault. In fact, these are the majority of abusers."[4] This is an important point to be made because there is a tendency to only consider the acts of physical violence as "abuse" when it is only one example of the many types of abuse a victim may endure at the hands of her abuser.

A client may share her meta-story of life in an abusive Christian marriage. However, there is one story in particular that still causes her some problems and she is seeking counsel for healing from its effects on her life. The concepts of Narrative Therapy will now be explored in detail and a counseling dialogue will be provided of the narrative process.

Client's Story

After becoming a Christian at age sixteen I was looking forward to one day raising a family of my own and raising my children with godly, Christian values. I felt called to ministry right away and, therefore, knew I would only marry a man who was also committed to full time ministry. I attended a Bible College, majoring in Missions, and spent a year teaching English overseas. While there I met a young man who was a pastor of my mission board's church plant. After returning to the states my fiancé joined me and we were married. We moved to Kentucky so he could attend Asbury Seminary and pursue a Masters of Divinity degree and we could later return to his home country to serve in ministry together.

However, the marriage was very difficult and involved aggression, verbal abuse, and the use of fear and intimidation including punctuated incidents of violence over the years. My final straw came the night my ex-husband flew into a rage and picked up our five-year-old son, swinging him in the air by one arm, screaming at him, hitting him, then holding him above his head and hurling him into his bed (which, at that time, was simply a mattress that sat on the floor), reaching to pick him up again, still screaming— holding him over his head and hurling him down a second time. My son was in the fetal position—sobbing, trembling, bright red, sweating, and terrified. I was yelling for my husband to put him down and

3. Bancroft, *Improving Court Response*, 2009.
4. Ibid.

chasing him during the entire incident. I never felt so helpless; I didn't know how far he'd go. I finally reached my son, scooped him up in my arms and cradled him, warning my husband to 'get away from us.' He stood back in the hallway panting because he had exerted himself physically and needed to catch his breath.

I tenderly held my trembling, whimpering son in my lap, rocking him, resigned to letting the tears fall from my eyes. I remember feeling tears of my own stream down my face. My husband said, "Oh, come on— it's not that bad." I did not respond. I had no words. I simply cried . . . quietly. In those moments, I willingly surrendered to my reality: Christian or not, minister or not, my husband was abusive. And, abuse is abuse.

Up until that point I had comforted myself by choosing to believe he would never hurt our children. So, when he did, and despite our years of counseling and making every effort to make changes, I lost every bit of faith that things would ever improve. From that day on, I knew the only way I could live with myself in integrity was knowing I had a 100 percent guarantee that something like that would never, *ever* happen again. I no longer believed his apologies. His professions of "repentance" and pleas for forgiveness no longer moved me. My quiet streaming tears represented the heartbreak I felt as I wholeheartedly accepted the realization that my marriage was over. It had to be. I knew I could never again live through another one of his rage episodes, or put my children at risk.

I have been divorced for six years and never once regretted leaving the marriage. However, this memory still haunts me more than any others. As time has progressed, it has gotten better, but there is still some pain in my heart when I remember it. It is my responsibility to protect my children from harm. And the fact that I could not protect my son in his own home, from his own father, made me angry and very sad. The fact that I felt my son *needed* protecting from his father made me angry and very sad. I could not believe I had created this kind of family for my children. I wanted better for them, and somehow . . . *somehow* I had given them worse.

Narrative Approach Defined

Narrative Therapy began in the late 1980s and was introduced by Michael White and David Epston. French postmodern philosophers, existentialism and relativism heavily influence their theory. The philosophical underpinnings of this therapy include a strong emphasis on the individual's experience and the power of language. The founders of this theory believe if one can control language, one can control how reality and truth are defined.[5] Therefore, the Narrative approach is very sensitive to and aware of the use of language throughout the counseling process.

Narrative Therapy uses the word "narrative" to describe the extensive use of stories and their effects on the lives of the client. It is human nature to tell oneself a story about a particular experience. Individuals tell themselves good and bad stories, and each of these stories enable clients to interpret themselves, their families, and their cultures through the experiences they have and the meanings they attach to them.[6]

The main goal for this type of therapy is to establish a therapeutic alliance, maintaining that the client is the expert of her own life and help her use her stories to "explore and re-vision her past and reconnect with her social and cultural resources while focusing on addressing current interpersonal problems, personal decisions, and plans and hopes for the future."[7] In this way the client feels empowered and satisfied knowing she is capable of making and maintaining the necessary changes in her life. The process of change begins by learning where the client currently is and the story she is using.

INTERNALIZED CONVERSATIONS

According to Narrative Therapy in Practice, *Internalizing Statements* "locate whatever problem the person has been experiencing deep in some unchanging aspect of the individual's nature and therefore make it hard to change." By internalizing, an individual cannot see the external social constructs that "promote, sustain, and nurture" the life of the problem.[8] Many clients use the phrase "I am . . ." when describing their problem with Internalized Conversation. Their actions are defined in relation to the person and they seek the opinions of outside help (i.e., a counselor) to explain their behaviors.

Internalizing Conversations lead the client to describe the problem inwardly, speak about the problem as it is a part of them or within them, and often leads to negative effects in their lives that result in thin

---

5. Yarhouse and Sells, *Family Therapies*, 266.

6. Ibid., 265.

7. Matima, *Narrative Therapy*.

8. Monk et al. *Narrative Therapy*, 164.

conclusions.[9] A client who internalizes a problem sees himself or herself as different or abnormal because they view themselves as an individual with a deficiency as opposed to an externalized viewpoint that sees the problem as a separate issue from the client. When using Internalizing Conversations, it is difficult for the client to separate himself or herself from the issue. The client is likely to view the opinions of the counselor as the expert opinion because they have associated the problem as a part of his or her identity. Internalizing Conversations can make an individual feel weak or sick and unable to access any personal power to make meaningful changes and lived a preferred life.[10]

In terms of domestic violence, research indicates that women and men differ in how they narrate, or tell the story of, what happened during the violent episodes. Women tend to focus on the consequences of the violence such as fear, feelings of helplessness, and any injuries that were sustained. Men describe the motive for using the violence citing examples of wanting to end a verbal argument or prove a point. It has also been theorized that masculine and feminine identity issues are being communicated through the narration of these events.[11]

The following are examples of statements of my internalized dialog.

"I am a failure because I should have been able to stop it."
"I'm a bad mother because I couldn't prevent it or stop it."
"I let harm come to my children, particularly my son."
"I let his father hurt him."
"I am afraid I will let their father hurt one of them again, particularly my son."
"I am often afraid I will let someone hurt my children, particularly my son."
"I have failed in my job to protect my children."
"I doubt I'm a good Christian since I couldn't prevent it."
"If I were a better wife, I would have kept my son safe."
"I feel it's my fault because I chose to marry him."
"I married the wrong person."

9. Morgan, *What is Narrative Therapy?* 17–18.

10. Monk, et al., 191

11. Boonzaier and Rey, " Woman Abuse" 443–63.

"I am afraid to commit to another man, because he may be harmful to me or my children."

"I am afraid I may choose another violent partner."

"If another man hurt my children, particularly my son, I couldn't handle it."

NAMING AND EXTERNALIZING THE PROBLEM

Externalizing is the practice of separating the problem a client faces from the clients themselves. This practice allows the client to distinguish between their identity and the identity of the problem. Morgan emphasizes the importance of language and question formation to initiating Externalization. Through careful listening, the therapist is "hoping to hear a word or phrase that describes what might be getting in the way of the person's life."[12] It becomes the therapist's responsibility to use words and phrases that help to position the problem outside of the client's personality.

In addition, Monk stresses the importance of the therapist focusing on the themes that are central to the clients concerns, and not simply focusing on externalizing the first problems presented in the early accounts of the problem-story. As the client moves through his or her problem narrative, so must the process of Externalizing.[13]

One way the therapist goes about initiating the practice of Externalization is through Naming the Problem. The last thing the therapist wants to do is impose a name for the problem on the client, so it is necessary for the therapist to move the client from Internalizing language to Externalizing questions so that the client can Name the Problem for him or herself. By Externalizing the Problem, new opportunities are created to examine and interact with the problem without the client feeling paralyzed by fear and self-blame.[14] This technique helps to personify the problem and give it an identity, and by doing so, the therapist, client, and perhaps the client's family can strategically work together in collaboration against a common enemy.[15]

Narrative Therapy values externalizing language because it enables the individual to separate him or herself from the problem and make it

---

12. Morgan, 18.

13. Monk et al., 100.

14. Ibid., 99.

15. Ibid., 101.

a more tangible construct to examine and create strategies for change.[16] Otherwise, the individual sees him or herself as the one with the problem and, therefore, does not believe living free from the problem is possible.

Client and Counselor Dialogue on Externalization

Client: It's so interesting to me that out of all the bad memories I have from my marriage—this one sticks out the most.

Therapist: Okay. So, what is it about this memory that makes it different from the others?

C: My son getting hurt.

T: That sounds like it was a very difficult experience for you?

C: Yes, the worst.

T: How often do you remember it?

C: Not as often anymore.

T: When was the last time?

C: Well, I notice it comes up for sure whenever my son expresses some concern to me about his visitation with his father.

T: What do you experience when that happens?

C: Oh, I experience a whole range of emotions! It's gotten better over the years, but it is still way more problematic for me than I would like.

T: What are some of the feelings?

C: Fear. Anxiety. Guilt. I feel fear because I am concerned his father may escalate again and hurt him and I won't be there to step in this time.

T: Okay, that makes sense. What does the anxiety do?

C: It makes me worry about what may or may not happen. I worry if I should even worry! I don't want to make things any worse by my son picking up on my anxieties. If I worry, and it complicates things for him, I feel I'm not being a good mother—I'm not protecting him, shielding him from all this. If I don't worry and something happens again, I failed him because I didn't anticipate him being harmed.

T: It seems this anxiety is causing you to feel like you may be failing your son? That you're not a good mother? Is that correct?

C: Yes. Well, I know I'm a good mother. But, I feel this is one area I've failed him. I feel so guilty that it happened to him in the first place. Guilty that he even has a father that he is afraid of. He's a kid. His parents should protect him.

16. Ibid., 191.

T: So, if we had to give this problem you're experiencing a name, what would you call it?

C: Hhmm, a name. I think I would call it "failing my son."

T: Okay, so tell me more about how "the failing your son" makes you feel?

C: Well, I feel that failing my son is not an option so, maybe I feel like I'm a bad person because I did? I dunno, I'm not sure. And, that maybe I have to work doubly hard now and in the future so that it never happens again.

T: So, the feeling of "failing your son" tells you you're a bad person and that you have to work really, really hard to make sure it never happens again? Is that correct?

C: Yes. That is correct.

T: What else does the feeling of "failing your son" tell you?

C: You know, I think it also tells me not to trust others, especially other men, and to always be cautious.

THE STORY UNFOLDS

Context is very important in understanding the fullness of any story. This is especially true in Narrative Counseling. Scaffolding is the term used to describe the method of tracing the history of the problem, including finding its origin and learning about its progression in the life of the client.[17] During this phase, the therapist will work to unpack the ways the symptoms have affected the client in terms of relationships, beliefs, and views of him or herself.[18]

Former victims of domestic violence commonly experience feelings of guilt. These guilty feelings center on variations of the theme of not leaving the abusive relationship sooner. This is especially true if the woman has children and the children are having problems related to being exposed to domestic violence.[19]

---

17. Ibid., 133.

18. Yarhouse and Sells, 275.

19. Kubany and Ralston, *Treating PTSD*, 161.

Client and Counselor Dialogue on Scaffolding

Therapist: Okay, so far we know that the feeling of "failing your son" tells you you're a bad person and that you have to work really, really hard to make sure it never happens again. It tells you not to trust others, especially other men, and to always be cautious?

Client: Yes.

T: That's a lot. It sounds to me like that can be exhausting.

C: It can be, yes. I think that trusting other men effects me when I'm dating, but not in other areas of my life. But, feeling hyper vigilant of my son's well being is still with me in general, and especially in regards to his relationship with his father.

T: What about it telling you you're a bad person?

C: Well, I'm not so aware of that one, I guess. I don't really think of myself as a bad person in my everyday life . . . just when I think back on my marriage and it leading to that event with my son.

T: How long do you think you've been experiencing all of these symptoms?

C: Oh, for the past six years. It happened in March 2005. The first couple of years were really bad. I had trouble sleeping. I would startle awake at night thinking someone was trying to break into my home to hurt my children. The first six months or so I had to have a half a glass of wine before bed to fall asleep. I just couldn't believe that I let that happen to my son. I know I didn't do it to him, but somehow, I just feel like I should have known it would lead to that one day.

T: So, by not being able to foresee your ex-husband's actions, you failed your son?

C: Yes.

T: Okay, let's talk more about your symptoms. On a scale of one through ten, one being the best and ten being the worst, how much is the feeling of "failing your son" affecting your life?

C: I would say a six. It used to be a ten.

DECONSTRUCTION

Deconstruction is the process of challenging assumptions that contribute to the formation of the original problem story. Cultural pressures are involved and an unwritten code of conduct is present for most forms of identification to which a client ascribes, including gender, sexual orientation, familial role, religious faith, culture, ethnicity, etc.[20] The process of Deconstruction enables a discourse to open up between counselor and client and sometimes for the first time, the client becomes aware of the influence these constructs have had on one's identity and actions. This is also the critical part in the Narrative process where the counselor will help the client find exceptions to their problem story.[21]

A significant part of the domestic violence research community considers cultural and religious norms and their definitions of masculine and feminine identities to be a strong contributing factor to power-based violence. As cited in Boonzaier and de la Rey's article, O'Neill found that "the beliefs and values surrounding masculinity, femininity, the family, and violence within the culture are seen to shape and constitute the problem of woman abuse." For example, many women who have survived abusive relationships feel they stayed too long and it has been argued that one of the reasons is related to "her positioning within traditional constructions of femininity as patient, selfless, and long-suffering."[22]

Client and Counselor Dialogue on Deconstruction

Therapist: Okay, so what are some things that made it go from a 10 to a 6?

Client: Well, in some ways, I think time helped—getting some space between the event and my present life.

T: Okay, so time . . . what else?

C: Oh my . . . I've done a lot of internal work, I think. I've separated out some of my stuff from my ex-husband's stuff. I've done a lot of reading on forgiveness of self. I've talked about the event a lot and processed it with different people in my life. I started a support group for single moms who have come out of abuse. I've acknowledged myself for leaving the relationship. I think that was a good thing. To be honest, for a long time I was really scared to be a single parent. But, after that happened, I didn't really care what was on the other side of that fear, because now I was too afraid to stay. I decided to face my fear and forge ahead.

T: So, I'm hearing you say that some of the things that have helped you get relief from the feeling of "failing your son" are facing your fear to leave the

20. Monk et al., 47.

21. Ibid., 95.

22. Boonzaier and Rey, 454.

abusive relationship, finding resources on your issues with forgiveness, and starting your own support group.

C: *Yes. All of those things have helped.*

T: *Have you always had those skills and abilities—facing your fears, being resourceful, bringing people together, and offering support?*

C: *Mmm, yeah. I guess so.*

T: *What are some other examples you might be able to tell me about?*

C: *Well, I wouldn't leave my marriage until I turned over every rock. We went to three marriage counselors in five years. I sought out help from pastors, older Christian couples, prayer warriors, and our mission board. I read books, I searched the Internet, and I insisted he see a medical doctor so he was prescribed some antidepressants.*

T: *Wow, that's a lot. You have a lot of perseverance.*

C: *(laughs) Oh, yeah. I've always had that!*

T: *Do you think your son benefits from some of these qualities you have?*

C: *I do.*

T: *Okay, in what ways?*

C: *Well, I've been really resourceful with finding ways to support him through finding a play therapist for him after the divorce. He was really angry and really frightened by the incident and then the sudden absence of his father. Plus, I'm sure he picked up on my anxieties. It was a lot for him.*

T: *I'm sure it was. But, you found a way for him to process it and get better.*

C: *Well, yes, better. But, there are still some residual effects.*

T: *Okay, how else has your son benefitted from these skills and abilities we just mentioned?*

C: *I feel like I've given my son a voice when it comes to his father. Soon after our divorce his dad remarried and my son's anxieties went through the roof because he said they were arguing a lot and he thought someone might get hurt. I negotiated with his father for my son's visitation to be reduced.*

T: *His dad agreed?*

C: *Yes, he agreed.*

T: *So, you've made a huge difference for him there.*

C: *Yes, I believe so.*

T: *Is that the first time you've advocated on his behalf?*

C: *No, I've always done it.*

T: *Okay, tell me about a few other times.*

C: *Well, during my marriage I felt I was always watching his father's interactions with him like a hawk. He was so easily irritated with the children and I felt he had unrealistic expectations of them for their age and developmental stage.*

T: *So, from the time he was born you were protecting him.*

C: *Absolutely.*

T: *It seems to me that you were a very good mother all along. Is it possible your husband made a very bad choice that night and hurt your son and you could still be a good mother?*

C: *Hhmm, I guess I've never thought of putting those two things together like that. Yes, of course it's possible. I guess I just felt if I was a better mother, or maybe a different sort of person, I never would have married him in the first place.*

T: *So, you feel you should have been able to predict this behavior before the marriage?*

C: *Looking back now, I can see there were signs. He had a quick temper, he didn't like any of my family or friends, and he would indirectly belittle my thoughts or theology.*

T: *But, you didn't see any signs of violence?*

C: *No, none. Verbal aggression, maybe.*

T: *Is it possible he was trying to hide his volatile nature from you and you were a good person who unknowingly married a violent man?*

C: *It was absolutely unknowingly!*

T: *So, it seems to me that it's hard to hold someone accountable or responsible for something they simply didn't know. What do you think?*

C: *Yeah, I guess I can see your point.*

REAUTHORING

Re-authoring is the process used in Narrative Therapy to enable clients to create a new, more empowering and supportive story for their lives. Just as individuals play an active role in creating the current problem story, they also play an active role in Re-creating or "Re-authoring" their story. Beliefs, presuppositions, and cultural assumptions can all be changed. This process guides the client in how to do this.[23] Re-authoring gains momentum

---

23. Wimberly, *Recalling Our Own Stories*, 73.

when the client gains "a stronger sense of what it is like to be positioned by the alternative, favored story rather than the problem-saturated one."[24]

Client and Counselor Dialogue on Reauthoring

T: So, despite having unknowingly married and lived with a violent man, you've been able to show tremendous courage and dignity. How did that happen?

C: Well, sometimes I do think about the courage I had . . . and still have. I dunno, I guess I have some resilience in me.

T: I agree. And, I think it's that same resilience that has enabled you to protect your son. Do you think it's possible that your ex-husband is the one who failed your son and not you? And, that you're the one who has been the constant source of protection, love, and comfort for him?

C: Well, yes, it's possible. And, I actually like that way of thinking. You know, sometimes I feel that maybe there is still this part of me who is concerned with putting to much blame on the abuser, and carrying it myself.

T: I think that's an interesting idea. So, you feel that you are carrying the blame?

C: Yes, I do.

T: Is it possible that the blame doesn't belong to you, but to the one who was abusive?

C: Yes, exactly. I'm just trying to pick up the pieces and minimize the damage. But, you're right, I didn't hurt my son. It's kinda sad when I think about it. I'm sorta doing to myself what he used to do—blame me for his actions. That's kinda wild.

T: Ok, so let me ask you this: If you woke up tomorrow morning and the feelings of "failing your son" were completely gone, how would your life look? How would it be different?

C: That is such a good question! Let me think . . . I guess the opposite of my issues. I would feel more carefree in how I shared my son with the world. I would have an easier time letting him and his father figure out their relationship together. I wouldn't worry so much! And, maybe I would have an easier time dating and letting good men into my life.

24. Monk et al., 110.

DEFINITIONAL CEREMONY

Narrative Counseling takes a very definitive stand on challenging assumptions from all sources of influence. Therefore, the influence of others is a strong consideration in two ways. The first way is in terms of the problem-story. The therapist's role is to help the client identify some of the key players who have encouraged and supported this problem in his or her life. The second way the influence of others is a strong consideration is in terms of the preferred life story or Alternate Story/Re-authored Story. The client is guided through the process of identifying an audience in his or her life who can acknowledge and support him or her in the changes being made toward the new preferred life. This audience can include the counselor, loved ones who have passed away, and the client him or herself. The Definitional Ceremony helps to cement the changes the client has been making by creating an opportunity for his or her supportive audience to witness the new story and thereby substantiating its credibility and viability in the life of the client.[25]

Client and Counselor Dialogue on Definitional Ceremony

T: *Who are the people in your life who you think will support you as the resourceful, courageous, supportive, and good mother we've talked about you being?*

C: *My mother, for sure, and a lot of my friends. Good people surround me.*

T: *That's really great to hear. I think you might benefit from writing a letter to your mother and/or a few of your friends about how you see yourself now since we've worked through some of the feelings of "failing your son."*

C: *Okay, I will do that.*

Narrative Therapy is helpful therapeutic approaches to help women who are survivors of intimate partner abuse separate their experiences of abuse from their self-identity. The guilt described here is very common for survivors, particularly when their children have been severely affected. The victim story is only one story in the meta-story of the client's life.

25. Ibid., 110.

9

I Was Told I Would Be Okay

But Had to Face the Painful Truth Alone—Abortion

LORA GREGORY[1]

THE STORY

AS A TEENAGER IN high school, I struggled to fit into my own class. I had come from a middle school situation where I had experienced some trauma from a situation with a classmate. I switched schools, but still struggled with friendships. I finally became friends with some of the class members above me and eventually became very close with one of the guys in that class. His name is Darin. He shared with me that he thought he was gay. When he shared that, we grew even closer because he became a safe guy friend. I thought I didn't need to worry about the physical stuff in a relationship because of what he had shared.

We pushed the boundaries anyway and just before my senior year in high school, I became pregnant. I didn't tell anyone because I was going to a Christian school and would have been kicked out of the school. The situation was complicated by the fact that my mom was a teacher at the school. I was worried about her reputation if anyone knew what was going on with me. I chose to have an abortion. Looking back, if I knew the emotional consequences of that choice, I never would have chosen abortion. I

---

1. Names in this chapter have been changed

have struggled for years with guilt and grief. It affects me in so many ways. I struggle in relationships, with both family and friends.

I currently have no contact with Darin. We ended our relationship and have not talked since that time. I named my daughter Paige Renata.

NARRATIVE THERAPY

Our lives are filled with stories. Most people often tell stories throughout a typical day. Stories enrich our lives and help us to understand each other. We can gain some understanding of a person based on their stories. The goal of the counselor using Narrative Counseling is to assist the client in Re-authoring and gaining and Alternative Story, giving the client a new perspective and view of her story. "Narrative approaches to counseling invite clients to begin a journey of co-exploration in search of talents and abilities that are hidden or veiled by a life problem."[2]

Narrative Therapy begins with the client telling her story to the counselor. The story is a thin story, with little detail or understanding for the counselor. As the counselor begins to ask questions to gain understanding, the story develops and becomes a thicker story. This Mapping of the Problem gives the counselor a clearer understanding of the whole story. At this point in the process it is important for the counselor to see the problem apart from the person. This Externalization gives the ability to look at the problem from a new perspective, examining all sides and pieces to the problem. This also gives the client the understanding that they are more than just their problem.[3]

The next step in the process is to Name the Problem. "Narrative therapists will listen to the description of the person's experience, hoping to hear a word or phrase that describes what might be getting in the way of the person's life."[4] Naming is part of the Externalization process, placing the problem outside of the person.

Another important step in Narrative Counseling is Deconstruction. It is in this part of the process when we look for exceptions and begin to search for an Alternative Story. Once this story has been established and grown, it becomes the preferred story, replacing the initial Dominant Story. It is then that we begin the process of Re-storying or Re-membering. Re-membering allows the client to search through their life and find those

2. Monk, et al., *Narrative Therapy in Practice*, 3.

3. Ibid., 7–13.

4. Morgan. *What is Narrative Therapy?* 18.

people who can acknowledge their Alternative Story and support them in this. It also allows room for the client to distance himself or herself from someone who is not going to bring support. The safe environment of the counseling allows the client to explore the possible outcomes of various scenarios.[5]

The final step in the process is a Definitional Ceremony. This ceremony could look many different ways. It could be simple or complex, with many people or few. Ritual is important in Narrative Counseling and can be seen in these ceremonies.

In the following sections of this chapter, I will explain using my own story how this process works. I have included several portions of my personal journals that show how a person may express the different processes in Narrative Counseling. Before taking the Narrative Counseling course, I was unaware that when I went through counseling myself, I went through the process of Narrative Counseling. Re-reading my journals through that time allowed me to see the process clearly. I hope in sharing these pieces of my own story, the overall picture of how Narrative Counseling may look are clear.

INTERNALIZED CONVERSATIONS

In my experience, I had difficulty expressing these Internal Conversations. My counselor continued to ask questions to understand the story, but I was hesitant to go there with my spoken words. She asked me to write a letter to my daughter, expressing the feeling and thoughts I had related to the abortion. As I read it today, it is clearly my Internalized Conversations coming through as I write to her. For a long time, I defined myself in terms of my bad decision, allowing it to take over my life.

Dear Paige,

My heart is breaking tonight. I miss you so much. Sometimes I don't think I can take it anymore. It just hurts so much. I want you to be here with me. You were my very first child. The day you died will forever be the day that changed my life.

That day has played over and over in my mind. Certain times of the year my mind is there more often. For several years, I have rarely gone to that day in my mind. But lately, I stay there. It's as if it's a movie playing over and over in my head. I can't seem to let it go.

---

5. Ibid., 77–80.

I keep coming back to the moment I made the decision. The moment when there was no going back. How could I make that decision? I didn't want to! All I've ever wanted to be was a mom. It doesn't make sense that I would make that decision. My life at the time, and maybe still today, was all about keeping up appearances. I wasn't allowed to say when something was wrong, so when I found out I was pregnant, I felt like I had no one to go to. I was only 18 and only a senior in high school, but I wanted you more than anything. I just didn't know how to face it. I remember trying really hard to tell a few people. I always stopped just short of telling them. Had I told even one of them, you would be here today. I wish I had had more courage. I'm sorry.

I remember sitting in that awful waiting room, the faces of the other people sitting there with me. I wonder if the other people there that day thinks about it much. I've never been able to talk about anything that happened beyond that waiting room. I'm not sure if it just makes me too sad or if it's such a personal thing I just don't want anyone "there."

Walking back to that next room was one of the most terrifying moments of my life. I wish I could say I didn't know what I was doing. I wish I could say I believed what I was doing was right. I knew. I knew it was wrong. Deep in my heart I had already started to grieve the moment I made my decision. What I didn't know was that 10 years later my heart would still be grieving. I didn't know I would still long to hold you and that I would still miss you so much. I wish I would have known. I would give anything to go back and change that decision.

Someone came in and told me about all of the risks and things that could go wrong. What they didn't tell me is that I would cry myself to sleep every night for years. Or that seeing a child that is the same age as you would be still hurts. Or that I would always feel just a little jealous when I see someone who is pregnant. Or that being around babies and children would always be a little bit rough. Or that my decision that day would so strongly impact the rest of my life. I wish they had told me.

When the doctor came in, he barely said a word. Within a few minutes, you were gone. The doctor left quickly, without a word. My mind still can't seem to grasp how quickly your life was taken. One moment you were safe inside of me. The next, your life was over. I have wondered, even worried at times, about whether you were in pain. Was that moment as quick for you as it was for me? I fear it may have seemed much longer to you. I'm sorry.

I sat in the recovery area for a long time. The physical pain was intense, but it didn't begin to touch the pain inside. I wanted to die. Sometimes, in my dark moments, I still wish I would have. Those moments following were some of the worst. I heard that I would feel some relief afterward, but that feeling never came. It was only pain after that.

On my way home, I had to pull over several times because I felt so sick. The whole time, all I could think about was how much I missed you. My heart felt so empty. When I got home, I put a blanket on the floor of my closet and curled up. I don't remember why. Only that I didn't want to lie down in my bed. I didn't sleep that night. Actually, I slept very little over the next few months. I would lie in bed and the abortion would replay over and over in my mind. When I did sleep, it was for very short amounts of time. After a month, I couldn't handle it on my own anymore. The pain of losing you was too much. I told someone about you, about the abortion.

In the years that followed I reacted often to words, sights, and sounds that reminded me of the abortion. These things were an intense reminder of losing you. I have never been able to really describe the pain I've experienced since losing you. Sadness, depression, and despair . . . these words don't begin to describe the feelings from the last ten years. Sometimes, it's all I can do to make it through the day. To say, "I miss you" doesn't begin to describe what I'm feeling. I long to see you, to hold you in my arms. I don't want to feel wounded forever, but at the same time, I don't know how to let go of you.

So here I am after ten years. Why is that number significant? I have no idea. But a decade seems like a long time. It is as if I've lost the last ten years of my life because of my decision to abort. I will never get that time back. I feel so helpless. Maybe that's the wrong word. I want you here with me and that's not possible. I want to go back and change my decision. The pain of missing you and longing for you never go away. The pain of watching those who would be your age grow and mature is a constant reminder of that emptiness in my life. The emptiness seems to grow with each passing year. I sit here. Alone. Longing for you. Desperately wanting my child but unable to be with you. The words "it's not fair" sound so childish, but sometimes I want to scream them. I know so many people who yell and get upset with their kids every time I see them. Don't they know how precious those children are? Don't they understand that there are those of us who would trade places with them anytime? Why don't they love their children? The thing is, those parents have never hurt their children as much as I have hurt you. I go back and forth between wondering when it will be my turn to be a mom and wondering if you were my chance and I gave you up.

I love you, Paige.

Mom

The Internalization going on in this was clear. The problem and thickening story comes more into focus. I was longing for my daughter. In addition to the things mentioned in the letter, I also struggled with depression, cutting, and several major destructive relationships. All of these things are typical of someone who has experienced abortion. My problem was very much in control of my life, causing me to feel depression and grief for a very long time.

Naming and Externalizing the Problem

Naming and Externalizing is a process of taking the problem and giving it a name. The counselor asks the client to Name the Problem, perhaps suggesting a word or phrase the client has spoken multiple times. Externalizing the problem is the idea of taking the problem and talking about it separate from the person. This is specifically done in conversations where the problem can be examined using language that separates the person from the problem. Naming the Problem is a step in working to Externalize the Problem. In some settings, Naming or putting a word to the Problem can be difficult. In the counseling setting, it is a safe place to name and look at what the problem is. In relationship to the family, Jordan says this, "We often don't trust ourselves with naming and speaking the truth of what we feel and think, nor do we trust others to receive our vulnerable communications with tender acceptance and loving understanding."[6] This may be true in many settings. With family and friends sometimes we are not safe enough to allow our problem to be seen. Counseling allows that problem to be examined and worked through.

In my own story, I Named my problem 'Longing.' This came from a string quartet piece I wrote. The piece was written the year after the abortion and has a very forlorn sound to it. It was written for Paige and was an expression of what I was feeling at the time. It was performed for the first time without a title. My pastor came up after the performance and said, "I'd like to suggest a title for your piece—Longing." The Name is a perfect description of both the piece and my feelings at the time.

Longing kept me from enjoying life. It interfered with my ability to concentrate and complete a task. It created issues between those around me and myself. Longing made my life miserable. I became very depressed and ended up hospitalized for a few days because of it. I continued to cut myself through much of this time, not knowing how to handle Longing.

6. Jordan, *Reclaiming Your Story*, 25.

Longing lasted a long time and often it felt as if life was never going to be good again. I had major difficulties with friendships and family relationships through this time. Longing made me very irrational and difficult to live with, causing anger and sadness it seemed like I couldn't control.

The Externalization of the Problem allows for the problem to not only be examined, but also to be changed and molded into something new. Holding the idea out that Longing is out there and not inside of me allowed me to begin to seek to change my own life.

SCAFFOLDING

Scaffolding, which is similar to tracing the history of the problem, allows the counselor to begin to see different pieces to the problem. It may reflect in the history of the problem or in seeking further explanation about a missing piece. Scaffolding brings us to a window that we might see the problem a little bit more clearly.

In my own story, there are two examples of Scaffolding. The first is in the connection to my grandfather. He was extremely important in my early life and many of his stories and actions still affect me today. I lived with him for a while during the time right after my parents separated. He helped me at three years old to stabilize after the separation. Another scaffold is the following journal excerpt written on Paige's due date, that fell on Mother's Day that year.

When I was little, my grandpa was my only hero. I absolutely loved him with my whole little kid heart. He was amazing! Everything was an adventure for Papa and everyone a friend. I have several vivid memories. First, he used to take me with him when he delivered Meals-on-Wheels. Now, he didn't just deliver the food. I remember going in, sitting down, having a glass of juice, (or whatever was offered) and watching him talk with people. He absolutely loved people. And he loved to help them. Often, they would ask him to repair something or change a light bulb or something like that. He always did it willingly. I loved those times with Papa. I love knowing that I have a little bit of that sense of wanting to help people and, no doubt, it comes from him.

Papa used to let us play in the mud and catch tadpoles. Kids need to get muddy and just have fun sometimes. I remember going back into his townhouse, covered head to toe. He told us to stay on the porch, would go turn the water on in the kitchen, and come back to scoop us up in his arms to set us on the counter. He would help us get all of the mud off, so my grandma wouldn't get upset, before gently lifting us out and to the floor. Papa was kind and loving. He loved to see us happy and enjoying life. He enjoyed life himself.

Papa was an electrician. Every Christmas he wired the Christmas tree to a foot pedal that sat underneath his chair. He would bring the grandkids in and have us do different things to get the lights to turn on and off (like clapping or blowing on the tree, etc.) We all thought it was magical. Papa was fun! He made life enjoyable everywhere he went.

At family gatherings, we don't talk a lot about Papa. I think about him often and LOVE to hear stories, but that rarely happens anymore. Today, we told "Papa stories." Now, that may seem totally insignificant, and it may be. But, every time I dream about Paige, Papa is in my dream. He is enjoying life with her in some way, reading, playing, walking, talking—each dream is a little different, but he is always in them. I have no idea what I believe those dreams are, but I know they are a comfort. I know thinking about them eases the pain just a little bit. To be reminded of Papa and Paige today was a good thing.

The second example of Scaffolding has to do with why I felt so safe with Darin. When I was in counseling, we spent much time discussing this. The background eventually came forth. When I was in middle school, I experienced some trauma from a classmate who raped me. I did not tell anyone for nearly fourteen years. Sitting in the counseling room, I was able to express what had happened when I realized this was much of the reason I felt so safe with Darin after he told me he was gay. He was a male I did not have to fear. This piece of the puzzle allowed me, and my counselor, to see why I allowed the relationship to move to places I didn't go near in other relationships. This piece of information was the Scaffolding needed to see why I made the decisions I did.

DECONSTRUCTION

Deconstruction is the chance to look closely at the problem and find out the details. Does it really affect everything? Are there any exceptions to how the problem affects you? Beginning to point out these contradictions is a way to help a client see the problem in a new way.

In my experience, my exceptions came around anniversaries or holidays. When I would feel something positive unexpectedly I almost wouldn't know how to react. There were many examples of Deconstruction, but this journal excerpt is from Christmastime of 2007 when I was going through counseling. This is an example of an exception, where I had an experience with the problem, but continued to remain happy through thinking about the problem. This exception is part of the Deconstruction process.

Something has changed in me over the last year or so. I have always had a hard time dealing with this year's 3rd grade class. From the time they were in kindergarten, I have watched them grow up and wondered what Paige would be like, as she would be in that class. I watched these kids perform last night in their Christmas program. It wasn't until the end of the program that Paige even crossed my mind. Even then, my thought about Paige was just that. . . . a thought. One. That was it. It wasn't even a sad thought, just a thought. I felt so happy afterward that I had reached another clue that I truly am beginning to heal. Sometimes I doubt this. There are so many days when the struggle is still there, but as I look back, the struggle is much less than it used to be. The pain is less, and the good stuff begins to outweigh the bad.

I guess, as I continue to heal, life just keeps on going. I'm waiting for the day when I can say, "It's done. I'm all healed." Will this day come this side of heaven? I have no idea. But I keep hoping.

Deconstruction is an opportunity to bring truth and perspective to a client's actions or viewpoint. Asking for exceptions and getting a clearer picture of the problem's effects gives insight into the problem.

Re-authoring/Re-membering/Miracle Question

In my story there are two pieces that have been a Re-membering process. The first is in Naming my daughter. For a long time, my child didn't have a name. I simply thought of her as "little one." Then someone suggested that I name her. I poured through baby name books and came to the name Paige, that means child or young one, which is perfect for her. Because I love names and their meanings, I wanted Paige to have a middle name as well. Her middle name is Renata, that means reborn. I think it is perfect, Paige Renata, child or young one, reborn.

"When you have worked for years to keep the memory of the abortion away from your heart, thinking about the baby as a real human being is amazing."[7] My daughter became a part of my Re-membering process as I named her. She became more than just a mistake; she became my daughter. Giving her a name allows me to think of her and remember her. It allows me to bring her into other parts of my life as I speak about her.

---

7. Masse and Phillips, *Her Choice to Heal*, 86.

The second piece of Re-membering in my story is related to Paige's father. We parted ways soon after I became pregnant. I struggled for many years with the loss of both Paige and Darin in such a short period of time. This letter was written when I was ready to let go of grieving my lost relationship. It speaks of both the good times and bad, expressing finality to the friendship.

Darin,

I miss you. I came across an old picture of us tonight. We were both laughing. It's a beautiful picture that brings such sweet memories! I can't tell you how often you cross my mind. I wonder how we ended up in such different places. You, with your lifestyle choices and me, with my secrets . . . we really are two big messes.

I am back in my old room. The one where we spent so many hours studying and hanging out. As wrong as that was and as horrible as the places it took us, I treasure our memories together. Do you remember our recordings? And our dances? And all of the times we asked each other "Truth or Dare" questions, but ended up leaving out the "dare" ones because they were boring? You used to sleep in the "alcove," as you called it. It was the hallway, but you liked having your own space to call your own.

I loved how you used to make me laugh. You would get going on an improv thing and just keep going and going. You loved to make me laugh.

Remember how we used to read to each other? We would pick out something funny, or serious, or touching, or whatever we could find, and read so dramatically. We would laugh and cry together.

Remember your letters to me? I wish I had kept them. They were treasures that I have since lost. You would give them to me in the morning and tell me not to open them until after school, when I could read them out loud with you listening. How crazy?! But it sure made me curious. There were so many times when all I wanted to do was see what you had written to me that day. Sometimes, there were only a few words on the page, but by the end of the day, when I had waited and waited, those few words meant more to me than anything. I loved you for that.

Remember our dances? We loved to dance. Out in the middle of nowhere. Car radio turned up. Dancing on the dirt road. What moments we had!

Do you remember hearing for the first time about our daughter? Do you remember how you broke my heart by denying it? I remember how I broke yours. I'm sorry.

When I see your face, I am reminded of Paige, not because I know what she would look like today or what she would be like, but simply because she is yours, too. Whether you choose to acknowledge it or not, whether you think about it or not, she is yours.

Honestly, I love that. I love that she is also someone else's. I love that she's not just mine. Sometimes, I forget that she's yours, too. She would probably look and act a lot like you. No doubt, you would be reflected in her looks and abilities and actions and character. No doubt, she would want to know her dad.

As I write that, I am reminded of something I've been learning recently—that she is not only mine and she is not only yours. Ultimately, she is the Lord's. As are you. As am I. I miss her desperately. I miss you as well. But I am reminded that she is held by stronger arms than mine. And when I feel like my life is falling apart and that I am going to break because I miss her so much, I realize that I am held by those same arms. Darin, I pray that you will someday know those strong arms, too. I pray that someday you will grasp the truth I know you have heard. I pray that you will understand how much God loves you, no matter what choices you are making. I'm slowly, but surely, learning about God's love. I don't understand it all. No one has shown me that idea of unconditional love, which makes it a hard concept for me to grasp. But I am trying. I hope you someday are able to begin to grasp the depth of God's love as well.

I love you, Darin.

These examples of Re-membering in my story represent the addition and subtraction of people related to the story. There were other things I did as well, such as sharing my experience with my mother and grandmother. All of these things, and more, helped me to discover my Alternate Story. I believe this story is still developing and growing. Had I been asked the Miracle Question while going through this process, I do not believe I would have had an answer. My ideal was to go back in time and change my decisions. Today, though, I look at my life and it really cannot get much better. I love my job and the activities I choose to be involved in, including many mission trips that greatly impact my life and the lives of those around me. I have created my ideal life without Paige. This Alternate Story gave me a new perspective on my problem.

DEFINITIONAL CEREMONY

The Definitional Ceremony is very important in the Narrative Counseling process. In my story, this step has happened in several different ways, at different times over the years. The first was actually asking forgiveness from the Lord. The following journal excerpt is Re-membering that time in a special way. I had gone away for the weekend because it was the anniversary of the abortion.

I left on Saturday morning for a relaxing weekend to myself. I headed about two hours south and spent the morning shopping. I intended to go to the music store but I never got there. I felt like I should go to church the next morning where I attended through some of college. Understand that this church was about four hours from where I was and in a completely different direction than I had started out! But I felt so strongly that I needed to be there for church on Sunday.

I'm going to back up a little bit. My last semester in college this church did a sermon series that really impacted me. Right around Easter they did something that I have never forgotten. There was a wooden cross up front and we were each given a piece of tile. On the back of the tile we wrote something that we were giving up to the Lord. I wrote Paige's name and the word 'abortion.' Then, everyone in the congregation went and put their tiles on the cross. That week, the cross was made into a beautiful piece of art, demonstrating how God takes the broken pieces of us and makes it into something beautiful. The mosaic cross stood in the front of the church for the next month or so, but had been taken down by the time I moved away.

When I began worshipping yesterday, I noticed the cross. It was standing up in the front of the church. I immediately teared up. That cross is such a great reminder to me that God has forgiven me. I gave that to Him over four years ago in that church. I still struggled after that and didn't really begin healing for almost two years, but I was forgiven in that place. I keep trying to pick that burden back up again. I don't want to, but the memories and struggles are still there. Looking at the cross in the front of the church reminded me that God has already taken that and I know I don't want it back.

What is really cool about this cross is that it has not been displayed in that place since I was there over four years ago. I spoke with a friend of mine there and she said it has been stored since then and was just placed back out on the stage area. I think God knew that I needed that reminder this week!

There have been other rituals and ceremonies over the years. I have written poetry, songs, and created art. I have shared with specific people and opened up my life to those who were impacted or affected by my decisions. I have even returned to those I might have hurt through the process and asked for forgiveness. I find I need time in my life to both honor my daughter and celebrate my healing. What I thought would be the final Definitional Ceremony came nearly twelve years after the abortion. I was invited to be the keynote speaker at a conference. I stood in front of five hundred people and shared my story. I spoke about the struggle to make a decision, about the struggle since that day, and about how God worked in my life and healed my heart. It was terrifying and thrilling all at the same time. It was amazing to share and allow her few weeks of life to make an impact on people. It brought the closure I needed in order to really begin to move on and live my life. I will always miss Paige, but I know now I can enjoy my life here on earth until I get to see her again in heaven.

I continue to process, growing and changing in relation to Paige. I continue to find ways in which she is a part of my life and ways to honor her. In researching for this writing, I read a book by Wendy Williams and Ann Caldwell called *Empty Arms*.[8] It gives a voice to the unborn. It tells many of the stories of the names listed at the National Memorial for the Unborn. I am considering placing a plaque there in Paige's honor. This would be yet another ritual or ceremony as I continue through life.

Final Thoughts

As I think about the journey I have taken, I am reminded of how great God is to redeem those pieces of my life and make me whole again. I love the concept of Narrative Counseling because it seems as if it a picture of what God does in our lives. He takes our problems and helps us to find an Alternate Story. It's not always an easy task, but manageable with a little bit of help. I really like how Wimberly says, "These opportunities are part of God's creation, and of God's continued presence and work in renewing our lives as well as creation itself."[9] It is a continual process.

---

8. Williams and Caldwell, *Empty Arms*.
9. Wimberly, *Recalling Our Own Stories*, 142.

10

Narrative Healing with Scripture through the Agony of Postcolonialism

Sègbégnon Mathieu Gnonhossou

Introduction

The question that Christian religious educators should ask is not whether the Bible is literally binding; rather it is how best to bring God's life-giving message to God's people in their own culture, time, and place.

—Boyung Lee

The thrust of this contribution is based on the premise that the Bible is primarily a Christian Scripture and its authority is derived from God's with context-specific healing, judging, and recreating activities evidenced among God's people and in the larger world.[1] In the Republic of Benin,[2] as in many parts of the Africa continent, most intellectual elites and indigenous religious leaders are skeptical toward Christianity and are, at times, very critical of its progress, especially due to its colonial legacy. Rather than offering abstract apologetics in response to this situation, churches can respond to the increase of psycho-emotional and socio-spiritual difficulties as an opportunity to mediate God's authority through Scripture.

---

1. Wright, *The Last Word*, 36–43.

2. A francophone West African country, The Republic Benin, is located in the Westside of the Federal Republic of Nigeria, formerly called Republic of Dahomey.

The need for public Christian responses to those problems becomes more pronounced today than ever before. Such a situation calls for an urgent review of the non-pastoral approaches to Christianity adopted by some mainline foreign mission-related churches and movements in Benin.[3] Admittedly the situation also calls for a critical look at the tendency of neglecting Scripture as a resource for healing in the African context.

However, the manner in which the church is to respond to people's problems pastorally in a religiously pluralistic setting with a heritage of colonial Christianity such as Bénin[4] calls for a non-colonial approach to the praxis of pastoral care and counseling. In a context like this, what kind of hermeneutical approach to the realities of life and Scriptures consistent with God's vision for the world is cogent with the pastoral task of responding to people's problems? In this paper, I purport to respond to this question by arguing that the task of counseling and caregiving must be a religious conversation. Such an orientation is set against Western Enlightenment projects of secularism and imposition of outsiders' interpretations of and technical solutions to human problems. I will suggest that as Christian ministers engage in this religious and conversational task, despite the past colonial misuse or abuse of the Bible with its consequent current public discredit, there is still need to engage all people—not Christians only— with Scriptures. Providing practical responses to people's problems in a way devoid of Scriptural actions in people's lives is antithetical to God's design. However, Scripture requires a reading and use conducive to healing. For this reason, this study suggests that a Narrative approach is conducive to pastoral aims in Bénin context. The Narrative way of reading Scripture can be located within the perspective of postcolonial criticism, which seeks to recognize and critique the shadow of foreign empire in the lives of indigenous Bible readers, particularly those who have been trained and nurtured within the western modes of reading ancient—Judaist and early Christian—texts.[5] This chapter also argues for the importance to enter the narrative hermeneutical task of reading ancient texts conjoined with contemporary human narratives. This sort of reading is able to provide a

---

3. This study is interested in the praxis of pastorate that engages persons' lived realities and not just in pastorate as the holding of a professional administrative office.

4. The close cooperation between foreign missionaries and Western politicians was perhaps clearly evidenced from the 1860s by the Roman Catholic missionaries who worked side by side with French colonial interests. See Boucher, À Travers les Missions du Togo-Dahomey, 1926.

5. Segovia, "Biblical Criticism," 40–41.

healthy approach to using the Scriptures in the process of counseling and caring for both Christians and non-Christians alike.

SCRIPTURE AND SOCIOCULTURAL FACTORS IN HEALING

After completing the Masters Program in Pastoral Counseling at Loyola College in Maryland, where I learned many theories in counseling, I returned home to Ghana in West Africa with the hope of practicing the theories I had learned in the West. I realized, however, that though the theories I learned were good ones, most of them were not practicable in Ghana. Joseph K. Ghunney

Prior to the rediscovery of 'story', the field of counseling was largely pervaded by a rationalistic approach to life problems leading to the treatment of individuals "in strict isolation from the contaminating influence of environment, family and other variables."[6] As people's experiences proved this approach to be unsuccessful, family therapists got past it and began seeing pathology not in one individual as they used to do. Instead they observed all family members and studied family structure, interaction, behavior, and processes. They conceived 'pathology' not in any one individual but in the operations of the whole family system."[7]

Despite its helpfulness, compared to the old individualistic paradigm of counseling, the family system approach has come under several attacks—the basic of which being that its proponents "have unwittingly retained an empiricist epistemology regarding their own clinical observations and research."[8] One of the most prominent signs of this is the zeal of certain system-oriented family therapist to predict clients' futures based on clients' genograms, i.e., their family history. The predictions sometimes comes across as absolutes, whereas, not only because of Christian faith but other life issues also could well lead certain individuals to detach from their family pathologies, however recurring these might have been. Such is the contemporary belief regarding life problems:

> Assertion about the nature of reality no longer can be made with the same kind of absolute certainty or predictability as before. Knowledge of reality must be forthcoming about its inherent limitations and concede that it is finally always relative,

6. Bradt, *Story as a Way of Knowing*, 82.

7. Ibid.

8. Ibid., 83.

discontinuous, uncertain, indeterminate, containing potential complementarities and possibilities yet to be explored.[9]

Non-Narrative approaches have the power to confer foreign narratives embedded in theories and practices used for the counseling process to people of other cultures. Christians using those approaches are prone to using disconnected biblical portions as means of Christianizing those theories. I remember how, after having been taught a course in Pastoral Counseling, I went about teaching Eric Bern's Transaction Analysis approach to Christian healing in a village in Bénin. One memory related to teaching Bern's theory in that village was that because I was speaking in Goungbe, my native language, I could not find words to express some of Eric Bern's concepts such as Parent State, Child State and Adult State. I easily expressed the same concepts while teaching in French, but what a pity when I went further down in the village trying to explain to my people a theory based on foreign stories that they were not and could probably not be part of! A Narrative approach to life problems can better help pastors explore life problems in a way that fits an appropriate way of healing.

To this end, family therapists Michael White and David Epston, using deconstruction and social reconstruction paradigms, have developed Narrative Therapy as an alternative approach to helping people.[10] The name of the approach tells of the fact that counselors who work from that approach understand people's problems and walk alongside them *narratively* so that they could find and embrace alternative problem-free narratives for their lives. This approach to helping people is driven by important key narrative concepts. Proponents of this approach deny that the approach is one more technique or method of counseling. They maintain that it is rather an attitude that counselors can integrate their practice. When appropriated narratively, biblical texts find their place in the process and thus can be integrated into people's narrative world for a reconstruction of communal and personal living.

Working from the perspective of Narrative Counseling, Edward P. Wimberly advocates for the importance of *Using Scripture in Pastoral Counseling*, of course in a narrative mode.[11] Burrell D. Dinkins breaks from the non-narrative perspective of life in which he was domesticated even in Christian ministry, and argues for the importance of *Narrative Pastoral Counseling*, instead of a counseling practice informed by story-

9. Ibid., 95.

10. White and Epson, *Narrative Means*.

11. Wimberly, *Using Scripture in Counseling*.

less rationalistic principles and techniques.[12] Wimberly undertakes a growth-facilitative-authoritative use of Scripture instead of a stasis authoritarian use of Scripture.[13] His approach, while not neglecting the cognitive and moralistic aspect of life, has as its primary focus, "the interaction between the counselee and the counselor, the pastoral counselor, and the Bible story in question."[14] The model, because it takes seriously counselees' personal mythology, is, unlike other counseling techniques, willing to acknowledge their spiritual worldview and broadens it to provide a holistic approach to treatment.[15] This is a positive model that does not seek to communicate or impose foreign vision of life and secular methods of intervention on counselees. As a holistic approach, it genuinely takes into account counselees' life world and understanding of their situation while also challenging them about their narrow understanding of (Christian) life. To this effect, Wimberly presents cases through which counselees' concepts of grace, faith, and the nature of biblical narratives, which have been greatly challenged in a manner akin to 'speaking truth in love.' Wimberly's approach is based on a suitable pastoral theology of Scripture:

> Scripture contains within it a drawing, transformative power that has the ability to communicate to those who are oppressed and abused in ways that call them to wholeness. This power is contained in many narratives of the faith and encourages persons to be courageous survivors.[16]

Wimberly illuminates how the blending of role-taking theory and Narrative Theology allows Bible stories and biblical characters to shape one's perception of reality. Such blending also helps experiment how biblical narratives work to set persons free from "negative personal, marriage, and family mythologies and how this liberating activity can be blocked."[17] Wimberly's goal and method are worth considering for a contextual pastoral counseling practice in the post-colonial setting of Bénin. However, maybe because his method is germane of western conflict between religion and public life, Wimberly encourages the narrative usage of Scripture

12. Dinkins, *Narrative Pastoral Counseling*.

13. Ibid., 14.

14. Ibid., 32.

15. Ibid., 44.

16. Ibid., 64.

17. Ibid., 71.

only for counselors helping counselees with some backgrounds in biblical tradition within which storytelling is well appraised.[18] African pastors in general, and Beninese pastors in particular, cannot afford agreeing with this perspective for two reasons. Firstly, as argued earlier, pastoral praxes in Benin can naturally involve spiritual conversations, whether in the Church or outside the Church because the whole population has a spiritual tradition and many still interpret their lived realities with spiritual stories.[19] Secondly, Christian ministers ought to engage people into spiritual dialogues from the standpoint of the grand narrative of Scriptures while allowing particular biblical stories to encounter counselees' stories. As Gerard Loughlin argues, the Bible as a consuming text views other stories as partial renditions of the bigger story told in the Bible:

> Consequently, all other stories must be inscribed into the Biblical story, rather than the biblical story into any one of them. Insofar as we allow the biblical story to become our story, it overcomes our reality. We no longer view the world as once we did; we view it from the point of view of a character in the Bible's story.[20]

Besides, West Africans Christians have historically viewed the Bible as bearing witnesses to events performed by God; those events being so paradigmatic that people "can efficaciously apply [them] to situations of life."[21] Wynnand Amewowo

> expands on this idea: For the [West African] believer, the miracles and other mighty works that happened in the Bible can and will happen again. The Bible is potent for all conditions of humanity. The Bible therefore, is considered as an efficacious sign of God's active presence with salvific action.[22]

Given this perception of the Bible, its usefulness cannot be limited only to those who are or have been within the 'walls' of the Church as Wimberly suggests it. Aware of the history of mishandling of the Bible in relation to counseling,[23] however, African pastoral counselors ought not

18. Ibid., 9.

19. Adjido, "Links Between Psychosomatic," 265–78.

20. Loughlin, *Telling God's Story*, 37.

21. Amewowo, "Experiences and Discoveries," 16.

22. Ibid., 16. See also N. T. Wright, *The Last Word*, 36–41.

23. For a critical self-evaluation of the biblical counseling movement, see Powlison,

continue such tradition either by relegating Scripture to a document for scholarly explorations (with little to no connection to the grassroots), or by using it as a divine stick of moralization or as an instrument for spiritualizing western counseling techniques. Rather following an intercultural interpretative framework, Benin pastors can prayerfully employ religio-cultural and experiential givens "to examine the text of a given passage of the Bible in order to derive meaning suitable to . . . [our] context."[24] As such, the basis upon which African pastors can transmit the biblical gospel in local cultures in a deeper and transformative way becomes evident. Given that African religio-cultural heritage and current life experiences constitute windows for a thorough embrace of the Biblical message, an appropriate use of the Bible requires not just predetermined modern exegetical tools but a humble attitude that seeks to know those pre-existing cultural windows too, as well as and dependence on the Spirit to actualize God's message in context.

Burrell Dinkins is helpful in this regard in suggesting that helpers must enter Narrative Pastoral Counseling with an attitude of respect and humility marked by an inductive approach rather than a deductive approach.[25] An inductive approach to conversation starts from a genuine "not knowing" stage at which counselors offer sincere questions that help expand the presenting issue from a smaller (what the client presents) to a broader perspective. A deductive approach to counseling operates with stringent theoretical biases. Working with a medical approach, deductive counselors want to find and pick bits and pieces of information in the counselee's story that will fit into their predetermined theories about people's problems.[26] The inductive approach is more suitable for Narrative Counseling, whereas the deductive approach is a mechanistic approach to human problems.[27] An inductive approach ultimately leads counselors to a productive rather than a reproductive way of thinking. Reproductive thinking leads counselors, after they have listened to counselees, to refer to their repertoires to pick solutions that worked in situations similar to those recounted by their clients. It causes them to apply to the new situation what is in their repertoires as experts. In productive thinking,

---

The *Biblical Counseling Movement*, (2010), and Lambert, *The Biblical Counseling Movement After Adams*, (2011).

24. Manus, *Intercultural Hermeneutics in Africa*, 35.

25. Dinkins, *Narrative*, 24–25.

26. Ibid., 31.

27. Ibid., 24.

however, counselors, instead, referring to a repertoire of past knowledge, think "creatively about the many ways the problems could be viewed" and "try new ways of looking at the story."[28]

Instead of continuing to use modern non-narrative methods to handing life problems, African pastors would do better to re-appropriate their narrative tradition and use the Bible in counseling narratively, thereby putting an end to the rationalistic approach to Scripture that continues to deprive believers from the many transformative adventures in which biblical texts can launch them. Biblical texts are capable of a wide range of acceptable meanings[29] and "[d]ifferent people will respond to the Bible message according to their mode of reception, i.e. according to their culture, social background, environment, and education."[30] Even the cross of Christ, which evangelicals take as central to the Christianity, did not have and cannot be thought to have a preferred and exhaustive meaning for every culture and every age.[31] Therefore, in narrative practice, though pastors must hold biblical stories at a higher esteem, they must prioritize an inductive and productive attitude to interpreting persons' stories in counseling. Pastoral counselors must expect counselees to embrace a better life story by which to live. Yet, it is not necessarily our goal to routinely diagnose the "five common idols" in the lives of the counselees in order to "apply Scripture to the individual counselee" and to deal "simultaneously with the idol worship of the heart and with the lifestyle produced by living for false gods."[32] This approach can be unhelpful because it is likely to make counselors ready to provide 'biblical' diagnosis of 'dysfunctions' in their counselees whereas narrative counselors, together with their counselees, are able to broaden the sources of presenting problems. Particularly in post-independence African contexts, many presenting personal problems correlate with neo-colonial socio-economic and political injustices[33] that for counselors to go about searching for 'idols' in counselee's hearts only would amount to a colonial reading of Scripture. This individualistic and modernistic approach is opposed to the goal of Narrative Counseling,

28. Ibid., 62–63.

29. Green, "Scripture and Theology," 8.

30. Amewowo, "Experiences," 17.

31. Hooker, *Not Ashamed of the Gospel*.

32. Sigley, "Evangelism Implosion," 11, 14.

33. For descriptions of the psychological and socio-economic conditions in post-independence Africa and Benin, see Fanon, *The Wretched of the Earth* (2004); Nkrumah, *The Struggle Continues: Six Panaf Pamplets* (2001); Hountondji (ed), *Économie et Société au Bénin: d'Hier à Demain*, (2000).

which is to help counselees discover and embrace an Alternative Story to live by and to live it *together with* other people. When counselors approach persons with narrative perspective, they expect not only individuals' transformation but also that of their immediate networks, which also need to change toward counselees according to their newfound journey.

NARRATIVE CONCEPTS AND NON-COLONIAL USE OF SCRIPTURE FOR HEALING

I contend that to be a real Christian therapist one must become a practical theologian, in the sense of being able to contextualize the Imago Dei in different life contexts.

—KEVIN S. REIMER

David Tuesday Adamo[34] rightly laments the spiritual void that western missionaries left within African Christianity by teaching African Christians to discard their indigenous ways of handling daily problems like diseases, witches, enemies, and lack of success in life:

> Charms, medicine, incantations, divination, sacrifices and other cultural ways of protecting, healing, and liberating from evil powers were hurriedly discarded in the name of Christianity. Yet, we were not taught *how to use the Bible as a means of protecting, healing, and solving* the daily problems of life. The Euro-American way of reading the Bible has not actually helped us to understand the Bible in our own context.[35]

Concerns about how the Bible relates to existential needs are well established among African Christians. Yet, most African Bible scholars trained in the finest skills of biblical exegesis are incapable of engaging African life problems with them. The methods that they painstakingly learned have come to be powerless in helping church members engage life problems based on Scripture. To remedy this problem, African pastors must understand that the use of Scripture in pastoral counseling is a theological hermeneutic task, calling for an interdisciplinary engagement with both the contemporary world and that of the biblical text.

---

34. Adamo, *Exploration in African Biblical Studies.*
35. Ibid., 47, emphasis mine.

In relation to pastoral counseling Wimberly rightly discusses the concept of hermeneutic of engagement as a means by which in-depth exploration of full participation in 'inner history' affects the life of the counselee. The concept of 'inner history' is distinct from that of 'outer history,' which means, "Observation of God's activity in the past as it has been revealed in Scripture and in church history."[36] It is this outer history that becomes inner history "when a person or a community encounters God's unfolding and continuing outer history in the present. The person and community of faith move from observers of history to participants in history."[37]

The use of such a hermeneutic of engagement demands a blending of behavioral sciences (psychology of mythology, object relation theory, and role-taking theory) as analytical tools for assessing emotional and psychological difficulties that people face. To this effect, Wimberly aptly argues that these sciences must be used with the best practical theology method in conjunction with narrative biblical criticism as the method of observing God's activity in the past as revealed though Scripture and the Church.[38] This approach is suitable in the quest for an appropriate pastoral counseling approach in Bénin because it is integrative and transformative. In effect, in the post-independence Béninese context, with its neo-colonial structures, the use of the Bible must take into account such areas like socio-economic and political situations in which people find themselves. Such a theological and cultural engagement with the Bible is what West African biblical scholars are trying to do today:

> While our people grope for meaning and existence, the Bible remains their source of hope and solace. It speaks to our people in their situation. The West African sociopolitical realities urge us on to develop newer methods and make them fully operational to ensure that our reading of the Bible is relevant and responsive to the West African experience.[39]

This is a way of saying "no" to pervasive western modes of reading the Bible with overarching concerns being to derive same meanings before those can be applied "to my life" or to "my heart." Such readings pay little to no concern to how the church's reading of Scripture is affecting the overall socio-political situation, that entangles its members.

---

36. Wimberly, *Using Scripture*, 120

37. Ibid., 120.

38. Ibid., 119–28.

39. Manus, *Intercultural*, 17.

Key concepts of Narrative Counseling are able to convey such a reading, thus allowing for indigenous pastoral counselor to help individuals and communities to relate the Bible to their total life realities. They include *Internalizing Conversations, Naming* and *Externalizing* of the *Problem.* According to Narrative therapist Alice Morgan, Internalizing Conversations are those self-talks by which struggling people locate their problems inwardly resulting in thin descriptions (problematic stories and their meanings reached in the face of adversity) of their life situation.[40]

Taking this aspect seriously in pastoral counseling causes Wimberly to attend to the presenting problem and the stories that surround them in order to discover people's personal mythologies, i.e., their self-beliefs and self-convictions. This concept helps explore the counselee's self-beliefs and convictions, the symbolic and emotionally laden themes that make up the self and the self in relation to others, which includes the internalized ideas of significant others.[41] As counselors allow counselees to explore their stories, problem-saturated mythologies emerge. At this point, the counselor's active listening is crucial. Both counselees and pastoral counselors must engage in a conversational approach to counseling in which they "speak as naturally as possible, using everyday words,"[42] and seek to avoid professional counseling or theological languages in favor of down-to-earth language.[43] Active listening helps identify the content of the counselee's narratives beyond the presenting story.

The following tactics are used to this effect: Unique Outcome (anything standing in contrast to the Dominant Story such as a plan, an action, a dream, a commitment, or a cultural value), Landscape of Identity (experiences of events related to one another in the same plot), and Landscape of Action (interpretations and reflections made on Unique Outcomes and landscape of identity), which is constituted of self-identity, social contexts, interpersonal relationships, life events, life meaning, and story plot.[44]

These aspects are necessary because, contrary to the aim of diagnostic based counseling methods, personal experience of freedom in Narrative Counseling normally impacts multiples layers of one's life and not just one's individual's psyche only. Jesus seems to approach personal problems

---

40. Morgan, *What is Narrative Therapy?* 12, 18.

41. Wimberly, *Using Scripture*, 22.

42. Dinkins, *Narrative Pastoral*, 21.

43. Vernacular Hermeneutics discussed in, Ukpong,"Inculturation Hermeneutics," 17–32.

44. Wimberly, *Using Scripture*, 235–50; Morgan, *What is Narrative*, 51–61.

in this manner. For instance, he engaged the Samaritan woman at the well, actively listened to her, and helped her explore her personal mythology. Such an exploration shone a light not just on her psyche but also on her relationships, her people group, Jesus and the Jews as can be found in her statement: "You are a Jew and I am a Samaritan woman (for Jews do not associate with Samaritans) . . . I have no husband . . . Our father worshiped on this mountain, but you Jews claim that the place where we must worship is in Jerusalem . . ." (John 4:9, 17, 20). Indeed, without helping people become conscious of their present location, how can pastors walk alongside them confidently from their point of despair into a hopeful stage? To achieve this *Internalizing Conversations* help counselees externalize the problems they have deeply internalized for so long.

By *Externalizing the Problem* counselors help counselees separate problems from themselves. They thus empower counselees to rise above their life circumstances by allowing them to *Name* the problem by themselves or with counselors' involvement.[45] As a different way of handling people's issues, *Externalizing Conversation* is an important linguistic shift able to move the focus away from personalized attitudes (self-attack, recrimination, blame, and judgment) that work against productive and positive outcomes in the counseling process. In a collectivist context like Bénin, Externalizing Conversations help those involved in a problematic situation to dissociate problems from one another and "invite them to work together against the problem."[46] *Externalizing Conversation* is based on the conviction that people's problems are "manufactured in a social, cultural, and political context" thus inviting the belief that counselees' problems are the result not just of internal dysfunctions, but also of social and cultural influences that "shape their desires, ambitions, and purposes."[47]

The western method of diagnosing people's ills based on the rationalistic grasp of 'truth' locates the problem within counselees themselves and put the entire burden on them. This diagnostic approach ignores factors related to the societal, cultural, political, economic, and spiritual environments within which counselees live. For this reason, it is important to help counselees participate in *Naming* the problems they are faced with instead of forcing them to accept the name given to those issues by the very sociopolitical structures that might have been directly or indirectly involved in creating them in the first place.

45. Morgan, *What is Narrative*, 17–23.

46. Monk et al., *Narrative Therapy in Practice*, 28–29.

47. Ibid., 29.

In the Narrative process, the Naming of people's problems by coun-selees is a counselee's responsibility rather than the sole responsibility of expert counselors. Counselees often name their problems based on their cultural, spiritual, economic, and political conditions, which are usually unaccounted for in the Diagnosis Statistic Manuals. It seems to have been a pattern in the ministry of Jesus to allow suffering people to external-ize their problems although stereotypes of the populace might have made those problems stuck to the sufferers. Hence, his public presence frees people from social isolation and empower them to look for him for the purpose of detaching themselves from their problems. Some examples of people Naming their own problems can be: "Lord, if you are willing, you can make me clean," (Matt 8:2) meaning something like 'my problem is uncleanness with its social and religious consequences of isolation. Can you save me from this social death?"; "Lord, my servant lies at home para-lyzed and in terrible suffering . . . just say the word and my servant will be healed" (Matt 8:6–8). Or "Lord, have mercy on my son. He has seizures and is suffering greatly. He often falls into the fire or into water" (Matt 17:15).

Experts normally expected to work on these kinds of problems could have given diagnoses of despair, whereas the people immediately concerned express faith and hope in the presence of Jesus. Another case in point is the woman "who had been subject to bleeding for twelve years" and "came up behind him and touched the edge of his cloak," despite the impossible diagnosis she might already have from experts and the result-ing social ostracism she was enduring. Naming her Problem in light of Jesus' own story, she said, "If I only touch his cloak, I will be healed" (Matt 9:19–25). This is something experts—then and now—may not be able to affirm. Because Jesus allows those struggling to 'Name their Problems,' he does not appear to be solving identical problems with identical techniques in every case he faces, according to the gospel narratives. If Jesus allows people to express their problems with their own words, his servants who claim to render service to others after his likeness can do likewise in their various ministry contexts.

As the Narrative process enfolds, *Open questions* are critical because through them successful Internalizing and Externalizing Conversations leading to the naming of the problem can be reached. The Internalized and Externalized Conversations help attain a thin description of the issue at stake, that is, they help constitute the problem-saturated stories related to the presenting issue and their meanings as the person sees them.[48] The personal mythology discovered through these actions give a picture of the counselees' family memories, or birth stories, or preferred books, movies, or particular characters (biblical and non-biblical) with whom they identify. The counselor then takes that personal mythology in account in order to "guide the storyteller toward seeing hopeful directions and acting in ways consistent with that focus"[49] or in order "to assist" him or her "in the development of a more hopeful and future-oriented story."[50] Reaching a more hopeful story usually requires that counselors help counselees move from a thin description of their life to a thick description.

Thick descriptions appear in the Narrative Counseling process as counselees discern and accept an Alternative Story by which they want to live instead of the *thin description* with which they have been living. An *Alternative Story* is the new story co-constructed with the therapist's help by the counselees, the one on which they would rather want to build their life. As the therapist finds ways to enrich this Alternative Story, it gives place to the thin conclusion previously reached and becomes a thick description.[51] Narrative philosophy assumes that there are resiliencies factors in the counselee's life and culture that might come to play in the thickening process. Particularly as Beninese counselors engage indigenous people whose rich narrative tradition is well established,[52] Narrative counselors must be attuned to strengths embedded in personal stories as well as in Bénin cultural stories that could help present day Beninese build these preferred problem-free stories. Narrative therapists refer to *Sparkling Moments* to mean the ignored lived experiences that go un-storied because counselees usually do not notice or understand them while living under the burden of their problems.[53] Others refer to the same concept by using *Unique Outcomes* to mean, anything that the dominant problematic problem would not like or "events that shine or stand out in contrast to the Dominant Story."[54] One can find *Sparkling Moments* or *Unique Out-*

48. Morgan, *What is Narrative*, 12.

49. Wimberly, *Using Scripture*, 250.

50. Dinkins, *Narrative Pastoral*, 21.

51. Morgan, *What is Narrative*, 14–15.

52. Herskovits, *Dahomean Narrative*. For a more detailed account of the variegated narratives embedded within Dahomean way of life see Yai, "The Path is Open," in *Program of African Studies*, 1999.

53. Monk et al., *Narrative Therapy*, 13.

54. Morgan, *What is Narrative*, 52.

comes in the past, in the present or in the future of individuals, families, and whole communities. A Unique Outcome can be a plan, an action, a feeling, a statement, a quality, a dream, a thought, a belief, or a commitment. When Beninese religio-cultural heritage is attended to correctly, narrative counselors can help identify these *Unique Outcomes* in a great sufficient number for each issue in such a way that counselees themselves will embrace them as resiliencies. In a biblical/theological sense, narrative pastors can appreciate those resiliencies as God's grace at work in a prevenient manner through the Beninese religio-cultural narratives as has been the case with Paul in relation to Greco-Roman culture.[55]

These *Unique Outcomes* must be historicized through questioning the client about his contribution in producing valued experiences and virtues. This open questioning thus helps for the emergence of latent abilities[56] to face life problems. Alice Morgan calls the abilities and capacities that come at this point *Landscape of Identity*. Counselees arrive at such a reconstructed identity when they reflect on the meaning of the Unique Outcomes or Sparkling Moments and explore what the development of these moments mean in term of their desires, preferences, beliefs, hopes, personal qualities, values, strengths, commitments, plans, characteristics, abilities and purposes. The narrative counselor can discover in a context like Bénin not only the abilities and strengths of an individual but a whole cultural wealth that is being buried due to an overt westernizing of our way of life.

Narrative counselors enter in counseling relationship with a genuine inductive and productive perspective. Thus, they must allow counselees to arrive at their own preferred stories in the process of building alternative problem-free stories. From a pastoral perspective, Wimberly helpfully suggests that the use of the Bible again becomes critical at this stage:

> Here the pastoral counselor engages the counselee in a discussion of the significant Bible stories that have surfaced in the early stages of pastoral counseling. The aim of the discussion is to 1) compare the preferred story and the Bible story, and 2) to get a glimpse of how the Bible story is at work within the counselee to assist in developing the preferred story.[57]

Ann Streaty Wimberly, working from a Narrative perspective in the area of Christian education, has developed the concept of Story-linking

55. Flemming, *Contextualization.*

56. Monk et al., *Narrative Therapy*, 108; Morgan, *What is Narrative*, 61.

57. Wimberly, *Using Scripture*, 24.

for African American Christian education. Using this concept, the goal of Narrative counselors who use Scripture will be to connect counselees' personal and cultural stories "with the Christian faith story in the Bible and the lives of exemplars of the Christian faith outside the Bible."[58]

In the counseling process, Narrative counselors help counselees "link Bible stories by using them as mirrors through which"[59] they reflect critically on the desired healing, freedom, and wholeness. As a method that encourages "looking at Scripture through contextual lenses,"[60] story-linking is governed by the following guideline:

> The Bible story is disclosed; participants focus on the story or text as mirror; they enter into partnership with the characters of the Bible story; they envision God's action today; and they anticipate with their ongoing response to God.[61]

Dinkins aptly suggests that this process must be seen as a co-creation of stories between the counselor and the counselee.[62] The pastoral counselor doesn't showcase western biblical erudition upon the counselee.[63] To avoid such rationalistic scholarly temptation, Dinkins uses the metaphor of pastoral conversation "to move away from the notion that counseling is mainly advice or therapy" because "people are not objects to be changed by telling them to do specific things: they are not sick persons to be healed. They are individuals looking for a more hopeful story."[64] Within that framework of pastoral conversation, instead of clinical or biblical-expertise-show, the primary task will be "to develop a relationship that promotes dialogue" by promoting "narrative interchange" that incites counselees to carefully identify their stories and to tell them in a way that fosters healing and not just makes a point.[65]

As they handle narrative guidelines effectively narrative pastoral counselors, working with their counselees, can deconstruct ideas and perspectives that do not support God's design for healing. The idea of *Deconstruction* consists in considering and dismantling the contexts

---

58. Wimberly, *Soul Stories*, 39.

59. Ibid., 39.

60. Ibid., 43.

61. Ibid., 44–45.

62. Dinkins, *Narrative Pastoral*, 32.

63. Adamo, *Reading and Interpreting*, 41–42.

64. Ibid., 32.

65. Ibid., 33.

within which problems arise as well as the ideas and beliefs underpinning the presenting problem. As counselors consider these, they can help the person pull apart and examine the taken-for-granted assumptions. This examination may lead to challenging those assumptions and open the way for alternative stories that help people "to challenge and break from the problem's views and to be more connected with their own preferred ideas, thoughts and ways of living."[66]

This *Deconstruction* stage however, needs not be done with the Bible only. Joseph Healey and Donal Sybertz rightly recognize that there are many similarities between African and biblical wisdoms, making it, therefore, possible to integrate those wisdoms in the task of African practical theology.[67] Therefore, in addition to searching for and using positive factors in the counselees' own life, the task of Deconstruction must also embrace indigenous cultural resiliencies that many contemporary individuals and families might have—and indeed *have*—forgotten due to the legacy of the Enlightenment on African cultures. In order to arrive at this point, indigenous pastoral counselors can use what Chris Ukachukwu Manus calls the folkloristic approach to biblical interpretation. This approach "empowers the practitioner to engage in the retrieval of the values found in traditions handed down to posterity through folktales, poems, hymns, proverbs, riddles and art,"[68] and which inform about traditional legends, belief-systems, customs, and fables. Whenever such values do not oppose the Scriptural vision for well-being, narrative pastors accept and use them as significant helps alongside Scripture's own texts in the shaping of Alternative Stories.

In Narrative practice, the task of Deconstruction is followed by that of *Re-construction* whereby a new story co-constructed by counselees and indigenous pastoral counselors becomes the one on which counselees would rather build their life. Narrative counselors thus attempt to seal the new story through the tactic of *Re-authoring* or *Re-storying* the counselee's life. *Re-storying* consist in pulling together the Unique Outcomes and using them, together with counselees, to form a new plot or an alternative story that will be richly described. This new story will be a means by which people's skills, abilities, competencies and commitments, which have been

---

66. Morgan, *What is Narrative*, 49.

67. Healey and Sybertz, *Towards an African Narrative*, 45–52.

68. Manus, *Intercultural Hermeneutics in Africa*, 22.

overshadowed by the dominant plot, will come out and constitute a new non-problematic story.[69]

The tactic of *Re-storying* comes from the belief that the new chosen story is precious enough for counselees to hold on to it and to stay connected to it. But since "community is the given condition of life" and "individuals exist only in so far as they are members of a group,"[70] it follows that Narrative counselors must encourage *Re-storying* of counselees' lives by involving those who are part of their communities. Hence, the Narrative practice of inviting outside witnesses around a *Definitional Ceremony* in order to seal and celebrate the Alternative Story must be taken very seriously.

Within biblical narratives similar rituals or events akin to *Definitional Ceremony* served to seal the newfound faith or newfound story. Stories of such characters as Zacchaeus (with whom Jesus ate to the knowledge of everybody, Luke 19), the Samaritan women (who invited the whole city to come and hear Jesus and her new story, John 4:39–40), and the healed demoniac (whom Jesus ordered to go back home and tell people what God has done for him, Luke 8:39), are a few. It also seems to be a biblical pattern that the new story received from the working of Christ through his Spirit is a communal gift and not an individualistic affair.

Gerard Loughlin addresses this corporate nature of the working of Christ through the Bible. According to him, looked at from a narrative perspective, salvation in Christ has a different meaning than the individualistic, abstract, and non-involving ones often assigned to it. It is not enough to understand the identity of Jesus with the words written about him in the Gospel. One needs faith in him, which is not simply a propositional ascent, "for faith is finding one's story in his."[71] Hence, salvation in Christ "consists in establishing a *storied* relation between Jesus *and* those who are saved."[72] This is so because those who are saved are included in his story, which "continues in the history of the Church, in the life of the community to whom Christ returns always."[73] When we are thus saved, our old stories are "enfolded within a new story, which, by promise of a different future, changes the past"[74] and gives us a new sense to our present

69. Morgan, *What is Narrative*, 52–53.

70. Sundermeier, *The Individual and Community*, 17.

71. Loughlin, *Telling God's Story*, 210.

72. Ibid., 211, emphasis added.

73. Ibid., 214.

74. Ibid., 217.

and releases us from past and present burdens. Instead of the currency of salvation as one-time event merely guaranteeing one's safety in a rather other-worldly heaven, salvation is narratively conceived of as "the process of *embracing a life-world*, a conversion of the imagination, on display in the Christian community,"[75] or "as an *incorporation into a new community*, including adopting the rituals and behaviors peculiar to or definitive of that community."[76]

Indigenous Pastoral Counselor, in their Narrative approach to helping people can prayerfully help them find real meaning in a Christ-shaped new story lived within the community of those who perform Christ's story. As such the Narrative concept whereby new stories are sealed through rituals or ceremonies is not only biblically appropriate but also culturally sound in Benin. As Theo Sundermeier argues, in Africa "the communal, the normative and the religious form a unity. They are renewed and made effectual in ritual."[77] Given such a heritage African narrative counselors can find ways to thicken Alternative Stories with the counselees as the latter abandon their previous thin conclusions to the profit of richer and thick descriptions of life.[78] This aspect of communal dimension of healing is cogent with Beninese culture and with the biblical nature of salvation. Yet, it is an important missing in the modern theories of counseling with their Christianized versions, a corrective of which we find in P. R. Holmes's integrative works on therapeutic discipleship in Trinitarian communities.[79]

In the process of Deconstructing unhealthy stories and reconstructing Alternative Stories, indigenous Pastoral Counselors skillfully engage in the pastoral task of narrative theology, using both biblical materials in a way that brings Good News to people. They make use of indigenous narratives or wisdoms in a way that communicates to people that God's presence was in some way with them. These indigenous resources are important because in those remembered stories counselees can find positives and negatives elements that may be influencing their life today. Taking them in account in the reading of biblical texts leads to the 'folklorizing' of biblical stories in pastoral conversations.[80]

75. Green, *Salvation*, 117, emphases original.

76. Ibid., 117.

77. Sundermeier, *Individual and Community*, 98.

78. Morgan, *What is Narrative*, 14–15.

79. Holmes, *Becoming More Like Christ*.

80. Manus, *Intercultural*, 29.

David T. Adamo rightly cautions with regard to this approach in his careful analysis of how West African indigenous cultural hermeneutics operate. He praises, as well as offers cautions about, the therapeutic use of the Bible, particularly of the book of Psalms by indigenous West Africans Christians: "Admittedly, care must be taken so as not to have the wrong impression that all aspects of African cultural tradition are good. African Christian must be able to perceive what is good and compatible, and throw away whichever is not compatible."[81] In order to approach the task of pastoral counseling in this way, the Church in Benin needs to choose approaches to Scripture and to local culture that aid towards a healthy handling of both.

Of the three main approaches to biblical interpretation currently used in biblical scholarship,[82] the literary approaches and the contextual approaches[83] are suitable for African post-colonial contexts. Justin S. Ukpong believes so because the point of departure of these two approaches "is the context of the reader, and they are all concerned with linking the biblical text to the reader's context."[84] The linkage resonates well with Story-linking in the Narrative approach as discussed earlier in this paper. The cultural, religious, social, and economic milieu in Benin today demand that Christian ministers embrace these approaches for the sake of Re-constructing or Re-storying our personal and collective lives. Since pastoral counseling is an avenue of ministry whereby practical questions of life are handled, Benin pastors better not be exposed to years of ministerial training with biblical and theological methods that attempt to answer questions will little bearing on people's lived realities.

CONCLUSION

Recognizing the dynamic religious and spiritual worldview of West Africa G. Parrinder remarked, "Many ill-founded superstitions will disappear before the teaching of scientific fact in the schools."[85] Yet, he warned, "It would be a pity if the African's spiritual and living worldview were replaced by a superficial and purely materialistic outlook."[86] The field of

81. Adamo, *Reading and Interpreting*, 36.

82. West, *Biblical Hermeneutics of Liberation*, 131.

83. Ukpong, "Development of Biblical Interpretation," 11–28, 25.

84. Ibid., 25.

85. Parrinder, *West African Psychology*, 16.

86. Ibid., 16.

psychology and counseling is one of the areas through which religious and spiritual perspectives can be quickly dismissed in Africa. Such dismissal can cause public Christian dialogues to become taboos, especially for those in mental helping profession, as is now the case in several western countries. Yet, consistent with Beninese religious heritage and with Christian calling, pastoral counselors can undertake the task of helping people integratively without discounting the spiritual and religious nature of their realities. For this reason the role of Scripture as provider of a distinctive spiritual life-world for counselors and counselees is critical.

While the use of Scripture in the pastoral praxis has been debated a lot in western circles of counseling, there is an increasing return to spirituality in order to fill the void deeply felt by people who seek therapeutic help. Hence Christian efforts are being made to think about the use of Scripture even in professional counseling.[87] As we think about the praxis of counseling in Africa, and particularly in Bénin, the pressing question before us should not be whether we should use Scriptures or whether we should engage in religious discourse. This question is unwarranted because most people, particularly those who have not yet been too westernized, are disposed to receive counseling that would engage them in religious dialogue. The pressing question should rather be how to appropriately use the sacred Scripture; how to introduce them in pastoral conversations in a way that avoids the abusive and neglectful uses it has known throughout Western colonial history in Africa.

The path before African pastors is to appropriate Narrative Counseling as the best framework within which an appropriate narrative use of the Bible can be located. This approach borrows from a wide range of other approaches to counseling but holds to a radical Narrative approach to life problems and to their solutions. It is an appropriate approach in Benin context due both to the richness of its indigenous Narrative approach to life and to the overwhelming narrative nature of the Bible itself.

---

87. Garzon, "Interventions that Apply," 113–21.

11

A Child's Healing Journey Battling Anger

JEANNIE CHAPMAN

NARRATIVE THERAPY: A CASE STUDY OF A CHILD WITH A PROBLEM OF ANGER

Case Example:

HARRY IS TEN YEARS old and has been referred for counseling by his school because of his continual disruptive behavior. He is reported to be aggressive with the other children and defiant and disrespectful to the teachers and administrators. Harry has been in numerous fights and is referred to the principal almost daily. His teachers report a lack of interest in his schoolwork resulting in failing grades.

His aunt, who is also his legal guardian, accompanies Harry. His parents were killed in an accident when he was five years old, and he has been living with his aunt and uncle since that time. His aunt is concerned about the reports from the school of Harry's behavior. At home she describes Harry as a loner, uninterested in being a part of the family, unwilling to complete chores or participate in the family in any way. She also reports that Harry does not display any of the aggressive or disrespectful behavior at home that is reported by the school. She is quite concerned for Harry and wants to help him to better adjust both at home and at school. When she has tried to discuss his problems at school, he runs out of the room or refuses to talk. He is unresponsive to any displays of affection or nurture, which she tries to give him and he frequently pulls away. She feels by now that Harry should be able to better respond to being a member of their family, but she admits that she does not know how she can help him. She is frustrated with Harry's rejection of her and his uncle and hopes counseling will somehow bring them closer together.

NARRATIVE THERAPY

People are the expert in their own life experiences. In order to heal, people need to learn to separate the problem from them. People have many resources, skills, and abilities to assist them in reducing the influence of problems.[1] Narrative Therapy encourages collaboration between the client and the therapist in rediscovering and reconstructing the favored experiences in life focusing more on the client as a courageous victor rather than a victim.[2] Michael White found his exploration with narrative methods with children so beneficial and valued by clinicians and parents, he decided to carry it into his work with adults.[3] Narrative Therapy focuses on the role of language in counseling. By listening to clients tell their stories and focusing on the language used to define the client's worldview, the therapist can help the client to become aware of the Dominant Story. The therapist can then ask pertinent questions helping the client to become aware of other possible elements that bring Alternatives to the Story to which the client is unaware because of their focus on the Dominant Story.

Initial Session with Henry:

Therapist: Good afternoon Mrs. Dursley and Harry. What brings you in today?

Mrs. Dursley: Harry's principal requested that he make an appointment with a therapist in order to address his behavior problems at school. He has received many discipline referrals for fighting with other students and being disrespectful to his teachers. At home he just stays in his room. He joins

1. Morgan, *What is Narrative Therapy?*
2. Monk et al., *Narrative Therapy in Practice.*
3. Bennett, "Narrative Methods," 21.1.

us for dinner, but is uninterested in conversation or family time. He has been a loner ever since he came to live with us after his parents' death.

Therapist: Harry, would you share with me what is going on at school. (Silence)

Therapist: Harry, I'm very interested in hearing what your feelings and thoughts are about school, would you be willing to share with me what is happening?

(Continued silence)

It is important to get an accurate description of the problem from the client and listen to the language the client uses to explain their experience of the problem. However, in working with children, this might prove to be a difficult task and may not be achieved during the first stage or even the first session.[4] Because of this, nonverbal ways of working with children are appropriate and these methods fit with children's needs for playful attitudes to serious problems. Puppet work, dollhouse play, sand play, drama, and art therapy all provide the means needed in helping children to tell their story in a comfortable, play-like atmosphere.

The therapist brings several puppets to the table and asks Harry if he would like to play with the puppets. After several minutes of observed play, the therapist initiates the conversation again.

Therapist: I wonder if one of the puppets might like to tell me about school.

Harry: I don't know if that's ok.

Therapist: Sure, it is absolutely ok.

(Harry chooses a wolf puppet)

Harry/puppet: I hate school and everyone at school hates me.

Therapist: What is it that makes you hate school?

Harry/puppet: I'm always in trouble. The kids are mean to me and I beat them up, and I always get sent to the principal. He hates me too.

Therapist: How are you doing with your class work?

Harry/puppet: I'm no good at that, so why even try. I just get yelled at even when I'm doing nothing; I'm no good. I'm just trouble.

The therapist allows Harry an opportunity to share his story, and Harry identifies himself as trouble. This description Harry has given of himself shows an assumption that he is the problem and that the problem is now his main identity. Conversations that locate the problem inwardly are termed Internalizing Conversations and usually have negative effects

---

4. Butler et al., "Using Puppets," 31.3.

on people's lives and result in thin conclusions.[5] It is important in Narrative Therapy to move the client from Internalizing Conversations to Externalizing the Problem. White developed the principle of Externalizing the Problem in his work with young children with the intent of engaging their imaginations. Puppets are an effective tool for Externalizing the Problem because they assist in objectifying the problem and creating distance between the problem and the client.[6] Narrative methods work with children's natural imaginative, playful approaches. By keeping fun in the process a balance is created for the difficult work of therapy. Taking the focus off the child's problem and placing emphasis on strengths and abilities helps in dealing with the problem. This approach also promotes interplay of the child and the clinician's imaginations in the coauthoring of meaning in the search for solutions.[7]

In the book *Recalling Our Own Stories*, the problematic story is termed a Personal Myth. Personal Myths form the basis of interactions and experience with others. They can lessen the quality of our interactions and our ability to interpret our experience.[8]

Therapist: So it seems there is some trouble happening at school and some problems with completing class work. I wonder if the puppet might be willing to give these problems a name. You may choose any name you wish.

(Harry spends some time looking over the puppets and chooses a fox.)

Harry (Wolf): I think I will call it "Mr. Fox" (puppet), because foxes are sneaky and they attack and eat other animals.

Therapist: Ok. We will call it "Mr. Fox". So, Mr. Wolf is there a time during your school day that Mr. Fox hides in his hole and doesn't come out to hunt?

Harry (Wolf): Yes, when I am in reading time Mr. Fox hides and I can get my work done.

Therapist: Why do you suppose Mr. Fox hides during reading time?

Harry/wolf: Maybe it's because I love to read and I am busy thinking about the story.

Therapist: How about that! There are some times that Mr. Wolf can keep Mr. Fox away. I wonder if you can think about some other times that Mr. Fox stays in his hole, so that Mr. Wolf can do what he needs to do?

5. Morgan, *What is Narrative Therapy?*

6. Butler et al., "Using Puppets," 31.3.

7. Bennett, "Narrative Methods and Children," 21.1.

8. Wimberly, *Recalling Our Own Stories.*

Harry/wolf: I went to the library yesterday and checked out some new books to read for my Accelerated Reader points.

Therapist: So you like to read?

Harry/wolf: Yes, I won the Summer Reading Program certificate at the library this summer.

Therapist: Congratulations! I'd say that is quite an accomplishment. Where was Mr. Fox while you were completing this task of reading so many books?

Harry/wolf: He was in his hole! I am a good reader, and he can't stop me.

Therapist: Sounds like Mr. Wolf knows how to handle Mr. Fox when he is reading, huh?

Harry/wolf: Yep, I guess so.

Therapist: Mr. Wolf, do you think you might be able to find some other times this week when you are able to keep Mr. Fox in his hole? Perhaps, you can think of times while you are at school or times when you are at home that Mr. Fox is hiding, because Mr. Wolf is about his business. How about at the end of each school day, writing down some times when Mr. Fox was in hiding that day, so that we can talk about them next week? Would you like to do that Mr. Wolf?

Harry/wolf: I'll see if Mr. Wolf would like to do that.

Therapist: That would be very helpful. Thank you, Mr. Wolf, for coming out of the forest to talk with us today.

The therapist begins the process of looking for meanings that are not readily apparent in the telling of the story. There may be hidden meanings or gaps in the story and evidence of conflicting stories. This process of listening for what is not said is termed "Deconstruction."[9] In the case example, the therapist recognizes the comment about reading that Harry made earlier in his story. There is a possible hidden meaning, in which reading is something positive happening in the midst of his school day. Recognizing this might be an opportunity to thicken the story, the therapist works to remove the problem from an Internalized state to an Externalized Conversation. The problem has been renamed "Mr. Fox" as chosen by the client and can be related to as something outside of the self. In using metaphors supplied by children to describe their problems, they are left with a feeling of relief that someone has listened and understood them and feel more empowered to solve their problems.[10] Harry's choice

9. Monk et al., *Narrative Therapy in Practice*.

10. Ibid.

of puppets gave him a sense of safety and control over his situation. It empowered him to tell his story using his own language. Children may be more apt to tell their story in the third person because of the distance and emotional safety it provides.[11]

Now that the problem has been named, the therapist works with Harry to further investigate his comment on reading and finds that reading is indeed something he enjoys and in which "Mr. Fox" is under control. The Deconstruction process will continue through the next session as they work together to uncover times when "Mr. Fox" has remained hidden in his hole. Following the therapy session, the therapist chooses to write a note to Harry recapping the work that was done and encouraging him to continue to externalize his problem and look for times of success.

> *Dear Mr. Wolf,*
>
> *I enjoyed our talk on Thursday and am glad to meet you. You are a very courageous animal in the forest, and you have survived many things! I am looking forward to more times we can meet in the forest and talk. We must be on the lookout for Mr. Fox. He is a sneaky one. Remember to be on the lookout for times that you have kept him in his hole. I recall that you enjoy your reading time and want to hear more about the stories you enjoy and how Mr. Fox remains in that hole while you are busy reading and during your other school activities. Until our next meeting in the forest...*
>
> *Your friend indeed,*
> *Mr. Lion (Dr. Hudson)*

Narrative Therapy is a collaborative effort between the therapist and client. The client is seen as the expert of their own story, while the therapist is a trained listener and has skills in asking questions, searching out meanings that the client may not be aware of within their story. The therapist seeks to understand what is of interest to the people consulting with him/her and how the journey suits his/her preferences.[12] This letter demonstrates the collaborative relationship sought out between therapist and child-client, and the support offered from the therapist in working through the journey.

(Harry has entered the therapy room and begun free play with the puppets. He has buried Mr. Fox underneath a pile of puppets and Mr. Wolf is playing in a friendly manner with Mr. Rabbit. He gives Mr. Lion to the therapist, a sign of acceptance and appreciation of the letter he received.)

11. Nelson et al., "Storytelling Narratives," 37.3.

12. Morgan, *What is Narrative Therapy?*

Therapist: How are things in the forest Mr. Wolf?

Harry/Wolf: It has been a long week.

Therapist: Would you like to tell me about it?

Harry/Wolf: On Monday, the Fox came and beat up Andy on the playground because he was talking about me. Wednesday I went to the library to pick out some more books so that I can stay at the top of the chart, but when we went to P.E. Mr. Fox snuck back out and attacked the PE Coach, because he wouldn't let Mr. Wolf sit on the bench and read.

Therapist: When Mr. Fox is out of his hole and sneaking around how does that affect your day?

Harry/Wolf: Mr. Wolf doesn't want to be at school and he gets upset. When Mr. Wolf gets home with the pink slip, the Aunt gets upset, and Mr. Wolf is sad, so he hides in his room.

Therapist: Would you like to draw me a picture of how that feels when the fox is sneaking out of his hole?

(Harry draws a picture of the fox with big teeth and Harry hiding in his room)

Therapist: Thank you for sharing that picture with me. It seems that Mr. Fox has a way of causing you to be very sad. I wonder if you would like to see Mr. Fox stay in his hole and not sneak out? (Harry nods yes) Were there sometimes when Mr. Fox was in his hole this week?

Harry/Wolf: Well, Mr. Wolf went to the lunchroom yesterday and Tommy took his pudding. Mr. Fox was about to come out of his hole, but Mr. Wolf told Tommy that he doesn't like vanilla pudding and walked away.

Therapist: Was Mr. Wolf alone with Tommy when this happened or were others around?

Harry/Wolf: Others were with Tommy.

Therapist: How did Tommy react to Mr. Wolf?

Harry/Wolf: He didn't say anything at lunch, but at recess Tommy invited Mr. Wolf to play kickball.

Therapist: Has Mr. Wolf spoken up before with Tommy?

Harry/Wolf: No, this was the first time.

Therapist: How did you feel about Mr. Fox staying in the hole and Mr. Wolf talking to Tommy?

Harry/Wolf: Mr. Wolf was glad Mr. Fox stayed in his hole and that Tommy asked Mr. Wolf to play kickball.

In this session, the therapist is exploring with Harry Landscape of Action questions, which allow the therapist to dig for details and actions involving events in search of Unique Outcomes. Next an exploration is undertaken into what the Unique Outcome means in terms of the person's beliefs, expectations, values, etc. and these are what are known as Landscape of Identity questions.[13] The therapist is beginning the process of Scaffolding by mapping out the history of the problem, trying to fill in gaps that might have developed in the story, and making a connection between the past and present. Then the therapist explores the effects of the problem. In the following scene, the therapist will focus on the Unique Outcome

Therapist: Is having Mr. Fox stay in his hole something you would like to happen more often with other students and with your teachers?

Harry/Wolf: I like when Mr. Fox stays in his hole.

Therapist: And did Mr. Fox stay when you were in the library choosing your books?

Harry/Wolf: He always stays in his hole in the library.

Therapist: How are you able to keep Mr. Fox away in the library?

Harry/Wolf: The library is my place. The other students know that I have the most reader points and they don't bother me.

Therapist: Could that be because they know you are a good reader and a smart young man?

Harry/Wolf: Maybe, I never thought of that.

Therapist: Do you like the way the other kids treat you in the library?

Harry/Wolf: Yes, I wish it were like that all the time.

Therapist: This week when you are at school, can you think of some ways that you might keep Mr. Fox in his hole like at the library.

Harry/Wolf: Mr. Wolf could walk away like he did in the lunchroom, or let Mr. Wolf talk to the teacher if someone is bothering him.

Therapist: I think those are good ways to keep Mr. Fox away.

(Following the session, the Therapist contacts the school consultant and asks for teachers to be on the lookout for positive changes in Harry's behavior and to work diligently to acknowledge those positive changes with Harry. He also confers with the PE teacher and they establish a plan to reward Harry after four days of positive behavior with one day to go to the library during PE.)

The Scaffolding process, which includes mapping out the problem, is an important step in preparing the client for recognizing areas of competence for which they have become unaware. Some clients are so beaten down and disheartened by the struggles they are facing, it is difficult for them to believe they even have competencies to help them tackle the

13. Ibid.

problems. It requires tenacity on the part of the therapist in order to identify these competencies.[14]

The next step in the Narrative process is Re-authoring or Re-storying
the problematic story. Wimberly defines Re-authoring as a change in the
personal, marital-family, and ministry myths. By transforming the beliefs
and convictions held about ourselves, we are not at the mercy of our childhood experiences, unconscious processes, and cultural conventions.[15]
Through the Re-storying therapeutic process, the client is assisted in creating a sense of empowerment, self-efficacy, and hope.[16]

When Re-storying with children it is important to offer structure
and guidance consistent with their cognitive abilities. It is important to
first allow the child to describe the problem from their own perspective
and ask the child to identify ways they engage with the problem to lessen
its influence. Using these ideas given by the child helps to co-create new
meanings about ways to manage the problem. This type of dialogue provides evidence of Unique Outcomes and serves as the entry point for the
Re-storying and affirms the child's ability to effect change with respect to
the problem.[17]

Certainly with the right support and opportunities, a child can Re-
story a problem story by replacing it with a story that details strengths
and resilience. Having a diagnosable condition such as ADHD (Attention
Deficit Hyper Disorder) is only one aspect of a complex individual. Rather
than a description of "I am ADHD", the story can be Re-authored to a
description of "I am a strong and courageous individual, and I can deal
with ADHD." In other words, the totality of the person's identity is not
being ADHD; rather, the person has a problem with ADHD. There are
always aspects of a child's life that show how they are competent, caring,
or a contributor to the welfare of others. These new stories can be told and
their volume increased so that others come to know the youth differently.
In the following scene, the therapist will begin the Re-authoring process
with Harry.

*Therapist: Harry, I brought out my sandbox again, which contains
many forest friends including a wolf and a fox. I wonder if you might share
with me your experiences with the wolf and the fox this week.*

---

14. Monk et al., *Narrative Therapy in Practice.*

15. Wimberly, *Recalling our own Stories.*

16. Monk et al., *Narrative Therapy in Practice.*

17. Bennett, "Narrative Methods and Children," 21.1.

(Harry plays in the sand box, but begins to tell his story more in the form of a personal narrative)

Harry: This week I won a prize for my reading report and the whole class cheered for me and we had a pizza party!

Therapist: That's awesome, Harry! Tell me, how in the world did that happen with Mr. Fox lurking around.

Harry: Mr. Fox was not happy about it, but I don't care, because I like it when the class cheers for me. And Friday, I got to spend a day in the library during my PE time, because I was good in PE all week.

Therapist: How did it feel to receive a special reward like that?

Harry: I really like my PE teacher now.

Therapist: Did Mr. Fox stay in his hole all week?

Harry: There was one time when someone on the playground kicked some dirt up at me, and I got really mad. Mr. Fox tried to come out, but then I remembered Mr. Wolf could choose to walk away and Mr. Fox went right back into his hole.

Therapist: Sounds like you and Mr. Wolf are really working well together at keeping Mr. Fox under control. Tell me, Harry, what is like to be a boy that can control his anger and stay out of trouble?

Harry: I like it that I can make good choices and make friends at school.

Therapist: What effect is that having on your schoolwork and your teachers?

Harry: I am finishing my homework now, and my teachers are helping me each day. I even get a turn to be the teacher's assistant now.

Therapist: Did you know you could be that strong and keep Mr. Fox in his hole?

Harry: I didn't think so, but now I know I can.

Therapist: What would be different and what would it look like if you and Mr. Wolf stayed strong and kept Mr. Fox under control?

Harry: I would be able to concentrate on my schoolwork and make friends at school. My teachers would be happy about that.

Therapist: I'm glad to hear that, and so happy to know that your PE teacher and your classroom teachers are supporting you. Is there anyone else who will support you?

Harry: My aunt and uncle are happy that I didn't get any pink slips this week, and they promised me ice cream this afternoon for my reading report grade.

Therapist: Harry, do you think your mom and dad would be proud of you if they were here today?

Harry: Yes, I know they would

Therapist: Would you like to write them a letter and tell them all about how you are keeping Mr. Fox in his hole and tell them about your reading report?

Harry: I would like that very much.

After the Re-storying process, the Re-membering process begins. In the Re-membering process, the therapist asks questions such as the ones in the scene above which allow the client to notice themselves from the perspective of another, such as a significant person from the past or a family member. These questions allow other relationships into the room and put clients into a position where they see themselves the way the therapist and others see them. By bringing these people into the therapeutic environment, a powerful audience is developed for the development of an alternative story.[18] In Harry's case, the therapist is assisting him in developing an audience that includes his family, his teachers, and his schoolmates. Harry is also encouraged to include his deceased parents as way to bridge from past to present. To have new stories heard, they must have a powerful audience in order to applaud the child and give power to the new story he is telling about himself. The more people who hear the Alternative Narrative and show support, the more likely the new story will stick.[19]

The therapist enlists the support of the teachers and school system by having them keep a special record of the times Harry is successful at keeping the problem under control. They agreed to also send him to the principal's office for some positive reinforcement rather than just for those times when he was having difficulty. The next session the therapist invited Harry's aunt in to the room to speak about her experiences with Harry's new story and to offer support and affirmation for him. The therapist also gave Harry the opportunity to share the letter he wrote to his deceased parents if he chose, and they planned a time to visit the cemetery to send the letter away through a ritual. The therapist planned a ceremony to celebrate Harry's success with his support audience after ten positive reports from his school contact. In conclusion, Harry was asked to be a consultant to other children who might also struggle with the problems Harry faced. He agreed to create a video that other children can view.

Rituals and Celebrations are important in order to recognize the significant steps in the process of moving away from a problem story to a new, preferred story. Rituals and Ceremonies are as unique as the

18. Zimmerman and Dickerson, *If Problems Talked.*

19. Little et al., "Practical Applications, 37.

people who come to therapy and can be performed with or without the therapist. The therapist and client collaborate on the timing, the scope, and the content of the rituals and the appropriate audience. The telling and performance of the new story in settings such as rituals and celebrations can be transformative.[20] In the case of Harry, the therapist worked closely with the school to build a support system, that could be included in a closing celebration. He included a ritual to emphasis the importance of Re-membering the support Harry would have received from his deceased parents, and the therapist included Harry's legal guardian, his Aunt. All of these plans would have been made under Harry's guidance giving him the authority to direct his celebration.

Through the use of Narrative Therapy, children and adults realize the power of their personal stories. In collaboration with the therapist, clients are able to address the problems in their lives. Children become aware of the effects of problems in their lives and can decide to mobilize efforts against those problems. The client decides what the new story will be and why it is important to them. The key elements of the new story are what these changes mean to the individual's identity, about the kind of individual he/she prefers to become, and about people's experience of them.

20. Morgan, *What is Narrative Therapy?*

12

I Am Only 12 and Have to Parent

Child Headed Families' Stories of Survival

Tapiwa N. Mucherera

WHAT A GIFT IT is to have parents. Many children don't realize what a blessing it is to have parents who care about their welfare and wellbeing. Greater is the gift of one having caring parents being physically present during the early precious formative years of one's childhood. Many young children today no longer have the "luxury" of having parents who will see them grow through their infancy or to their teenage years. The HIV/ AIDS pandemic has wreaked havoc on many families, especially children on the African continent. No child expects to be parenting their siblings by the age of twelve or even fourteen years of age. Worse still is a child at this early age having the responsibility of taking care of their ailing parents, as well as burying their parents at their death. It has, however, become the norm for many children around the world, and many wonder why God chose them for such a role at such a tender age where they themselves are looking for someone to parent them at this early stage of the journey called *life*.

Children in these roles quickly discover that they have to maneuver through the world of adults and are expected to act as adults. At the same time, when these children try to live into the world of adults they are reminded that they are still children and are expected to act as other children. Even with these mixed messages they have to grow up fast, yet there is not a place for them to fit in. They can't afford to act as children because it means no one will take care of them and/or their other siblings. While living in the world of adults at this age also often means abuse or being marginalized by a society ran or managed by adults.

This is true in many parts of the world today, especially South Central parts of Africa due to the HIV/AIDS pandemic.[1] In this chapter, the author presents interviews of families that are child headed. The children narrate their struggles, pain, and the grief of losing parents at a young age. Many of the children report the pain of having to deal with the way the community and extended families treated them—the very people from whom they expected support treated them in an abusive manner or deserted them. In the midst of these hopeless and bleak situations these children found much hope and support, especially given by church people and individuals who took interest in their daily affairs. In the normal world of humans, it is abnormal for young children to raise or be fully responsible for the welfare of their younger siblings. The children reported that they found their ultimate hope in God, the One who created and sustains them day in and day out. God is what kept them hoping for a brighter tomorrow. In presenting their stories, some of the orphaned children reflect theologically on evil, the meaning of forgiveness and reconciliation, and grace and hope in God as reflected by their narratives. How did these children find God in the midst of their suffering? How did a sense of community through the lenses of narrative become a "cloud of witness?" It is only through sharing their stories in light of the meta-narrative (Scriptures) and experiences of God's daily saving grace that these children found hope to continue the journey called *life*.

The use of the Narrative Approach works well with these children because it allows them to tell their stories. Some of the stories the children told were shared for the first time. These orphaned children wished they would have more such informal times with adults to share about their struggles and as a way to help them make informed decisions about life—that is, a palaver[2] with people just willing to listen to their concerns. Excerpts from the interviews are presented. The goal of the chapter is to use the Narrative Counseling approach while letting the children's stories self-present. In other words, the stories are "in their own words," that is, in the words of the orphaned children.

1. MSNBC "Scientist Make Curing of HIV a Priority."
2. Mucherera, *Meet me*, ix.

Survivors with Hope:
Enala and Her Two Siblings (Zambia, Lusaka)

At the time of the interview Enala was a twenty-three-year-old single woman who was taking care of two of her siblings. They lost their mother when Enala was twelve-years-old. The father, who was already ill and bedridden, died two years later. Enala had two older sisters. One married when the parents were still alive and the other, older sister got married as soon as the father died. At age fourteen Enala was left with a younger sister (twelve-years-old) and a younger brother (eight-years-old) to take care of. She took the role of being the head of the household soon after the father's passing in 1999. The older sisters were never concerned about Enala and the welfare of the other younger siblings. They told Enala to be responsible since they had their own families for which to care. At first she thought they would reconsider their decision and they would come help. Eventually, she realized both of them were not going to help with Enala and the other sibling's wellbeing and it meant she had to take charge as head of household right away.

Note that from this point on the conversation turns to "Externalizing Conversations."[3] The interviewer intentionally asks questions in an externalizing manner, so as to help Enala narrate her story in a way that helps "distance her" from the story and pain. In the interview, Enala answers the questions in third person and the interviewer also asks the questions of Enala in third person. As indicated in the introductory chapter, Externalizing Conversations allow room for a person to talk about oneself. Enala talks about "Enala and her siblings" as if they were other people, but she is talking about herself. This is a Narrative Approach that works very well when people tell painful stories or experiences about themselves.

What are the words that would best describe "Enala and her two siblings? *Enala would say, "survivors with hope." At that young age Enala and her siblings learned to survive and to simply have hope even in the face of a bleak life. There were days they would pray for food when they had nothing in the house left and somehow the Lord provided. A lady at the church they attended would once in a while give them a few things such as food items and it tended to happen when there was nothing left to eat in the house. Many times Enala and her siblings survived on thick porridge and peanuts. For some, peanuts are nothing or not that important, but for Enala and her siblings at this young age they saw the hand of God in their lives in providing*

---

3. Morgan, *What is Narrative Therapy*, 17.

them with the peanuts. *They could not have made it through life without the hand of the Lord providing for them in times of need. God created them and it was God who was going to see them through, to survive life, and that's what gave them "a future with hope."*

Their house was four roomed and at that young age it dawned on Enala that they could rent some of the rooms for survival. Enala decided to rent out two of the rooms to sustain themselves. It was not always easy for her to get the rent money on time since she was dealing with adults as a child. Somehow, God always provided her with the skills and patience to work with the adult renters. She used some of the rent money to buy food, clothes, and pay for their school fees. She learned basic budgeting skills early. Enala saved some of the rent money until she had enough to start building two more rooms to rent out. By the age of sixteen, Enala had managed and supervised the completion of two more rooms. This was added income to the existing two other rooms, helping with much needed income since school fees is always higher as you move from one grade to another.

A Day In The Life of An Orphaned Child

Can Enala describe a day in the life of "Enala and her two siblings" or if you could tell about a day in the life of an orphaned child,—either what Enala has experienced or what she has seen/observed? *Life in the day of an orphan is bad. Many of the orphans drop out of school. You find kids on a daily basis engaged in prostitution to survive. They engage in these behaviors not by choice but for survival. Some men take advantage of this and abuse these young girls. These kids are abused, neglected, and some end up on the streets stealing from people just to survive. Just as we did, many of the orphans can go for days without food, just drinking water. If they go to school, they sleep in class because they are hungry and can't pay attention to the teacher. Some drop out of school because their uniforms are so tattered and they are ashamed to wear them to school. You also find others who end up addicted to drugs such as inhaling glue, drinking, and smoking marijuana as a way of escaping the suffering and/or stresses of life at such a young age. Enala actually counts her brother and sister blessed since they were left with a four-roomed house to live in. Other orphaned children might belong to parents who were renting and the day the last parent dies those kids are thrown out of the rental property onto the streets. Can you imagine, one day you have a roof over your head and the next you have nowhere to go, but just open air? All that belongs to you is what you can carry in your bag. You may have been the brightest in your class but it won't matter anymore since you are pre-occupied by where to get food and where you are going to lay your head. Those who used to call you a friend now avoid and shun you. As many children are not always well informed about HIV/AIDS some might actually think that since your parents died of "the disease" you also might have it and they don't want to catch it from you. Due to lack of proper nutrition many of these children may lose weight fast and appear sickly and be suspected of carrying "the disease." Literally, one becomes an outcast of the community and/or society in general.*

What are some of the things that "Enala and her two siblings" and/or other orphaned children would hope for, that they could use on a daily basis? *People such as "Enala and her two siblings" who have been orphaned need to be trained in skills that they can use such as tailoring, building, raising poultry, etc., things they can use their hands in order to survive. These are things that they can lean on and use for their daily survival. Feeding them for a day is not enough even though sometimes it may be necessary. They need education and as indicated before, skills such as carpentry, building, and sawing, for example. The type of education they need is not just book knowledge but also an education that provides them with skills to survive life, and to be able to self-sustain. If they can have a way to start up a project such as gardening or raising a few chickens this can help them with providing food at the table, and they could also sell some in order to buy more. What Enala has experienced is that hard times force one to be creative and innovative to survive. That's why "Enala and her two siblings" are survivors with hope." One uses the God-given gifts from birth, with the hope that God will bless what one does. God has never failed Enala and her siblings. Enala used to be angry with God but realized she was biting the hand that had fed her, was feeding her and would continue to feed her. She had to forgive herself and had to ask God for forgiveness for such misguided anger. Enala realized that she responded to things out of anger and that having an unforgiving spirit was making her immobile spiritually, emotionally, and relationally. As she grew older, Enala concluded that someone made a choice and brought the illness into the family that killed both their parents, not God. She realized that she had to forgive the parent responsible in order to move on in life. Once she took the step of forgiving herself and the parent, she experienced much peace and felt a weight had been lifted from her shoulders. Enala has much more peace with God than when she was younger.*

So what plans does "Enala and/ or her two siblings," have for the future? *Enala has chosen to go to school majoring in social work and* psychology. *Enala wants to do psycho-social work, especially working with other orphaned children so she can help them in counseling and encouraging them in obtaining hands-on skills. Many of the orphaned children are finding out that they need skills to be self-sustaining since they cannot always depend on their relatives who already have the burden of taking care of their own families on limited resource.*

Enala hopes that her siblings will keep focused and continue to go to school as they are doing. Parenting one's siblings is a challenge, however it has been amazing that the youngest sibling treats Enala more like a parent and it might be because of the age difference. They are both in high school and the older is about to write her ordinary level exams. If she qualifies, the older wants to be a teacher and the youngest sibling wants to be a doctor or nurse. They pray, talk, and thank God always for how He has given them the resilience as an orphaned family. They also try to make it to church every Sunday as much as possible.

Spiritual and Emotional Needs

What are some of the spiritual and emotional challenges that "Enala and her two siblings" have encountered? *It is hard to be upright as a Christian when you are a young person with no adult supervision. As a child, one needs the support of others, especially adults. As the older of the other two siblings, Enala felt she had the freedom to do whatever she wanted. She, however, soon realized that the younger siblings looked up to her for guidance and if she chose the wrong path they would likely follow. Knowing that the siblings depended on Enala made her reconsider her choices. The habit that had helped Enala the most is going to church. At church people have helped Enala find some of the answers about life for which she was searching. This does not mean she has found all the answers, but the few she has found have been helpful. Being told that what she was going through would come to pass encouraged Enala. She has been taught to walk by faith, not by sight, and that it was not necessary to have all the luxuries of the world and lose one's soul by being involved in prostitution, etc. Being content with the basics that God has provided would give them so much joy; hope and strength to carry on against the challenges that life might through their way.*

I realize the following is a tough question for Enala and she does not have to answer it. Was there any moments when Enala wished to end it all? *Enala says that she des not want to answer the question. She however, expresses that most of what she wished was all the suffering to pass way.*

Enala used to think that she was wrongly placed—that is born in the wrong family. Why did God leave her to take care of her younger siblings at such a young age? What evil did she commit for her to bear such suffering and responsibility as a small child. She was the one to provide them with food, school fees, and clothes at that young age? Why her? And what about her own childhood? She can't ever say she ever experienced the "play-full and care-free" years of childhood, because from when the parents became bedridden and died she was one of the responsible ones to take care of them. As soon as both were gone by the age of fourteen years she was thrown into the adult role raising her siblings. Once she accepted Christ and these responsibilities, she stopped asking, "why Enala?" to "what's next?" which led her to learn to live one day at a time.

The people who were most helpful to Enala, emotionally, were some of her friends (her age), especially those from church. They kept sharing with Enala about what the Bible says and that all would come to pass someday. Some men and women at the church helped them a little bit financially, especially soon after the father's death, and it helped to know that there were some people that still cared.

Enala tried to seek help from the extended family. She went to one of the close uncles (father's brother) once to ask for help and he told her to do what the other girls were doing, which meant he was telling her to go into prostitution. It baffled Enala's mind since this uncle seemed to be the one that cared the most before Enala's father died. Through it all, Enala became independent and gained self-respect and it made her stronger. Enala thanks the church for what they have been able to do to help them as a family.

Enala became very protective of her siblings, especially when they turned into their teenage years; she kept a close eye on them. She wanted to make sure they were not emotionally, physically, and sexually abused. Enala made sure they were well informed about how people contracted the HIV/AIDS virus and how to self-defend if someone tried to touch them inappropriately. Enala and her siblings started or ended most of their days with prayer whenever possible.

What Enala missed out in life the most is that she did not get the opportunity to be a child. She had to raise her siblings and had to mature fast. In addition, she had to find ways to defend them from emotional abuse from people and to teach whom not to trust. Church is central in their life and they are finding that some of the extended family members are starting to take interest in them, probably because they have realized that "Enala and her sibling" are independent and self-sustaining materially, and that God loves them.

The Tale of Two Brothers: Collins and Fungai

Fungai is a sixteen-year-old male (Form 3, 11th Grade) and his brother Collins is seventeen (Form 4, 12th Grade). Their father died in 2001 and the mother died in July of 2008. This conversation with the brothers happened in October of 2008. Before the mother died in 2008 she had been bedridden and the boys had to work to supplement the family income. Until the mother's death they were allowed to stay in the company house for which the mother worked. Soon after the mother passed away, they were kicked out of the house. They have since been hopping from place to place trying to buy time for the older brother to sit for his exam in November. They have an Auntie who is trying to help, but she is also renting and they all can't stay at her place. They sometimes end up staying with neighbors or some of their friends from school. In short, they have no place to call home. The Auntie has paid the fees for Collins to write his O'levels (ordinary level exams).

The Conversation Turns to Externalizing Conversation from This Point

Collins, can you tell me how "Collins and his brother" have managed and who has become the pillar of support for them in their struggles to make it through life?

One of the most important persons in their life is their friend Evans. They usually go to him to talk issues out if both of them need someone to talk to. Evans is only twenty-two-years-old, but he has become like their emotional support if they need it. Evans helps both Fungai and Collins with homework. It is critical at this time, especially this year, since many of the teachers are on strike and those who are sitting for exams are not receiving any tutoring. When Fungai and Collins go for tutoring with Evans, most of the time he usually asks them about their day and this gives them a chance to "empty out" emotionally if they were not feeling well that day.

Fungai and Collins see Evans as someone who was placed in their life by God. If it were not for Evans, they do not know where they would be today. Collins and Fungai wish there were more people such as Evans in their community who could help orphaned children. When many people in the community see orphaned children, they just assume they are going to ask for money or food, etc. Yes, that might be the case in many instances, especially if the children are young, but it is not always that they are looking for food or money. Sometimes it is a matter of thirty-minutes for these children to share their burdens. Many people miss the opportunity to minister to these children because what they see written on the children's faces is "material needs." Others miss the one-time opportunity God presents them thinking if they listen to children like Collins and Fungai, they will keep coming back and bother them. Yes, they may come back if you open the door for such, but sometimes they don't want to come back, they just need someone to talk to at that moment.

So what are some of the things Fungai wishes or wished for in life, had things not turned out the way they are?

Fungai grew up wishing he could have gone to a boarding school. He hears stories from friends about boarding school and it sounds more fun than staying and going to school from home. When their father died, the only option mother could afford was for them to attend school from home. Fungai appreciates what mother did and hopefully next year, God willing, he will be able to sit for his "Ordinary Level Exams—12ths Grade). Another wish that Fungai has is if the extended family had supported them materially, especially as it pertains to school fees and such.

As the youngest, Fungai has always and still wishes their parents were still alive. Spiritually, this was one of the hardest things with which Fungai struggled. It was hard for Fungai to accept Mom and Dad's deaths. He cried all the time. Collins would go to church but Fungai did not go. Fungai and Collins did not talk much about the parents' deaths since every time the subject was brought up Fungai would always cry. Fungai was very angry with God and wanted God to show how He was the Almighty but let their parents die. He would tell Collins that he (Fungai) identified with the story of Job in the Bible. The only difference for Fungai was in the Bible, it was Job's children who died. Sometimes Fungai wished he were the one who had died, not the parents. It is hard to be children alone without parents; sometimes one goes without food, care, or hope, and just the basic needs.

Some of the toughest times for Fungai are those when he needed someone to talk to and there was no one there. When the mother was alive she provided for them, but they are now struggling with material needs not always being met, it is hard. Yes, most of all Fungai always wished his parents were alive. Fungai now also talks to the pastor, but the pastor is not always available. One of the reasons why Fungai stopped going to church was because during the early stages of losing both parents, some people did not want to talk to them. Collins and Fungai would be excluded from some of the youth church activities. It was hard that some grown ups would say painful things such as, "you are reaping and paying for your parents' sins, and God is punishing you for the 'soar grapes your parents ate." Things are changing for the better at church and my hope in God the Almighty is growing. One day I hope to be a medical doctor.

The Determined Nomsa and Her Four Siblings

Nomsa (seventeen) is raising her four siblings, Panashe (twelve), Jacob (nine), Simbiso (seven), and Sam (five). The interview took place in 2008 and Nomsa's mother had died in 2006. She reports that her father died in Mozambique and was not sure of the exact dates. He had built a house for the family but it was taken away from them by the extended family when the mother was still alive. The mother in 2005, started going to beer-halls. Nomsa tried to confront her mother about these behaviors and the mother responded by saying Nomsa did not understand about life and that some day when she is grown she would. Soon after, the mother became pregnant with twins. The twins died and Nomsa found out later they died of HIV complications. The mother continued with her lifestyle and became pregnant again. She gave birth to another sibling who died and the mother's health deteriorated.

(Note: From here on the conversation is in third person to allow Nomsa to talk about herself and her siblings and how they have survived).

Tell me about the time Nomsa started caring for her Mom when she became sick.

Our mother revealed to Nomsa and the family after the twins died that she was ill from HIV. Nomsa dropped out of school to help raise the other children. Mother died in 2006. Nosma tried to ask for help from the extended family, especially the two well-known uncles (father's brothers) who play soccer and basketball. They acted as if the relationship was "a borrowed one" or existed because it "had been bought." Both of the uncles indicated that Nomsa and her siblings would become an expense to them with school fees and everyday up-keep, therefore, the uncles were not going to help. It was shocking that as young as Nomsa was, the uncles advised her to prostitute in order to take care of the other siblings. They asked her when was she going to grow up, and if she didn't remember what her mother was doing, as an example of what to do—that is going to beer-halls to prostitute and to do likewise, if she and the siblings were going to survive. Nomsa told them that they were telling her to do things that had caused their mother to be ill in the first place and sarcastically thanked them for their wise advise and their trying to kill off the only person old enough to take care of the rest of the remaining family. At the time when Nomsa went to talk to her uncles looking for help, she had an older sister who was accidentally run over by a car but survived. The sister was placed under the care of an organization called Lighthouse.

When Nomsa and her siblings had nothing to eat at the house, and the mother was bedridden most of the time, she realized she had to find help somewhere. Nomsa went to Simukai (an organization that helps orphans and street kids) to ask for help. Nomsa did not tell them the full truth and told them that they did not have a mother. When the Simukai people came to visit us, the mother acted as if she was a next-door neighbor. The mother had a hard time that day trying to get out of the house to their next-door neighbor's yard where she lay under a tree shed. Simukai started helping Nomsa and her siblings with some of the basic needs, mostly food. Nomsa went to look for work and started working at Red Cross and Hobehouse.

When their grandmother would come to visit, she would not use the utensils used by their mother. As much as their mother was bedridden, she would try to cook for grandmother, and grandmother would refuse to eat any food that our mother prepared for fear of being infected by the virus. It was as if a person who is HIV positive is no longer a person or infectious just by touching her or anything the person touched. People have these banners about "love" hanging on their walls in their homes, but really do not know what love is all about. They just utter the words, but its not coming from the heart. Our Mom died Dec 18th 2006, the same day her best friend, who used to be our emotional support, also died.

Nomsa and the young sister (next in age) started having problems (sibling rivalry). She had to tell the younger sister that if she wanted Nomsa's birthright she had to drop out of school and start taking care of everyone. They had a three-year-old brother who needed constant care and supervision so the birthright came with that responsibility as well. This helped to calm the relationship and they started respecting one another. Simukai also assigned a Guardian for them who would come and check on them at least once a week.

Can you tell me about some of the experiences of "Nomsa and her siblings" or even things that you have seen orphans go through? *Nomsa's experience is that, as an orphan one never knows who to tell one's problems,* especially people from the community. Some of the Guardians take the food for themself that they are supposed to give to the orphans and belittle the orphans. When you tell some of the Guardians about the struggles as a family, they just laugh it away and say to be thankful that at least we are alive and not dead or infected like our parents were. Just being alive is not enough to go through life. We need all the basic stuff to survive, plus everyone needs human relationships, especially as young as we are.

Right now we have a sibling who is HIV positive, but we do not tell anyone other than the doctors and nurses who know. Some children mock us and say we look like people who suffer from kwashiorkor or people who are not fed. Others ask whether we have a mother at home even though they know that our parents are dead. They will continue to say that "you have a dead mother, you forsaken things, pfutseki" (this is a word usually used to chase away dogs). When people found out that our mother was bedridden and would be sleeping in the house (and even after she passed way), some people would throw rubbish into our house if we left the door or windows open. Nomsa and her siblings have been told many times by others that they smell, they are dirty and filthy even though Nomsa makes it a point that every sibling takes a bath everyday and that their clothes are washed and clean. Children can be very mean spirited and it is surprising because the same kids don't realize that tomorrow they may be in our shoes. In this life one should never laugh at someone, because what goes around comes around.

Nomsa struggles with migraine headache since her mother died, and experiences them especially when there is a lot of tension with the siblings or the Guardian. Nomsa is very protective of her siblings, especially the younger ones. She tries to fill the mother's void or absence even though she is not always successful at it.

What keeps Nomsa and her siblings hopeful? *God is the One who keeps Nomsa and her sibling hopeful. Without God they would have died a long time ago. There are times when there was no food and someone, through God's grace, would bring some food. Do you remember the story of the old woman in 1 Kings 17, where the bowl of flour was not exhausted nor the jar of oil became empty? Great was that woman's faith and that is the way Nomsa and her siblings have lived their life. Even though there are days they have gone without food, it has never been too long. The Lord has always been on-time in re-filling the "bowl of flour" and "the jar of oil." Our cup, through God's grace, always runneth over. God has always been our hope and our refugee.*

Our pastor has also helped Nomsa and her siblings many times, not necessarily with material things but with emotional and spiritual matters. At church, we have heard our pastor preach about respect for the elders, widows, and orphans, and to treat each other as people created in the image of God. Once in a while, when Nomsa is "overloaded" emotionally, she goes to talk to the pastor. She just needs someone who will listen to her, without necessarily giving any advice. Nomsa's pastor is great at this and this has helped much. The Guardian has been good as well in talking to Nomsa and her siblings as a whole family. As children, we have disagreements and the Guardian helps Nomsa and the siblings to see each other's perspectives. It's a rough road, but we will travel through it with God's help. Thanks for asking Nomsa all these questions because just sharing these burdens that she had hidden inside of her helps take away much weight from her emotional shoulder. Maybe, she was able to open up because you seem to care and that she needs to be truthful to you and to Nomsa. (The other siblings who were playing outside in the yard came in and they were introduced). They looked healthy except for one, anyone could tell that he was not as healthy.

The Least of These: Peter and Daniel

In 2008, Peter (eighteen) and Daniel (fourteen) are living in a one-room they are renting. They have a little two-plate stove, one bed, and a wardrobe in this tiny room they've called home since 2003. Peter and Daniel started living in this room just before the mother died. They had a place at the market where Peter helped his mother sell fruit and vegetables. When the mother was bedridden, Peter continued to go to school and operate the market to raise money for rent and to live on. Their father died in 1997 and the mother died in 2003. After the mother died, her body was in the mortuary for four and a half months because they did not have any relatives to help them with the burial processes and money to buy a coffin. Peter went to the rural areas to ask for help from the relatives and no one was willing to step up to help. Peter went to a neighbor, Mr. Samuriwo, who was a carpenter and they agreed to trade with Mr. Samuriwo, getting one of their wardrobes and he making a coffin in which to bury their mother. Peter was thirteen-years-old at that time. Peter and Daniel went to the mortuary to claim the mother's body even though they were not sure what to do when they were given the body. When they got to the mortuary, a soldier happened to be there outside the building. They did not know the man but he took interest in two young boys carrying a coffin.

They told the soldier their story of how their mother's body had been in the mortuary for four and half months and how they finally managed to get the coffin and they were going to bury their mother. The soldier took over from there and helped them bury their mother.

When the mother died, the two brothers had a three-year-old step-brother living with them, and an only sister who got married a week after. They did not know the father of the stepbrother. The sister left the three year old with Peter and Daniel to take care, and she left with her new husband.

The Conversation Shifts to Externalizing Conversations from This Point

So, Peter, tell me how Peter, Daniel and the three-year-old sibling survived after the mother passed away.

Peter would go to collect plastic bags from dumpsters and garbage cans, clean up the plastics bags and resell them at the market. While digging in the garbage for the plastics, if he found fruit that was partially rotten, he would cut the bad parts out, wash them, and take them home for dinner. At the market, some people threw away partially bad cabbages and Peter would also take that home and cook them for dinner. Sometimes, if there were no food from the garbage, Peter would go around begging. Many times however, it was as if God knew that Peter would be going to the garbage and there would be something they could use to take care of "the least of these," us the orphaned three children. The money Peter had he sacrificed to pay for his school exams fees for 7th grade so as to qualify to go to secondary school. This left them with no money to trade at the market except for re-selling the plastic bags. 2003 was the toughest year for Peter and his siblings and looking back, he even wonders how they made it through.

Despite all the hardships they were facing, Peter managed to sit for his exams and passed with flying colors. Knowing that there was no way to proceed with school, even though he had passed the exam, in January 2004 Peter and his siblings turned to Simukai for help. Simukai started supporting them with rent money and the Lighthouse church offered to pay for Peter's school fees for secondary education. Meanwhile, the stepbrother became very sick. Peter and Daniel continued to take care of him until one day he died in Peter's arms. This was one of the most painful losses for Peter and Daniel since the three had bonded and were very close. A few months after the step-brother died, they received word their only sister got sick and died as well.

Daniel, we have heard what Peter had to say, what is your side of the story about you and Peter.

Now that Daniel is fourteen, he has grown to realize how Peter had to work hard to maintain our family. At young age, Daniel did not worry at all as long as Peter brought something for them to eat no matter how small. Sometimes, he thinks Peter would go without food to make sure us (the young brothers) got a little something in our stomachs. Daniel would ask Peter if he had eaten and he would always say, he was fine and for Daniel and the stepbrother to eat. Daniel grew up not seeing Peter as a brother, but as a parent, provider, and support. The pastor at the church also helped us a lot when we wanted to talk. There are times when other people or kids from the community would scorn and tease Daniel for being orphaned, and that we would follow our parents soon in death. These are the moments when Daniel, especially, wished the parents were alive. Daniel was happy living with his brother, Peter, but society told him there was something wrong with whom they were. Daniel came to conclude that it was God's will to be whom they were and not to listen to those who were trying to put them down.

So Peter, tell me how Peter and Daniel were able to handle the grief of losing a father, mother, brother, and sister in such a short period of time.

Peter has struggled much with grieving and he has always sought out the pastor and Auntie Nancy at the church to share when he feels burdened. He is very choosy on who he shares his hurts. Some people don't have a sense of confidentiality, thereby, they are not trustworthy. One of the main questions Peter struggled with was why God was putting all these people into his life and then taking them away. Recently, the struggle has been whether God will take Daniel away from him as well and/or he's afraid that if Peter were to die first, what would become of Daniel? There are no answers, but the pastor and Auntie Nancy have assured Peter of God's love, care, and grace for them. It is by God's grace that Peter and Daniel are alive, and that's what gives Peter hope even with all these unanswered questions. Peter and Daniel are very careful of the type of friends they have, because friends have influence on decisions about the future.

Does Peter have anything he wished the church or community could do to help children in these types of circumstances?

Children in Peter and his brothers' circumstances need mentors. If no one mentors them, they end up on the streets, influence each other negatively, and end up smoking glue, and doing drugs as a way to deal with their problems. They are seen as "nobodies" and they behave as the community perceives them. Orphaned children need to be taught skills and be able to be accorded education. Many of the children would like to be able to have skills so they can be self-sustaining. Adults in the community need to sit down and just listen to these children and help if they can, otherwise, we are going to end up with a generation of thugs. Many of these children know about the word love, but they have not experienced true love because people don't share it with them. The last thing Peter would say is that orphans are children first, not just orphans. Treat them as children, created in the same image God created those who are blessed to have surviving parents. It hurts to be treated like a dog or a wild animal. Orphaned children's hope, however, lies with the few who care about them, and in that it is God who created them in the first place. Peter's hope is to get a secondary education first, then go to a theological college and become a minister. Hopefully, Peter will someday be ministering and creating opportunities for "the least of these," the orphaned children.

These are the stories of these gallant children who survived against the odds and continue through faith in a few who took interest in them, and in their relentless faith in God. This is a challenge for the many of us who can afford to minister to "the least of these," so they can also have "a future with hope." Why don't you join the cause if the opportunity presents itself?

13

The Tragedy of Divorce and the Hope
Found through Narrative

ERIKA MAYERS

MY STORY

I HAVE SOME PERSONAL experience with Dominant Stories and the fallout of identity crisis when reality or circumstances proves that the Dominant Story is false. I lived life by one narrative with a dominant theme and then one evening in 1996 I discovered information that left me with a shattered narrative. At that time, I did not even have a beginning to an Alternate Story, I had what felt like a floor scattered with shards of a story I could no longer put together. I then spent time trying to find out who I really was and what story to live by.

I was married in 1990 to a man that I thought I loved and whom I thought loved me. I had expectations about what that marriage and love would do for me and how it would guide and complete my life. What I had blinded me to the red signal flags of truth. When my husband was my boyfriend he still had not quite broken up with his previous girlfriend, at least not in the beginning of our relationship. My husband did not want me to have friends outside our relationship and frowned upon my working late. It was not until I found evidence of what my husband's time off from work looked like that I was forced to face the facts and the reality of the true story of my married life. My husband was cheating on me. Before this day I had created a Dominant Story that was grounded in my identity of being a wife; being a good wife in a good marriage that would someday end in our growing old together and rocking on the porch in our rocking chairs. This changed when I learned what my world really was, which in turn made me doubt who I really was. I did not have the good marriage that I thought I had. I was not loved by my husband the way that I thought I was. I could no longer view myself as any kind of wife let alone a good wife. My Dominant Story became one of worthlessness and being less-than because I was not what I thought I should be—a good wife with a good marriage. I felt that I was less than everyone else because I did not have this anymore. Even though people would say that I did nothing wrong and that being single was okay, often their actions and the messages from social media said that I was a loser, less-than because I was without a family. For me, not being a wife meant that I would also not be a mother. The world was different and I was no longer confident that I knew who I was. And so the journey began.

Narrative Therapy is a skillful, intentional, and discerned approach to listening to people's problem-stories and collaborating with them in the pursuit of a hopeful and empowering Alternate Story. The Narrative counselor should possess certain skills of observation, persistence, respect, tentativeness, curiosity, and optimism; asking questions that he or she do not know the answer to.[1] Narrative Therapy is a collaborative approach where the client is the expert of his or her own problem and the counselor is the host of a therapeutic conversation that is set to the client's agenda. It is a co-creation that discovers the client's idle or unused "competencies, talents, abilities, and resources," in which the counselor helps to connect idle capabilities of the past to a present and potentially future overcoming of difficulties.[2] Narrative Therapy and its counselors have a positive view of human beings and their capabilities; it is about meaning-making and a hopeful future.

DIVORCE AND IDENTITY CRISIS

Divorce is one of those life changing events that not only changes a person's circumstances but also often leaves them questioning who they are in light of what has happened. Their identity is questioned. The causes of divorce, such as adultery, lying, manipulation, or criminal activity,

---

1. Monk et al., *Narrative Therapy in Practice.*
2. Ibid., 24.

contribute to the questioning of identity as much as the split itself.[3] I posit that some causes of divorce make a person feel as though the life they knew before was a lie. It is this feeling as though the life you were living was a lie that causes a person to also question who they think they are, at least this was my experience. I often heard similar stories from others in support groups that I attended. Hopper noticed that during the beginning of divorce proceedings the couples might be more ambiguous about divorce identities, but that after the proceedings start they almost always fall into assigning themselves the roles of either the initiator or the victim.[4] He also notes that the disorder of this life transition is a function of the lack of a social norm or rites-of-passage-type of guidelines that are usually associated with other life transitions. Not only do they have to rearrange and accommodate the changes in their daily lives and parenting responsibilities, but there are also adjustments that must be made to the way they view the world and themselves.

Divorce is not the kind of change that leaves one unscathed, even when the person is changed in a positive way it is nonetheless a change. There is a part of the divorce process that is a looking back over the relationship in hindsight to see what happened; this part may affect identity in that it highlights the difference between what you thought the relationship was at the time and what it actually was.[5] It also highlights that the other person may not have thought of you in the way that you thought they had. Even people who were quick to give complaints about their marriage could talk about the "security, safety, and comfort" that their marriage roles and its identity gave to them.[6] Olmstead, Futris, and Palsey found that divorce affects the role of father for men and, likewise, I propose, the mother role for women is also affected.[7] These roles are part of a person's identity, which is changed through divorce. Depending on the divorce settlement, the traditional roles within the family may also be blurred or changed altogether. Often both genders have to take on new duties and tasks of both roles at different times for their children. This transition can affect how one sees his/her own individual personal identity. Because these roles of mother and father are socially constructed, the view of these roles and related identity can change as divorce becomes more prevalent.

3. Hopper, "Oppositional Identities," 16.
4. Ibid.
5. Ibid.
6. Ibid., 141.
7. Olmstead et al., "An Exploration of Married," 249–68.

As the social norms are adjusting, it can be confusing for the individual as they no longer have a clear view of this part of their identity because of the "ambiguity and competing self-definitions [that] are exacerbated following divorce."[8] It can also change the meanings associated with such roles. Olmstead's study was limited to men and found that particularly with them their identity as fathers and what they perceived to be the obligations and responsibilities of that role was greatly hampered by the time available to perform those role functions.[9] This can hamper identity in that who you want to be and who you feel you are is limited by circumstances of divorce. It is this meaning-making or self-concept that Mummendey spoke of in regards to social identity and individual identity.[10]

Identity struggles due to divorce are not limited to the partners involved but also distills out to the children forced through the divorce as well. The consummate identity of a person, especially in the developmental years of teen and young adulthood, is affected by the person's identity-consistency, which is in turn affected by distress and chosen methods of coping.[11] This is a time when people are exploring identity choices affected by goals, values, and beliefs, which are further affected by the divorce proceedings of the adults in their lives. Depending on the choice of coping skills and other factors, such as self-differentiation and social support, one may either successfully resolve the natural developmental identity crisis or become subject to diffusion and insecurity in their identity. This can happen with all kinds of losses, but particularly with divorce loss as it affects a young person's secure base for life. It is suggested from the Mullis study that "college women who have experienced parental divorce tended to employ less adaptive coping strategies consistent with a destabilized sense of self."[12]

Teenagers and early adolescents are subject to the effects of identity conflict due to divorce, especially given their developmental stage. Erickson's stages put teenagers at the identity versus role confusion stage where the teenager is deciding who they are and developing a sense of belonging.[13] It can also cause teenagers to question the value of marriage and relationships and increase the chance of building an identity that leaves

8. Ibid., 251.

9. Ibid.

10. Mummendey, "Positive Distinctiveness," 657–70.

11. Mullis et al., "Relations Among Parental Divorce," 137–54.

12. Ibid., 150.

13. Devaris, "Family Therapy Issues," 242–47.

out the importance of family. Identity may be confused when one parent tries to draw a child into the divorce conflict; the forcing of taking sides or taking care of one parent or the other strains the roles and distorts the identity.

Part of the identity crisis and rebuilding after divorce is the realization that some of the process is out of your control; sometimes you have to "live out a bad decision that is made by someone else."[14] Identity is stretched in the adjustment of transition as daily life changes, new daily life is being established, going through disbelief, and accepting reality of what has taken place and that most things are now new. Going from being married to being single shifts a person's lifestyle and even social networks. "Divorce forces people to change."[15] A person cannot continue to live in the role of the old identity without discovering their new role or personal growth and their new identity will be stagnated. Accepting the new identity is easier with created space to experience that new identity. It is also detrimental to a person to let others force their vision of a new identity on them. The hope is that one can take time to grow emotionally, spiritually, socially, and as a whole person through the chaos of divorce.[16] While trying to resolve the identity confusion of divorce, submitting yourself to God is essential. It is imperative that one can see their "uniquely-created-in-the-image-of-God self" as part of a new identity.[17] Losing oneself in one's identity in Christ is to see one's self "perfectly reflected in the eyes of Jesus Christ, the one who loves me perfectly" and knows and can reveal one's true identity.[18] It is in this love that one can find true identity in the narrative of the Kingdom of God. Narrative Therapy's Alternate Story or Re-storying process is an excellent process to help in that way. Monk views identity this way, "that who we are is a constantly changing reality—a dynamic process of being rather than something essential or hidden somewhere inside us."[19] Our identity, our identity in Christ, is always changing as we live through the things and events of this world on our way to eternity where our identity will be perfected.

14. Smoke, *Growing through Divorce*, 11.

15. Ibid., 21.

16. Ibid.

17. Holeman, *Reconcilable Differences*, 110.

18. Ibid., 111.

19. Monk et al., *Narrative Therapy in Practice*, 47.

NARRATIVE PROCESS

Internalized Conversations

Internalized Conversations are the conversations that locate the problem internally making the person the problem.[20] Locating the problem internally, deep within the person, makes it difficult for the person to change.[21] Internalizing causes the problem to become more than a social construct; it can actualize it into the person as though it were a biological actuality.[22] The problem becomes a label, an identity. These internally negative conversations cause adverse effects and give the client very little room to think about or work out the problem. Internalized Conversations make the person the problem. It also gives the person a very narrow, shallow, or thin story for their life. A thin story is one that includes little other details of a person's life that does not fit their current Dominant Story.[23] It makes their life all about their problem.

A Dominant Story refers to the story theme that is translated into the story that dictates or overshadows the person's entire life, is usually the problem, and appears to be reality.[24] Often the Dominant Story is only one dynamic of the total reality, the other details like the person's competencies and skills are overlooked or discounted. The Dominant Story is often an incomplete story for the person, but it is the overwhelmingly controlling story. For me, my overwhelming story during and right after the divorce was that I was worthless and less than others in society that had marriages and families. I now no longer had a husband and that decreased my chances of having a family. I wanted what others had in a family and now I no longer even had what I once had, a chance at a family. Some of my Internal Conversations (built from past personal story and Morgan narrative questions):[25]

Erika: *"Now that I don't have a marriage because my husband cheated on me, I feel so worthless and alone. I am such a loser. I'm not good enough."*

Counselor: *"Tell me a little bit about why you do not feel good enough."*

---

20. Morgan, *What is Narrative Therapy?*

21. Monk et al., *Narrative Therapy in Practice.*

22. Ibid.

23. Morgan, *What is Narrative Therapy?*

24. Mucherera, *Class Notes.*

25. Morgan, *What is Narrative Therapy?*

Erika: "I'm not good enough to keep my husband. No matter how hard I tried to keep the house, cook, do things for him, even iron his clothes for work, or go fishing with him, or satisfy him . . . I guess it was not enough. Nothing I did was ever good enough."

Counselor: "Is "not good enough" the only feeling you are having?"

Erika: "No, I feel like I can't make my husband love me . . . There must be something wrong with me, I must be unlovable."

Counselor: "How did you try to make your husband love you?"

Erika: "By being a good wife, by making sure he could get the car he wanted and always having good meals and doing whatever he wanted."

Counselor: "Would you say that you lost yourself in the attempt to make your husband love you?"

Erika: "Maybe, because I don't really know who I am right now, I'm not even a wife let alone a good wife. I didn't do that right. And now I don't know what I like, what I want, or what life is supposed to be . . . I don't even know who I am."

At this time of my life I did not have a relationship with Christ yet, so I tried to derive love from human sources in a way that only God could supply. My Dominant Story, that I was less-than and unlovable, came from the actions and reactions of others. Fortunately, at this time a friend I had just met as the time of my husband's revealing of infidelity led me to Christ. Honestly, I have no idea what dark road this Dominant Story would have led me down had it not been for God's intercession. Even with salvation I still had the competing identity of being less-than and unlovable. Church was full of families, families who did not mind me joining them, but the pity was too much at the time. Sometimes families treat older single people like teenagers instead of adults and it just adds insult to injury by implying that adults have families. So even the church, no matter how well intended, supported my social construct of worth coming from having a family.

Naming and Externalizing the Problem

As the person's Internalized Conversations are being revealed, the counselor is not only allowing the client to express him or herself but is also listening for key words. These key words can be used in Naming the Problem. Even though the counselor can help prompt with these key words, the client must be the one to choose their name for their problem.[26] It is best

26. Monk et al., *Narrative Therapy in Practice.*

if they own the name.[27] This personification of the problem with a name that the client feels is appropriate is the beginning of not only relief, but also space. It makes the problem the problem instead of the person.[28] It gives them space to be able to breathe and work with the problem. It does not take away their moral accountability for the problem, but it relieves them from being the problem and makes the problem something to be dealt with.

Monk points out that Externalizing is a rhetorical device that allows the person a different way of speaking about their life, not just the problem.[29] It gives the person power in their own lives. It gives a person a different view of the discourses, or underlying assumptions, of our social constructs or ecosystem. Externalizing can put an ironic twist on the problem and/or discourses a person has been viewing as true but can now see through a different view or perspective. "Externalizing Conversations attempt to move the focus away from self-attack, recrimination, blame, and judgment—attitudes that work against productive and positive outcomes in counseling."[30] It can also give the counselor a way of working with clients that are respectful. Within Externalizing Conversations it is most important to pay attention to language used, take care to not use language that inadvertently supports the dominant/problem story.[31] The tongue holds the power of life or death, particularly to a person's spirit. Here are some of my Naming and Externalizing Conversations (built from past personal story and narrative questions):

Counselor: "If you had to give a name to your problem, what would you call it?"

Erika: "I don't know."

Counselor: "I've heard you use the words "less than" and "unlovable", do one of these sound right to you? Or do they spark an idea for another name?"

Erika: "I think that "unlovable" is what it is, it probably covers all of what I feel best."

Counselor: "So, what are some of the other feelings that Unlovable has caused you to have?"

27. Mucherera, Class Notes.

28. Ibid.

29. Monk et al., *Narrative Therapy in Practice.*

30. Ibid., 6.

31. Morgan, *What is Narrative Therapy?*

> Erika: "Mostly that I'm worthless, I feel like I shouldn't even try"
> Counselor: "Unlovable makes you think you shouldn't try what?"
> Erika: "It makes me think that I should not try to be loved, or get a new job, or try to date. It makes me feel like I can't live on my own or do life by myself, but that I can't do life with others either. I don't know, I'm not even sure what I want to do"
> Counselor: "Sounds like Unlovable has talked you into fearing living life and trying new things."

Having conversations like these, especially where the most overwhelming problem can be named really helps to give some breathing room. This would immediately make me feel less pressured and more like 'Unlovable' was a problem that was causing me distress. There is hope for dealing with this. This infidelity and divorce fed into my personal myth of unlovability.[32] And the start of being able to change such a myth is to move that problem from inside of me to outside of me.[33]

Scaffolding, Mapping the History of the Problem

Scaffolding is a Mapping of the influences and events in the history of the problem. Mapping the influences of the problem gives insight to the meaning that the client is assigning to the effects of the problem.[34] It helps the counselor understand the client's perspective of the effects of the problem. It can also make the client's perspective personally more clear.[35] Morgan purports Mapping can limit the spillover of the problem onto the Alternate Story. Scaffolding can be used fairly early during the beginning Externalizing process. It is similar to the Scaffolding on the outside of a building; it lets you look through "the windows [and] enable [you] to peak into the different rooms of the client's life and the connections between them."[36] It fills in the hollow spaces in the client's story to thicken it and gives it life. It connects the past to the present and in doing that it brings to the forefront the client's strengths and abilities that they used in the past that can be used again in the present situation and adapted to the future. Scaffolding looks at not just how the problem has affected feelings, but also beliefs, daily life, relationships, ecosystems, and the views the client

32. Wimberly, *Recalling Our Own Stories.*

33. Morgan, *What is Narrative Therapy?*

34. Ibid.

35. Ibid.

36. Mucherera, *Class Notes.*

has of self. This conversation is built from past personal story and narrative questions.

> Counselor: "When did Unlovable first show up in your life?"
>
> Erika: "I think that it has always been there, it is always plaguing me."
>
> Counselor: "When would you say that Unlovable was the strongest?"
>
> Erika: "Unlovable is probably the strongest ever right now. My husband's affair and the failing of my marriage has left me not knowing which way is up or what is reality and what isn't, my whole world is upside down."
>
> Counselor: "When would you say that Unlovable was the weakest?"
>
> Erika: "Probably when I was getting married, I felt like "finally someone to love me, now life will be great." But now it seems like I couldn't be more wrong and it, Unlovable, is making my heart hurt and filling up my mind with thoughts of worthlessness and stealing my life."
>
> Counselor: "Was there a time in the past when Unlovable did not affect you as much or that you were able to overcome it?"
>
> Erika: "There was time in college when it took a back burner. It was probably my sophomore year of undergrad, I was able to make friends, we were a group of friends and Unlovable didn't show up much at all."
>
> Counselor: "How long ago was that?"
>
> Erika: "Four years ago."
>
> Counselor: "Was there another time either since or before that you overcame Unlovable?"
>
> Erika: "Maybe my junior year of high school, things just seemed to be going right then. I had friends and life seemed normal."
>
> Counselor: "It seems as though Unlovable has caused you to be pretty miserable."
>
> Erika: "It has robbed me of life."
>
> Counselor: "Anything else? What has Unlovable told you about yourself?"
>
> Erika: "Probably that I'm nobody if somebody doesn't love me. Yeah, Unlovable has told me that I'm nobody on my own, that I have to have someone."
>
> Counselor: "Though there were those two times at least when you were able to overcome Unlovable. How did you do that?"
>
> Erika: "I think that those times I was just thinking less about who I was and just enjoying what was happening in life."
>
> Counselor: "Do you think you could try that again?"

DECONSTRUCTION OF THE DOMINANT STORY

Deconstruction concentrates on the problem and not the person in that it takes the label off of the person and makes the problem the problem.[37] In Narrative Therapy Deconstruction starts with finding out what social constructs are underlying the person's problem.[38] Social constructs are the ideas, beliefs, and values that a person perceives based on social practices or norms of the wider culture. They may seem to the person to be their own ideas. Or the person may not even know that they exist; they are taken for granted. Deconstruction reveals hidden social constructs, helps the person acknowledge that they exist, and helps to dismantle constructs that are promoting the problem story. Social constructs can keep a person stuck in unhealthy practices that they think are normal or right. Bringing the problematic social constructs out into the open gives the opportunity to question their validity and work to change them. Changing the underlying problematic foundation opens the way for the new Alternate Story to come forth and solidify without the invisible opposition of the problematic construct. Faulty social constructs may include ideas about being a single parent, being a workingwoman, or sexual relationships to name a few. These social constructs will have a history in the person's life; it is beneficial to not only expose the construct but to also map the history. History will give a thicker view of the exact construct the person is using and how it has affected them. Morgan notes that Deconstruction is one of the "central components" of this process and is the "pulling apart and examining of 'taken-for-granted' truths."[39] Deconstruction, like Naming the Problem, removes the problem from the person. When a social construct is revealed and shown to be untrue, there is then the chance for a person to be able to examine and adhere to his or her own personal beliefs and ideas. This also opens the way for creating the Alternate Story. This conversation is built from past personal story and narrative questions.

Counselor: "Tell me a little more about your beliefs of the role of a wife."

Erika: "Well a wife should be able to take care of her husband, make a nice home for him to come home to. She should know what he wants. Just overall be able to satisfy him."

Counselor: "Where do you think that your idea of an ideal wife came from?"

37. Monk et al., *Narrative Therapy in Practice.*
38. Morgan, *What is Narrative Therapy?*
39. Ibid., 46.

Erika: "I don't know, I guess that's what I've seen happen. Well, you see it in magazines all the time."

Counselor: "Were these ideas helpful in your relationship? Are they working in your life now?"

Erika: "Definitely not"

Counselor: "Do you think that there may be a different view of a good wife? A different perspective of what a wife is? Maybe it is one role that a person has among many in life?"

Erika: "Had not thought of that, you mean instead of being a wife and that is who you are, that maybe a wife is only part of who a person is?"

Counselor: "It's something to think about."

This is a conversation that would take some time to explore; 'taken-for-granted' beliefs are sometimes deeply ingrained in the worldview of a person. It would take time to move from false beliefs to more healthy ideas. I think that I was living the myths of the "ideal mate" and "the knight in shining armor."[40]

RE-AUTHORING, RE-MEMBERING, AND CREATING THE ALTERNATE STORY

Wimberly points out that we are not held captive to social constructs or Dominate Stories, change is possible.[41] The paradox is that the fact that a person who has held onto a Dominant Story or myth has shown the same ability to interpret and make meaning of events and ideas that shows that they can create or Re-author an Alternate Story. Re-authoring is a collaborative process as the transformation is effective if the client can see their past through a new perspective, and this opens the way for a new Alternate Story.[42] Wimberly further notes that certain phases of Re-authoring include discovering themes and their influence in personal myths, discerning God's presence and power for transformation, and making plans to change the themes.[43] God's presence and power makes the most dynamic transformations that last in terms of breadth and depth.

Re-membering is important to Re-authoring. Re-membering is deciding who will remain as part of a person's life and who will not—healthy relationships with significant others stay and unhealthy relationship

40. Wimberly, *Recalling Our Own Stories*, 34.

41. Ibid.

42. Ibid.

43. Ibid.

usually are removed if even for a time.[44] During Re-authoring and building an Alternate Story, it is important to discern whether the social support you currently have is positive or negative and adjust those people to support your new story. It can increase the success of living out the Alternate Story. The Alternate Story blossoms out of the Unique Outcomes and can be thickened as more client strengths and more overcoming moments are discovered. This Alternate Story can be named as well making it more concrete and more easily called to memory while the client is living it out outside of the session.[45] This conversation is built from past personal story and narrative questions.

Re-Membering Conversation

Counselor: *"You spoke of a time when you were effected less by Unlovable, when you were thinking less of who you were and enjoying life. Who do you think would not be surprised to hear this?"*

Erika: *"I think my old friend, Danielle. She would believe it."*

Counselor: *"Is there anyone else?"*

Erika: *"Oh, definitely, my friend Judith. Don't know why I didn't think of her at first."*

Counselor: *"Are these people in your life now?"*

Erika: *"Judith is—she led me to the Lord and is now my best friend as well! Danielle and I lost touch after I got married."*

Counselor: *"Would you be able to reconnect with her and include her in your life now?"*

Erika: *"Yeah, I think I could do that."*

Counselor: *"Is there anyone in your life now that is not supportive of you living life without worrying about who you are?"*

Erika: *"My ex-husband, but he's gone now. I really don't have a lot of friends."*

Counselor: *"Would you like to re-member Danielle back into your life and continue to dismember your husband then?"*

Erika: *"Yes."*

At this time in my life, a counselor did point me in the direction of a divorce support group and encourage the building of my support network. I see both of these things as contributing to building an Alternate Story. I participated in the divorce support group and was able to benefit from the

44. Morgan, *What is Narrative Therapy?*
45. Ibid.

normalizing that others provided and also learned new things about single life as an adult. I began to make friendships at my new church and joined a Bible study group. I think that I unofficially named this new budding Alternate Story "the great adventure." I took risks and expanded my social network, taught myself some social skills, and toned down my survival skills to something useful for daily life. I am still living this Alternate Story and it feels great. I have times where the old Dominant Story would like to enter back in even now, usually starts with a bit of self-doubt. But I take a look at who is in my life, to those voices I am listening, and I do some Re-membering of my Alternate Story and maybe some Re-membering of who is in my life.

OUTSIDER WITNESSES

Outsider witnesses are those people, two or more, who watch and listen to the counselor and more importantly the client as they re-tell their Re-authoring conversations.[46] The client knows and approves of the witnesses being there. The client then watches as the outsider witnesses are interviewed and tell of what they heard from their perspectives and what caught their attention. This usually leads to insight into the client's strengths and abilities and is very encouraging. The client may gain tremendous support through this process. They may also see areas of their Alternate Stories that they want to modify.

I had at least one outsider witness that was able to objectively listen to me, my friend Judith who led me to the Lord. She discipled me and was honest with me in obedience to the Lord whenever I needed reproof, guidance, or just a new perspective. At the time, I think that my baptism served as a Definitional Ceremony.[47] She is still my outsider witness, but I have also grown into one for her.

CONCLUSION

The Narrative Therapy process is a good way to live life. We all at some time or another have times where problems seem overwhelming, even if for a short time. When these times come, if we are able to step back and Name the Problem and have space to think about when it started and how

46. Ibid.
47. Ibid.

we have overcome before or other strengths that we have had or have currently to solve the problem and look to readjusting our story when necessary then Narrative Therapy can become a way of life. It is always good to evaluate who are your important people and who is less than healthy for you. I also think that a good community group can serve as a good group of outsider witnesses. I think this is not only an effective therapy but also speaks to how to keep a healthy perspective of self and life.

14

Just One to Hold

A Narrative Counseling Approach to Living with Infertility

MARCI HANNAH BOURLAND

CASE STUDY

A THIRTY-SEVEN-YEAR-OLD FEMALE CAUCASIAN presented today along with her spouse complaining of concerns of infertility. Patient reported an early miscarriage in a previous marriage at age twenty-five and has no biological children. Patient is considered advanced maternal age (>thirty-five) and is nine months into a second marriage, that has produced no pregnancies or live births. Patient meets standard definition of infertility. A complete work-up, evaluation, and treatment plan has been ordered.

In one simple paragraph buried within a medical file and devoid of personality and warmth, the narrative of my life was changed forever. But it was more than the narrative of an individual; it was also the narrative of our family and larger community of support. Our lives were now intertwined and defined by, to greater or lesser extents, the labels and effects of "infertility." That journey began more than three years ago and has yet to reach its final destination of resolution. It is with this personal case study in mind that I began to think through the recently learned principles of Narrative Therapy. This is my journey through the lenses of Narrative Therapy in search of any resolution toward the problem of infertility. The following is an account of therapeutic conversations between a woman named 'Ruby', who sought counseling for infertility, and her counselor, 'June.'

DEFINING NARRATIVE THERAPY

In order to utilize the principles of Narrative Therapy in her work with Ruby, June first sought to explain some of the basic principles to Ruby. As June began working with Ruby, Ruby gained a better understanding of Narrative Therapy, its various applications, and primary components.

Narrative Therapy, while relatively young as a therapeutic model within Western cultures, is actually a model that has existed organically within the culture of many indigenous communities for generations. Narrative Therapy involves the idea of working together with clients to help them Re-author some aspects of their lives that have been problematic through the use of personal narratives from the client's life. In Narrative Therapy it is assumed that the client, rather than the therapist, is the expert in discovering solutions to difficult life patterns or themes. Alice Morgan in her book, *What is Narrative Therapy?*, gives a helpful overview of Narrative Therapy by discussing some of the "ground rules" for successful Narrative Counseling:

- Narrative Therapy is a non-blaming therapeutic approach that distinguishes the person from the problem; in other words, we seek to differentiate the person as unique and separate from the problem they are seeking to resolve.[1]

- The client, rather than the counselor, is established as the "expert" in terms of his or her ability to resolve the problem. It is assumed within Narrative Counseling that the client best understands the problem and has the needed knowledge, skill set(s), resources and beliefs to solve the problem. He or she enters into counseling to receive assistance from the counselor in co-authoring a new story in response to the presenting problem story.[2]

- It is the job of the therapist to be curious as to the nature of the problem and ask appropriate questions that will allow the client to

1. Morgan, *What is Narrative Therapy?* 4.
2. Ibid., 4.

discover new or re-discover old stories and develop new ways of viewing and dealing with the problem story.[3]

UNDERSTANDING INFERTILITY

In order to successfully apply Narrative Therapy principles to one who is experiencing problems with infertility, it is helpful to have both a general understanding of infertility within the larger cultural population as well as recognize the personal effects of infertility upon the individual or family unit seeking counseling. According to *Resolve*, the National Infertility Association, infertility is a disease that results in the abnormal functioning of the male or female reproductive system.[4] *Resolve* also lists the official diagnostic definition of infertility as the inability to conceive after one year of unprotected intercourse (six months if the woman is over age thirty-five) or the inability to carry a pregnancy to live birth.[5] It is believed that infertility affects one in six couples, or approximately 7 million people.[6] Of those affected, about one-third of infertility is attributed to the female partner, one-third is attributed to the male partner and one-third is caused by a combination in both partners or, is unexplained.[7]

GRIEF & LOSS DYNAMICS

Additionally, it is important for those working with clients to have a general understanding of grief and loss factors that often accompany those struggling with issues of infertility. According to Dr. Alice Domar in her book, *Conquering Infertility*, clinical depression is a major factor for women experiencing infertility.[8] In her initial research for a 1994 National Institute for Mental Health (NIMH) study, Domar discovered some astonishing links between depression and women experiencing infertility. Among her initial findings:

---

3. Ibid.
4. Resolve, *Fast Facts on Infertility*.
5. Ibid.
6. Nair, *Understanding Infertility*.
7. American Society for Reproductive Medicine, *Reproductive Facts*.
8. Domar and Kelly, *Conquering Infertility*, 28.

1. Infertile women are more depressed than fertile women are.

2. Their depression levels peak two to three years after they start trying to conceive.

3. Infertility has as great a psychological impact as does a potentially terminal illness.[9]

The potential terminal illnesses compared with infertility in Domar's findings were: heart disease, cancer, HIV positive status, and chronic pain.[10]

A second critical factor to consider in working with those struggling with issues of infertility is Elisabeth Kubler-Ross' five stages of grief and loss. First identified in her 1969 groundbreaking book, *On Death and Dying*, Kubler identified five stages of grief and loss that every human being goes through in grieving the loss of a dream, an ideal, another human, or a beloved animal. While research has evolved and new grief and loss models have since emerged, Kubler's pioneering work is still a useful model in grieving the losses of infertility as sited in Axlerod:[11]

1. Denial or Shock and Isolation

   Often, this is the first reaction to learning about the illness or death of a loved one or the sudden loss of a hope or dream. It is a normal coping mechanism to deny the reality of the situation or rationalize overwhelming emotions. It is a temporary defense mechanism that buffers the immediate shock of our loss and enables us to endure the first waves of pain as we hide from the tragic and devastating news.[12]

2. Anger

   As the effects of our denial and shock begin to lift, the reality of our pain reemerges before we are psychologically able to cope with the pain. Our pain is redirected as anger and can be aimed at inanimate objects, strangers, family or friends. In fact, we may even direct our anger toward our loved one who is terminally ill or recently deceased. Our anger is not bound to rational thoughts as we may resent the object, dream or person for leaving us and causing us pain. This

---

9. Ibid., 28.

10. Ibid., 28.

11. Axelrod, "The Five Stages of Loss and Grief."

12. Ibid., 4.

misplaced anger may cause us to feel guilty about our emotional response, which often adds to our own anger.[13]

3. Bargaining

Bargaining is a normal reaction to feeling helpless or vulnerable and is often utilized in an attempt to regain control with thoughts such as:

- If only we had sought medical attention sooner . . .
- If only we got a second opinion from another doctor.
- If only we had tried to be a better person toward them.

Privately we may seek to make a deal with God in order to postpone the inevitable or see a miraculous turn-around in events. It is another attempt to protect us from the painful reality.[14]

4. Depression

There are two types of depression associated with grief and loss. The first type of depression involves our reaction to practical matters related to our loss and is dominated by sadness or regret. For example, in the case of a miscarriage, a woman may worry about what to do with the maternity clothes she recently purchased or feel deep sadness over a newly prepared nursery that now occupies unusable space within the home. This type of depression can be eased by the cooperation of others in offering practical help, reassurance, or understanding words. The second type of depression is less obvious and, generally, more private. This type of depression involves our ability to work through our losses by acknowledging them and separating ourselves from the object of our loss or saying goodbye to a loved one.[15]

5. Acceptance

Although this is not a period of happiness, it should be distinguished separately from depression. This stage is often marked by a sense of calm withdrawal for the grieving person. Acceptance provides an opportunity to grieve alone and experience the emotions of grief as they come; recognizing that while others may be able to provide you

---

13. Ibid., 5.
14. Ibid., 8.
15. Ibid., 11.

comfort, ultimately the grieving process must be worked through individually to bring about healing.[16]

Each of the steps within the grieving cycle is intended to provide a general guideline for the way in which humans most often work through their issues of grief or loss. Because everyone grieves differently and will spend varying amounts of time working through each of the steps, it is important to recognize that there is not a right or wrong way to grieve and the five stages of grief do not necessarily occur in order. In fact, it is likely that one will move between the stages before coming to a place of acceptance of the loss. In Western cultures, the grieving period is often cut short and individuals do not have the luxury of completely working through the grieving cycle and, therefore, may need to revisit individual stages over a longer period of time to come to a place of acceptance. It is not necessary to view the stages as a process that one must go through sequentially; rather it is more helpful to see the stages as a guideline to validate the individual grieving process and give perspective and location to your current place of grief and loss.

Internalized and Externalized Conversations

Now that a general overview of the problem of infertility has been identified as well as the stages of grief and loss, it is important to establish the therapeutic conversation between the client, Ruby, and her therapist, June, in order to effectively deal with the problem of infertility. For June, discovering the use of Ruby's Internalized Conversations is the first key in beginning to co-author a new story against the problem of infertility. Internalized Conversations are the internal messages and labels, usually negative, that clients ascribe to themselves as a way of making sense of the problem or problems that generally cause them to seek out counseling.[17] Clients often believe they are part of the problem or incorporate themselves within the problem. For example, in describing the problem for which the client is seeking help, the client may say: "It's my fault. If I'd gone to the doctor sooner, things would have been different."

In their first session together, June was intentional about making Ruby feel welcome and was genuinely curious to hear from Ruby what brought her into therapy. Although June had an initial understanding of

16. Ibid., 12.
17. Morgan, *What is Narrative Therapy?* 18.

Ruby's problem with infertility, as disclosed within the initial intake paperwork, she wanted Ruby to share about the problem in her own words:

June: Ruby, why don't you begin by sharing with me anything you feel I should know about you and the problem that brought you into counseling with me today?

Ruby: You're already aware of why I'm here. My husband, Ryan, and I married later in life and we have been trying to get pregnant since marrying more than three years ago. For the last year and a half we've been seeing a doctor for infertility. My husband and I have both been tested and have undergone five failed invitro-fertilization procedures (IVF). The doctor constantly says, "Your eggs are old; if I'd gotten ahold of you five years earlier it would be a different story." I feel like it's my entire fault. I feel like such a failure. For years now we've been consumed and overwhelmed by infertility treatments followed by one loss after another. We're never going to be parents because of me! I feel guilty that I can't give my husband children, but mostly I just feel numb right now, like life is passing by and I'm just watching it in slow motion.

June then explained to Ruby the concept of Internalized Conversations and explained that Ruby is not the problem; rather she has entered into counseling because she has a problem with infertility. June explained that the problem is the problem and although Ruby is experiencing the effects of the problem, Ruby is not the problem, rather she has a problem with infertility.

June went into greater detail to explain some of the differences between Internalizing Conversations, which Ruby engaged in with statements such as, "It's all my fault!" or "We're never going to be parents because of me!" versus using Externalized Conversations, which locate the problem outside of Ruby.[18] June explained that Internalizing Conversations are often negative statements or messages that locate the problem within the person and causes the individual to believe there is something "wrong or deficient" within their lives.[19] June gave further explanation that 'wrong' or 'deficient' mindsets often lead individuals to lose hope that things could ever change, inadvertently leading some to adopt a victim mentality of hopelessness. Furthermore, those who do seek relief from their problems often look to trained professionals as experts who will fix

18. Ibid., 17.
19. Ibid., 29.

their problems, not realizing that they, too, must actively engage in the process of healing.[20]

Sensing Ruby's interest in learning more about the Narrative Therapy process, June continued to explain how Internalized Conversations can be problematic when the individual erroneously views the problem as a 'deficiency' within their character, primarily because it often leads to a 'thin conclusion' while examining or re-defining the individual's entire life through the lens of this one problem. After explaining a little bit about the concept of Narrative Therapy June modeled for Ruby another possible description of the problem:

June: Ruby, in light of what I've shared with you about my practice as a Narrative therapist and the difference between Internalized Conversations versus Externalized Conversations, I'd like to go back to your earlier description of the problem. Would that be okay?

Ruby: Sure.

June: Here are some of the comments that I recall you saying: "It's all my fault. I feel like such a failure. We're never going to be parents because of me! I feel guilty that I can't give my husband children . . ." Would it be alright if I suggested another way to express some of those ideas in an externalized way that would make it easier for both of us to understand some of the dynamics you are currently experiencing?

Ruby: That would be great! It's all so overwhelming; I'm not really sure that I do understand all that I'm experiencing. If there were a way to get some of these thoughts outside of my head—for even a moment—it would be such a relief!

June: Okay, instead of blaming yourself for all these problems, would it be an accurate statement to instead say something like this: "The diagnosis of infertility is interfering with our ability to have children?"

Ruby: Yes, I suppose that is the real problem!

June: Could you also say that 'infertility' is trying to convince you and your husband that you will not be able to raise children together?

Ruby: Yes, I'm afraid that 'infertility' will win that argument. I'm also afraid that infertility will stand in the way of my husband and me, disrupting our marriage.

June: That's a great observation Ruby; I think you're beginning to see the importance of separating yourself from the problem in order to better look at it. If you could change your earlier internalized statement, "I feel like

---

20. Ibid., 3.

such a failure." to one of externalization, what do you think you would say, instead?

Ruby: Well, if I understand the idea of externalization as the problem being the problem rather than me, then maybe I would rephrase it to say, "When infertility is present in my life, it tells me that I'm a failure."

June: Yes, Ruby, I think you're beginning to see the importance of externalizing language in locating the problem outside of yourself in order to better examine its effects on your life. So far we have been addressing the problem as 'infertility.' Ruby, in thinking about the many aspects of infertility and the numerous ways it has impacted upon you and your husband, do you think using the name 'infertility' to describe the problem is a good name, or can you suggest another name that would best fit the problems you are experiencing?

Ruby: Well, in terms of describing what the problem actually is, I'd say that 'infertility' is a good name. But if we're talking about what it has actually done to me and to our dreams of family, then I don't think it is a very good descriptive name of the problem.

June: Okay, well I'd like you to come up with a name for the problem of 'infertility' that best describes what 'infertility' has done to you and your dreams of family.

Ruby: Well, the first name that comes to mind is 'baby snatcher' or perhaps 'the thief' . . . maybe I'd even call it 'the dream smasher.'

June: Wow! Those are some excellent descriptors of how 'infertility' has affected your family. I see that the problem of 'infertility' has really stolen a lot from your family. Is there one of those phrases that you identify with more than another?

Ruby: Well, I guess I'd have to say, 'the thief' because he has stolen so much from us—our children, our hopes and dreams, and even my motivation for living life!

NAMING THE PROBLEM

Naming the Problem often times is a natural outgrowth of the process of Externalizing the problem within Narrative Therapy. Because Ruby had received a medical diagnosis named 'infertility,' she and her therapist, June, were initially able to use the word 'infertility' to Externalize the problem until an opportunity arose for Ruby to give infertility a name that most represented its entire effects upon she and her family. Ruby chose to name the problem of infertility as 'the thief.' According to Morgan's book,

What is Narrative Therapy? therapists assist their clients in Naming the Problem by listening " to the description of the person's experience, hoping to hear a word or phrase that describes what might be getting in the way of the person's life."[21]

SCAFFOLDING

Now that Ruby had identified the problem by name, 'the thief,' June was interested in discovering more about the history of 'the thief' in Ruby's life as well as discovering what 'the thief' had stolen from Ruby and her family. 'Scaffolding' is a simple term for describing the process of taking one's history. The word 'Scaffolding' is representative of the temporary structures that are erected around buildings to give workers better access to complete necessary repairs. In a similar way, 'Scaffolding' in Narrative Therapy represents the process of accessing a client's history at multiple points through open-ended questions for the purpose of helping the client co-author a new, problem-free story.[22]

June: Ruby, would it be okay if we began to take a closer look at 'the thief?" I'd like to know a little more about 'the thief.' Has he always been a part of your life or have there been periods of time when 'the thief' has not been present? Also, maybe you could share with me when you were first aware of 'the thief's' intrusion in your life and share with me what kinds of things 'the thief' has stolen from you over the years. Would you be willing to share with me how 'the thief' has affected your life and family?

Ruby: Sure. I think I can do that. Where should I start?

June: Well Ruby, this is your story. You can start anywhere you'd like. What do you think is important for me to know about 'the thief' and what he has stolen from your life?

Ruby: Ah, that's easy! The 'thief' has stolen my hopes and dreams, even from childhood.

June: I'm listening.

Ruby: Well, I remember as young as age eight deciding that when I grew up I wanted to get married and have a family. I didn't grow up in a very nurturing home, so I remember thinking that I wanted to provide the love and nurture for my children that I did not receive. I wanted to have both natural and adopted children with my future husband.

June: So you believe 'the thief' was operating in your life as a child?

21. Ibid., 18.
22. Mucherera, Lecture.

Ruby: No, not exactly. But I believe my desire and commitment to have children was established in childhood because I wanted to model the right way to love and nurture a child, unlike my own childhood experiences that were largely devoid of emotional connection.

June: So you believe that 'the thief' began making plans to rob you later on in life?

Ruby: Exactly! I mean I wasn't necessarily aware of it as a child and I certainly didn't want children until I married as an adult, so I knew that children would not be in my immediate future as an eight year old, but I anticipated their eventual arrival, even as a child. I looked forward to the day when I could shower them with the emotional warmth and love that was bottled up within me with no expressive outlet because of my own family dynamics.

I know that sounds weird, but if we're going with this whole 'thief' motif of speaking about infertility, it's almost like the 'thief' studied my every move the way a bank robber would research a bank he was planning to steal from. The 'thief' targeted me from a young age. He knew all about my hopes and dreams and waited for an opportune time to strike—as a young, married adult!

June: You sounded a little unsure of 'the thief' as a way of talking about the problem just now. Is there another word you would prefer instead? Is there a word that might seem less weird to you?

Ruby: No, I think 'the thief' is a great word to describe the problem; it's just a little odd though. After all these years of trying to get pregnant, I'm used to believing that it's my entire fault rather than a stranger by the name of 'the thief!"

June: Yes, initially it can feel a little awkward to Externalize a problem we're used to Internalizing as our own.

If you're still comfortable Naming the Problem 'the thief' I'd like to follow up on your statement that 'the thief' kind of marked you as a child and waited to attack you once you married. Is it okay to continue talking about that?

Ruby: Sure. I still don't understand the point behind all this Externalization, but I'm willing to try anything to feel better about life right now.

June: Okay. Well, I was curious. Were you aware of 'the thief's' presence in your life prior to getting married? Did you feel 'marked' by 'the thief' as a child?

Ruby: No, not at all. I assumed I would grow up, get married, and have children, although I do remember having a small fear those things might not work out that way.

June: So is it fair to say that the presence of 'the thief' was largely absent from your childhood?

Ruby: Well, when you put it that way, yes. I was raised to believe that sexual relationships were reserved for marriage so it was not a concern of my childhood.

June: Are there other times outside of childhood that you can think of when 'the thief' was largely absent from your life?

Ruby: Well, yes. Although I've wanted to have children since childhood, I never wanted to have them outside of the marriage relationship, so I guess I can say that 'the thief' really wasn't present much after my first husband and I divorced. Being single did cause me some doubts regarding whether or not I would have children, but I was mostly able to ignore 'the thief.' Being single and celibate meant 'the thief' could not steal what I did not own—a marriage relationship with the possibility of children.

June: Well said. So to clarify, in both your childhood and after your divorce it sounds like you experienced significant periods of time in which 'the thief' was not a factor in your life.

Ruby: Yes, I guess I'd have to agree with that.

June: Can you tell me what it was like living without 'the thief' constantly intruding on your life and stealing from you?

Ruby: Wow! That was really helpful for you to phrase the question that way.

June: Why is that?

Ruby: Well, talking about infertility now as 'the thief' makes me realize that I wasn't as affected as I might have once believed I was as a single person.

June: What do you mean?

Ruby: Well, now I realize that I was pretty free from the effects of 'the thief' as a single person. Yes, it's true that I wanted children, and I guess part of me did feel that being single meant 'the thief' —infertility—imprisoned me since marriage offered me the only possibility of having children. But now I realize that I really was free from 'the thief' in those years.

I was free to spend time with friends and had no major responsibilities other than providing for my own needs. The 'thief' was absent from my relationships and did not cause any fights between those I loved and myself. The 'thief' didn't try to tell me what to eat or drink, how much to exercise, or what kind of prenatal vitamins I should take. Wow! This is kind of freeing to realize. The 'thief' had no say in whether or not my husband and I were sexually intimate, or how often. 'The thief' was barred from attending doctor's appointments with me and never once as a single person did 'the thief' demand that I take daily injections of hormones or require close gynecological monitoring and numerous surgeries! I really was free from infertility, 'the thief!'

June: It sounds like you're beginning to recognize how much 'the thief' has consumed your current life as a married woman in comparison to the times in your life when you were single.

Ruby: Oh, yes! In both my first marriage and in my current marriage, infertility, I mean, 'the thief,' was always present, snooping around in our personal lives and stealing anything he could get his hands on.

LANDSCAPE QUESTIONS

Michael White first introduced the concepts of 'Landscape of Action' and 'Landscape of Identity' questions into Narrative Therapy in the early 1990's. 'Landscape of Action' questions are designed to bring the focus on untold stories that could replace the negative, problem-stories that a client currently believes.[23] Some examples of 'Landscape of Action' questions might be:

- What did your friend say when you told him/her?
- When did this happen?
- Where were you when this happened?

'Landscape of Identity' questions seek to help clients narrow in on their true commitments and gain a greater appreciation of their unique gifts and talents.[24] Examples of 'Landscape of Identity' questions might be:

- What does this say about you as a person that you would do this?
- What does this say about what you were planning?
- Help me understand, what does this say about what you believe in or value?

June continued the conversation by asking a 'Landscape of Identity' question in order to discover stolen aspects of Ruby's identity. June

23. Monk et al., *Narrative Therapy in* Practice, 107.

24. Ibid.

understood that discovering the stolen aspects of Ruby's identity would eventually enable Ruby to reclaim or develop a new story with regard to her stolen identity and the problem of infertility.

June: What kinds of things has 'the thief' stolen from you and your family?

Ruby: Well, I could go on for days probably, but I'll just mention some of the first things that come to mind for now; I'm sure this won't be the only day that we talk about 'the thief.'

June: No, I'm sure it won't.

Ruby: 'The thief' has stolen so much from me: my identity as a woman, my childhood dreams of loving and nurturing children, the dream my husband and I shared together of raising children that share our DNA—children that look like us. 'The thief' has drained our finances and strained our marriage. 'The thief' has ruled our lives and held us captive in our decisions, big and small. Smaller decisions such as what I eat or how much I can exercise and larger decisions such as whether I can travel for a family holiday, take a job without medical insurance for infertility or even my recent life changing decision to quit my job. 'The thief' has caused me to experience extended periods of depression and overwhelming grief at the loss of each of our children. (Ruby begins to cry now)

June: The 'thief' has stolen so much from you and yet somehow you have continued to fight against him.

Ruby: Yes. It has been so hard. Many times I wanted to give up, but I kept fighting back against 'the thief' to protect my children.

June: How many children have you fought 'the thief' for?

Ruby: All of them. I lost a daughter to miscarriage in my first marriage. She would be fourteen now. Ryan and I married three years ago and immediately began trying to get pregnant. We were unsuccessful on our own and began seeing a reproductive endocrinologist. We got pregnant with twins on our first try with invitro-fertilization (IVF) and lost them both at five weeks. We lost three children in our second IVF attempt, three children in our third attempt, two children in our fourth attempt, and one child in our fifth and final IVF attempt.

I fought against 'the thief' every time and we lost twelve children. Ryan and I lost eleven children in eighteen months and that has been overwhelming. I fought 'the thief' for them and lost. Now we're through fighting with medical intervention, but if God supernaturally grants us another opportunity to fight against 'the thief,' I will fight with just as much determination as before and God will win that battle for us. Faith is very important for me.

And in fact, all this talk about infertility as 'the thief' just reminded me of one of my favorite Bible verses found in John 10:10: "The thief comes only to steal and kill and destroy; I came that they may have life, and have it abundantly (NASB).

DECONSTRUCTION

As Ruby began to get in touch with her grief over the loss of her children, June recognized this would be a good place to wrap up their first session together, ending with prayer in recognition of Ruby's strong faith. June was impressed with Ruby's willingness to engage in Externalized Conversations and felt confident much progress was made in Naming the Problem externally. June also felt that Ruby had done an excellent job of laying out an initial history with regard to the problem of 'the thief.' While there was still more history to uncover with regard to 'the thief,' June was pleased that they were well on their way to Deconstructing the problem-story and had even managed to discover a 'Unique Outcome' to the problem-story of 'the thief.' June remembered from her training that Deconstructive questioning and Unique Outcome questioning often occur "simultaneously" as one stage rather than two.[25]

Deconstruction is the process in Narrative Therapy interested in "disassembling the taken-for-granted assumptions that are made about an event or circumstance."[26] In other words, Narrative therapists are interested in 'taking apart' the ideas, beliefs, and practices of a person's culture that gives legitimacy to the problem or problem story the client presents.[27] The benefit of Deconstruction is that it allows the client to reassess the problem story, 'the thief,' outside of traditionally assumed values or cultural norms in order to better examine the problem story and see if new insights can be discovered in solving the problem.

When Ruby initially entered into Narrative Therapy with June, the Dominant Story Ruby presented was one of being overwhelmed and consumed by the issues of infertility. Her life felt permanently defined by failed treatments and heart-breaking losses of life. And although June did not gather a complete history of the problem in their first session together, initial steps were taken toward the Deconstruction of the problem-story of infertility, or 'the thief.' The process of Deconstruction was initiated when

25. Ibid.

26. Ibid., 95.

27. Morgan, *What is Narrative Therapy?* 45.

Ruby began to shift her beliefs that 'the thief' had always been present: in childhood, as a single woman, and in both her marriages. As those beliefs were gently questioned by June, Ruby began to recognize that, in fact, she had been relatively free from the effects of 'the thief' in childhood and as a single woman.

Thin to Thick Description

After June's initial session with Ruby she reviewed her session notes and began to think about whether or not she would like to write Ruby a therapeutic letter. This caused June to think of some Narrative Therapy concepts she would like to explore with Ruby in their next session together. One of those concepts would be to focus on developing a 'thicker description' of the problem than the 'thin description' that Ruby seemed to hold. 'Thin descriptions' are the meanings that people ascribe to problems in their lives based on surrounding circumstances and are often created by others who observe their actions or behaviors.[28] In Ruby's case she had believed the doctor's words, "Your eggs are old; if I'd gotten ahold of you five years earlier it would be a different story" and had developed a thin description of herself as an infertile woman incapable of giving her husband children. June hoped to be able to expand Ruby's 'thin description' of herself into a 'thicker description' in their next session. A 'thicker description' for Narrative therapists simply means that the client is able to begin describing their lives and relationships in a way that is richer or provides a more full and complete description of themselves rather than being identified solely by the problem-story.[29]

Unique Outcomes

This shift in Ruby's beliefs led to what June would call an exception, or a 'Unique Outcome', in Narrative Therapy. Unique Outcomes are described as "anything that the problem would not like; anything that does not 'fit' with the Dominant Story."[30] For Ruby, the 'Unique Outcome' was discovered as she began to think about all that 'the thief' had stolen from her in both marriages. As she began to relate all that 'the thief' had stolen in

28. Ibid.
29. Ibid.
30. Ibid., 52.

marriage, she got a revelation that 'the thief' had been unable to steal those things in earlier periods of life as a single person. The realization that 'the thief' had not been present throughout her life began to challenge her current feelings that 'the thief' would always intrude upon her life.

RE-AUTHORING & RE-MEMBERING

June was hopeful that in their next session together Ruby's ability to identify one or more Unique Outcomes within the problem-story of 'the thief,' would ultimately result in Re-authoring a new story, without the presence of 'the thief.' June was well aware that for Ruby to experience a new, problem-free life without the intrusion of 'the thief,' their work together would likely involve the use of Re-membering Conversations as well as the use of the Miracle Question and perhaps even a Final Ceremony to bear witness to 'the thief's' absence from Ruby's new life.

Ruby's Re-authoring of a new story, absent from 'the thief's' presence would begin to emerge as more Unique Outcomes were discovered that were in contradiction to Ruby's current experiences with 'the thief.' Narrative therapists attempt to co-author or help the client to 'Re-author' a new story by tracing the history of Unique Outcomes that are in contradiction to the problem-story. According to Alice Morgan's work, as "more and more Unique Outcomes are traced, grounded, linked, and given meaning, a new plot emerges and an Alternative Story becomes more richly described."[31] It is this emerging new Alternative Story, free from the effects of 'the thief,' that eventually becomes the new Dominant Story. Narrative therapists refer to the new Dominant Story as a Re-authored story.

The Re-authoring of a new, problem-free story would also require a conversation in which June questioned Ruby as to whom she would like to join her in this new story. 'Re-membering' is a Narrative Therapy concept that involves purposefully choosing the people you would like to include, or give membership privileges to, within your new story. Re-membering Conversations therefore are intended to "powerfully incorporate and elevate significant people's contribution in the lives of those consulting the therapist."[32] In Ruby's case, June could imagine that Ruby would want to Re-member her twelve children into the new story emerging against infertility and 'the thief' and looked forward to discovering others that Ruby would also want to Re-member into a newly Re-authored story.

31. Ibid., 59.
32. Ibid., 77.

THE MIRACLE QUESTION

In their next session together, June was able to ask Ruby 'the Miracle Question.' The Miracle Question is a simple tool that involves asking the client an open-ended question about how his/her life would be different without the problem.[33]

June: Ruby, I don't have a magic wand, and I suspect if I did you wouldn't be too interested anyway, as a Christian. But I am curious, if God were to perform a miracle in your life right now and tomorrow morning you woke up totally free from the effects of infertility and 'the thief,' what would your life look like?

Ruby: Well, I suppose at first my life may not look or feel any different— assuming God performed a miracle without first letting me know! Initially, I would be unaware of the miracle and might believe that I'm still bound by the effects of infertility and 'the thief.'

June: What a great observation. Some miracles are instantaneous and others we can only observe over time. Perhaps you are already experiencing a miracle without even knowing it.

What do you think would be your first clue that God had performed a miracle in your life and what would your life look like if you were free from the control of 'the thief?"

Ruby: Wow! That would be wonderful. I guess the first thing that I might notice is the absence of the barrage of unwanted thoughts I experience on any given day.

June: What kind of thoughts do you mean?

Ruby: Any and every thought you can imagine as it relates to having children. For example, when I'm in the grocery store and I see a child who has wandered away from a parent. Instead of focusing on grocery shopping my mind begins to wander. I wonder where the child's parents are. I question whether or not they are providing adequate supervision or if this child is just particularly adventurous. Those types of thoughts then lead into the many others that plague me such as: I wonder what kind of personality our children will have/would have had. What a cute little boy; I wonder if we'll ever have a boy. I'm sure we did have at least one boy. And the thoughts go on and on from there.

There are not very many moments in my day when I am not bothered by these kinds of intrusive thoughts that overwhelm and distract me from other tasks. So, I think that I would probably feel peaceful.

---

33. Mucherera, Lecture.

June: Great! What else would be different about your life if your life were miraculously free from the effects of 'the thief?'

Ruby: My mind would be at rest as I said. The most obvious sign of a miracle would be the day I received a positive pregnancy test. That would be a day I could never forget! I think I would experience such an indescribable joy!

June: Yes, I think I just witnessed some of that joy. Your face completely lit up just now as you spoke.

Ruby: Oh yes! I am excited just thinking about the possibility because it would mean far more to me than just the obvious. I would know beyond a shadow of a doubt that God had indeed performed a miracle for us because the medical professionals only gave us a 5% chance of achieving pregnancy with medical intervention. If we got pregnant without medical assistance, of course it would mean the obvious—a pregnancy, but it would mean far more to me than just a pregnancy.

June: (leaning in toward Ruby) Tell me more.

Ruby: Well, if it hasn't already been obvious to you, my Christian faith is very important to me. This miracle of a pregnancy, for me, would reassure me that God cares about the things that I care about. It would enhance my relationship with Christ and increase both my faith and my trust in Him. I've been pregnant before and lost children but I would not be afraid in this pregnancy. If I received this miracle I would absolutely know that it was from God and that would give me the ability to believe God for a healthy pregnancy and birth of our child.

June: So it sounds like this miracle would give you peace, great joy, the eventual birth of a healthy child, and it would really strengthen your relationship with God.

Ruby: Absolutely!

June: Is there anything else?

Ruby: Oh, sure! I'm just getting warmed up. This miracle would mean once and for all that 'the thief' is no longer controlling this area of our lives. Without having to worry about 'the thief' of infertility our lives would be free again. There would no longer be any anxiety, sadness, or depression about whether or not we could have children. The 'thief' would be kicked out of our doctor's appointments, our bedroom, and our marriage. We'd be free in our home, in fact. I would be free to eat, exercise, travel, and work without constraints of 'the thief.' We would experience peace and joy. This miracle would finally bring closure for me and allow me to pursue my lifelong dream of being a mom. Then I could pursue other dreams—like adoption!

June: I've enjoyed watching you and listening to you talk about this miracle. You've been so animated as you've spoken and your face is radiant. You look happy.

Ruby: I am. I feel so much better now. Suddenly I feel like I have hope. I've been living with nothing but discouragement, grief and loss for the past eighteen months. The 'thief' has stolen a lot from me. That reminds me of a scripture in the Bible about the consequences for a thief breaking into a house:

". . . if the thief is caught, he shall pay double" (Exodus 22:7 NASB).

Well, if 'the thief' is infertility in my case, and I woke up tomorrow to discover that God had indeed done a miracle for me, then I guess I just raised the bar for expectations. If God were to give me a miracle child and conquer 'the thief' once, I would fully expect Him to do it again. Infertility, 'the thief,' has been caught and I expect at least a double repayment! If God were to give me one miracle, why shouldn't I believe for two?

So yes, I think I do have hope now because I believe in a miracle-working God. And although I cannot control whether or not I am the beneficiary of such a miracle, I do believe it's possible, and that gives me hope. I will no longer allow 'the thief' to block that hope.

Ceremony

June continued working with Ruby in future sessions and found that her hope continued to grow as she began to gain victory over 'the thief's' presence in her life. As Ruby progressed in her work against 'the thief,' June began to wonder how Ruby would want to acknowledge the eventual defeat of 'the thief' in her life and its effects on her family. June often used and encouraged the use of Rituals and Celebrations in her work with clients as a way of acknowledging their progression away from the problem-story to a new, preferred story of life.[34] As she pondered what this final stage might look like for Ruby, she remembered Ruby's initial intake paperwork describing the event that triggered Ruby to seek counseling for the problem of infertility.

Two months after Ruby and Ryan lost their eleventh child to infertility, Ruby's sister, Marie, purchased three rose bushes for Ruby and Ryan to plant as a memorial for their children. Ruby wrote that it had been a kind gesture on the part of her sister and that she initially embraced the idea, but really struggled to pick out just the right roses at the nursery. Once

---

34. Morgan, *What is Narrative Therapy?* 111–14.

they brought the roses home neither Ruby nor Ryan had been able to plant them. It was too painful. After two weeks of staring at the neglected and withering roses on their back porch, Ruby called a friend to pick up the roses and care for them until they were able. Ruby entered into therapy with June the very next week.

June could not help wondering whether or not those roses might eventually be part of a Ritual Ceremony acknowledging Ruby and Ryan's progress toward the defeat of 'the thief.' For June's part she was mindful that "rituals do not focus solely on the problematic story and that Alternate Stories are performed in appropriate settings in front of especially selected audiences."[35] She also understood that the acting out of rituals that celebrate Alternative Stories were quite powerful and could be transformative in nature. With all of these thoughts and curiosities swirling in June's head, she picked up her pen to express a few of them in a therapeutic letter to Ruby as she anticipated their next session together.

35. Ibid., 114.

Bibliography

Adamo, D. T. *Exploration in African Biblical Studies*. Eugene: Wipf & Stock Publisher, 2001a.

———. *Reading and Interpreting the Bible in African Indigenous Churches*. Eugene: Wipf & Stock Publisher, 2001b.

Adams, Jay. *Competent to Counsel*. Grand Rapids: Baker Books, 1970.

———. *The Use of Scripture in Counseling*. Nutley: N.J: Presbyterian & Reformed, 1976.

Adjido, Clement T. "Links Between Psychosomatic Medicine and Sorcery," in *Endogenous Knowledge: Research Trails*, Paulin Hountondji (ed), Dakar: Codeesria, 1997.

American Society for Reproductive Medicine (1996-2011). *Reproductive Facts*. Retrieved from http://www.reproductivefacts.org

Amewowo, Wynnand. "Experience and Discoveries with the Bible in West Africa." in *Mission Studies*. Vol. 3, No.1, 12–24, 1986.

Arnett, J. J. "Emerging Adulthood: A Theory of Development from the Late Teens Through the Twenties." *American Psychologist. Vol. 55,* No. 5, 469–480. doi: 10.1037//0003-066X.55.5.469, 2000.

Arnold, J., and P. Gemma. *A Child Dies: A Portrait of Family Grief*. Rockville, MD: Aspen Systems Corporation, 1983.

Axelrod, J. "The 5 Stages of Loss and Grief." *Psych Central*. Retrieved on November 22, 2011, from http://psychcentral.com/lib/2006/the-5-stages-of-loss-and-grief/, (2011).

Baby Name Meanings. Retrieved June 25, 2010, from Babyhold.com: http://www.babyhold.com/list/Gaelic_Baby_Names/Seana/details/, 2006.

Bagley, R. "Trauma and Traumatic Stress Among Missionaries." *Journal of Psychology and Theology. Vol. 31*, No. 2, 97–112, 2003.

Bancroft, Lundy. "A Critique of Janet Johnston's Typology of Batterers." *Domestic Violence Report*, Vol. 4, No. 1, Oct/Nov 1998.

Basow, S. A., E. Lilley, J. Bookwala, and A. McGillicuddy-DeLisi. "Identity Development and Psychological Well-Being in Korean-Born Adoptees in the U.S." *American Journal of Orthopsychiatry. Vol. 78, No.* 4, 473–480. doi: 10.1037/a0014450, 2008.

Barbier, J. C. "Cohabitation et Concurrences Religieuses dans le Golfe du Guinee: Le Sud-Benin entre Vodun, Islam, et Christianisme." [Religious Cohabitation and Competion in the Guinea Golf : Southern Benin between Vodun, Islam and Christianity] in Pourtier R. (org.), Colloque. *Geopolitiques Africaines, Bulletin de l'Association des Geographes Francais*. Juin 223–236, 2002.

Bennett, Lorna. «Narrative Methods and Children: Theoretical Explanations and Practice Issus.» *Journal of Child and Adolexcent Psychiatric Nursing. Vol.* 21.1, 2008.

Besley, Tina. "Foucauldian Influences in Narrative Therapy: An Approach for Schools." *Journal of Educational Enquiry.* Vol. 2, No. 2, 2001: 72–93.

Bhugra, D., K. Bhui, R. Mallett, M. Desai, J. Sing, and J. Leff. Cultural identity and its measurements: A questionnaire for Asians. *International Review of Psychiatry, Vol. 11*, 244-249, 1999.

Bibliography

Boonzaier, Floretta, and Cheryl de la Rey. «Woman Abuse: The Construction of Gender in Women and Men's Narratives of Violence.» *South African Journal of Psychology.* Vol. 34, 443–463, September, 2004.

Boucher, A. *A Travers les Missions du Togo-Dahomey.* Paris: Librairie Pierre Tequi, 1926.

Bradshaw, Catherine P., Anne L. Sawyer, and Lindsey M. O'Brennan. "Bullying and Peer Victimization at School: Perceptual Differences Between Students and School Staff." *School Psychology Review.* Vol. 36, No. 3, 2007: 361–382.

Bradt, Kevin J. *Story as a Way of Knowing.* Kansas City: Sheed & Ward, 1997.

Braiker, Harriet. *The Disease to Please: Curing The People Pleasing Problem.* New York, New York: McGraw-Hill, 2001.

Briere, J. *Therapy for Adults Molested as Children.* New York: Springer Publishing Company, 1996.

Brindle, W. A. "*The Gospel of Luke.* By Joel Green." In *Journal of the Evangelical Theological Society.* Vol. 43, No. 1, 140–142, 2000.

Brodzinsky, D. M., and J. Palacios. *Psychological Issues in Adoption.* Westport, CT: PraegerCohn, 2005.

Brown, C. *Narrative Therapy: Making Meaning, Making Lives.* Sage Publications, Inc., 2006.

Bureau of Justice Statistics Crime Data Brief. February 2003, Intimate Partner Violence. 1993—2001

Burke, T. *Forbidden Grief: The Unspoken Pain of Abortion.* Springfield, IL: Acorn Books, 2002.

Butler, S., J. Guterman, and J. Rudes. Using Puppets with Children in Narrative Therapy to Externalize the Problem. *Journal of Mental Health Counseling.* Vol. 31.3, 2009.

Butler VI, John L., and Rhi Anna Lynn Platt. "Bullying: A Family and School System Treatment Model." *The American Journal of Family Therapy.* Vol. 36, 18–29, 2008.

Cabot, R. C., and R. L. Dicks. *The Art of Ministering to the Sick.* New York: Macmillan Company, 1936.

Capps, Donalds. "Pastoral Use and Interpretation of Bible." In *Dictionary of Pastoral Care and Counseling,* editor Rodney J. Hunter. Nashville: Abingdon, 1997

———. *Biblical Approaches to Pastoral Counseling.* Philadelphia: Westminster Press, 1981.

———. *Living Stories.* Minneapolis, MN: Augsburg Fortress, 1998.

———. *Pastoral Care and Hermeneutics.* Philadelphia: Fortress Press, 1984.

Carter, Dr. Les. "Learning About People Pleasers." Retrieved from http://www .drlescarter.com/pleasersone.asp, 2004.

Clinebell, H. *Basic Types of Pastoral Care and Counseling: Resources for the Ministry of Healing and Growth.* Nashville: Abingdon, 1984.

Cohn, L., J. L. Levitt, and R. A. Sansone. *Self-Harm Behavior and Eating Disorders: Dynamics, Assessment, and Treatment.* New York: Brunner-Routledge, 2004.

Committee on the Judiciary. "Violence Against Women, A Majority Staff Report." United States Senate, 102nd Congress, October 1992.

Crocket, K., D. Epston, G. Monk, and J.Winslade. *Narrative Therapy in Practice: The Archeology of Hope.* San Fransisco: Jossey-Bass, 1997.

DeRosier, Melissa. "Building Relationships and Combating Bullying: Effectiveness of a School-Based Social Skills Group Intervention." *Journal of Clinical Child and Adolescent Psychology.* Vol. 33, No. 1, 196–201, 2004.

Devaris, J. "Family Therapy Issues With Adolescents in Divorced Families." *Psychotherapy. Vol. 32*, No. 2, 242–247, 1995.

Dinkins, B. D. *Narrative Pastoral Counseling.* Xulon Press, 2005.

Dixon, Glenda, Maureen Bretherton, Mark Lynch, and Yvonne Perkins. "The Dunedin Safer Schools Safer Communities Initiative: A Narrative Approach to Community Collaboration." *New Zealand Journal of Counseling.* Vol. 26, No. 1, 1–15, 2005.

Domar, Lesch Kelly. *Conquering Infertility: Dr. Alice Domar's Mind/Body Guide to Enhancing Fertility and Coping with Infertility.* New York, New York: Penguin Books, 2002.

D'Onofrio, A. A. *Adolescent Self-Injury: A comprehensive Guide for Counselors and Health Care Professionals.* New York: Springer Publishing Company, 2007.

Drewery, Wendy and John Winslade. "The Theoretical Story of Narrative Therapy." *Narrative Therapy in Practice: The Archaeology of Hope.* Ed. Gerald Monk, John Winslade, Kathie Crocket, and David Eston. San Francisco: Jossey-Bass, 1997.

Durrant, M. K. *Ideas For Therapy with Sexual Abuse.* Adelaide: Dulwich Center Publication, 1990.

Edelman, Hope. *Motherless Daughters, The Legacy of Loss.* United States: Addison-Wesley, 1994.

Elshtain, Jean. "Reflections on Abortion: Values and the Family." In *Abortion, Understanding Differences.* Editors Sidney Callahan and Daniel Callahan. New York: Plenum Press, 1984.

Espelage, Dorothy L., and Susan M. Swearer. "Research on School Bullying and Victimization: What Have We Learned and Where Do We Go From Here?" In *School Psychology Review.* Vol. 32, No. 3, 365–383, 2003.

Figley, C. R. *Treating Compassion Fatigue.* New York, NY: Brunner-Routledge, 2002.

Flemming, Dean. *Contextualization in the New Testament: Patterns for Theology and Mission.* Downers Grove: IVP, 2005.

Forehand, Rex L., and Nicholas Long. *Parenting the Strong-willed Child: the Clinically Proven Five-week Program for Parents of Two- to Six-year-olds.* Chicago: Contemporary, 2002.

Freedman, J. *Narrative Therapy: The Social Construction of Preferred Realities.* New York, NY: W. W. Norton & Company, Inc., 1996.

Garzon, R. "Interventions that Apply Scripture in Psychotherapy." In *Journal of Psychology and Theology. Vol. 33, No. 2*, 2005.

Gerkin, C. V. "Interpretation and Hermeneutics, Pastoral." In *Dictionary of Pastoral Care and Counseling,* Editor J. Hunter, 1990.

Grief-Healing-Support.com. (n.d.). Complicated grief/prolonged grief disorder. Retrieved June 23, 2010, from http://www.grief-healing-support.com/complicated-grief.html

Green, J. B. "Scripture in the Church: Restructuring the Authority of Scripture for Christian Formation and Mission." In *The Wesleyan Tradition.* Editor Paul Chilcote. Nashville: Abingdon, 38–51, 2002a.

———. "Scripture and Theology." In *Interpretation: A Journal of Bible & Theology.* Vol. 56, No. 1, 2002b.

———. *Salvation.* Saint Louis: Chalice Press, 2003.

———. *Recovering the Scandal of the Cross: Atonement in New Testament and Contemporary Contexts.* Downers Grove: IVP, 2000.

Greer, R. C. *Mapping Postmodernism: A Survey of Christian Options.* Illinois: IVP, 2003.

Bibliography

Hamarus, Päivi, and Pauli Kaikkonen. "School Bullying as a Creator of Pupil Peer Pressure." *Educational Research.* Vol. 50, No. 4, 333–345, December 2008.

Hathaway, W. L. "Scripture and Psychological Science? Integrative Challenges and Callings." in *Journal of Psychology and Theology. Vol. 33, No. 2,* 2005.

Healey, J., and D. Sybertz. Towards an African Narrative Theology, Nairobi: Paulines Publication Africa, 1996.

Herman, Judith Lewis M. *Trauma and Recovery.* New York: BasicBooks, a Division of HaprperCollins Publishers, 1992.

Herskovits, M. *Dahomean Narrative: A Cross-Cultural Analysis,* Second Edition. Evanston: Northwestern University Press, 1998.

Hielema, J. S. *Pastoral or Christian Counseling: A Confrontation with American Pastoral Theology in Particular Seward Hiltner and Jay Adams.* Utrecht: "De Tille." 1975.

Holeman, V. T. *Reconcilable Differences: Hope and Healing for Troubled Marriages.* Downers Grove, IL: InterVarsity Press, 2004.

Holmes, P. R. *Becoming More Like Christ: Introducing a Biblical Contemporary Journey.* Milton Keynes, UK: Paternoster, 2006a.

———. *Becoming More Human: Exploring the Interface of Spirituality, Discipleship and Therapeutic Faith Community.* Milton Keynes, UK: Paternoster, 2007.

———. *Trinity in Human Community: Exploring Congregational Life in the Image of the Social Trinity.* Milton Keynes, UK: Paternoster, 2006b.

Hooker, M. *Not Ashamed of the Gospel: New Testament Interpretations of the Death of Christ.* Grand Rapids: Eerdmans, 1994.

Hopper, J. "Oppositional Identities and Rhetoric in Divorce." *Qualitative Sociology. Vol. 16, No. 2,* 133–156, 1999.

Jordan, M. R. *Reclaiming Your Story: Family History and Spiritual Growth.* Louisville, KY: Westminster John Knox Press, 1999.

Judith Lewis Herman, M. *Trauma and Recovery.* New York, NY: BasicBooks, Perseus Books Group, 1997.

Kluger-Bell, Kim. *Unspeakable Losses Understanding the Experience of Pregnancy Loss, Miscarriage, and Abortion.* New York: Norton & Company, 1998.

Kubany, Edward S., and Tyler C. Ralston. *Treated PTSD in Battered Women.* Oakland, CA: New Harbinger Publications, Inc., 2008.

Lee, D. C., and S. M. Quintana. "Benefits of Cultural Exposure and Development of Korean Perspective-Taking Ability for Transracially Adopted Korean Children." *Cultural Diversity and Ethnic Minority Psychology. Vol. 11, No. 2,* 130–143. doi: 10.1037/1099-9809.11.2.130, 2005.

Lee, R. M., H. D. Grotevant, M. R. Gunnar, and the Minnesota International Adoption Project Team. "Cultural Socialization in Families with Internationally Adopted Children." Journal *of Family Psychology. Vol. 20, No. 4,* 571–580. doi:10.1037/0893-3200.20.4.571, 2006.

LeMarquand, G. "New Testament Exegesis in (Modern) Africa," in *The Bible in Africa: Transactions, Trajectories and Trends.* Editors Gerald O. West and Musa W. Dube. Boston: Brill, 2000.

Levitt, J. L., and R. A. Sansone. *Self-Harm Behavior and Eating Disorders: Dynamics, Assessment, and Treatment, 2004*

Little, A, L. Hartman, and M. Ungar. "Practical Applications of Narrative Ideas to Youth Care. *Narrative Practice.* Vol. *20, No. 4,* 37, 2007.

Loughlin, G. *Telling God's Story: Bible, Church and Narrative Theology.* Cambridge: Cambridge University Press, 1999.

Manus, Chris Ukachukwu. "Methodological Approaches in Contemporary African Biblical Scholarship," in *African Theology Today.* Scranton: The University of Scranton Press, 2002.

———. *Intercultural Hermeneutics in Africa: Methods and Approaches.* Nairobi: Acton Publishers, 2003.

Marcia, J. E. Development and Validation of Ego-Identity Status. *Journal of Personality and Social Psychology. Vol. 3, No.* 5, 551–558, 1966.

Masamba, Ma Mpolo J., and K. Whilhelmina. *The Risks of Growth: Counseling and Pastoral Theology in the African Context.* Ibadan: Daystar Press, 1985.

Masse, Sydna, and Joan Phillips. *Her Choice to Heal Finding Spiritual and Emotional Peace after Abortion.* Colorado Springs: Chariot Victor, 1998.

Mathieu, F. *Running on Empty: Compassion Fatigue in Health Professionals.* Compassion Fatigue Solutions and Professional Development, Spring 2007. Kingston, Ontario. WWW.compasionfatigue.ca.

———. *Transforming Compassion Fatigue into Compassion Satisfaction: Top 12 Self-Care Tips for Helpers.* Compassion Fatigue Solutions and Professional Development, March 2007. Kingston, Ontario. WWW.compasionfatigue.ca.

Matima, Miriam. *Narrative Therapy and Abused Women: effectiveness of narrative therapy for sheltered/abused women.* Retrieved from www.brieftherapynetwork .com, 2009.

Mayo Clinic. Complicated Grief. *Foundation for Medical Education and Research.* Retrieved June 23, 2010, from http://www.mayoclinic.com/health/complicatied-grief/DS01023, 2009.

Miles, Al. *Violence in Families: What Every Christian Should Know.* Minneapolis, MN: Augsburg Books, 2002.

Monk, Gerald, John Winslade, Kathie Crocket, and David Epston. *Narrative Therapy in Practice.* San Francisco, CA: Jossey Bass Publishers, 1997.

Monroe, P. G. "Using the Scriptures in Counseling: Guidelines for the Effective Use of Bible in Counseling." *Biblical Theological Seminary.* August 17, 2004.

Morgan, Alice. *What is Narrative Therapy? An Easy to Read Introduction.* Adelaide: Dulwich Centre Publication, 2000.

McAdams, D. P. The Psychology of Life Stories. *Review of General Psychology. Vol. 5, No.* 2, 100–122. doi: 10.1037//1089-2680.5.2.100, 2001.

McKenzie, Wally, and Gerald Monk. "Learning and Teaching Narrative Ideas." In, *Narrative Therapy in Practice: The Archaeology of Hope.* Editors Gerald Monk, John Winslade, Kathie Crocket, and David Eston. San Francisco: Jossey-Bass, 82–117, 1997.

McNeill, John T. *A History of the Cure of Souls.* New York: Harpers & Brothers, 1951.

MSNBC article, "Scientist Make Curing of HIV a Priority" http://www.msnbc.msn .com/id/48308434/ns/local_news-anchorage_ak/t/scientists-make-curing-hiv-priority/#.UBbF-RyKu1Y.

Mucherera, T. *Meet Me at the Palaver: Narrative Pastoral Counseling in Postcolonial Contexts.* Eugene, OR: Cascade Books; A Division of Wipf and Stock Publishers, 2009.

———. *Pastoral Care from a Third World Perspective: A Pastoral Theology of Care for the Urban Contemporary Shona in Zimbabwe.* New York: Peter Lang (2001, 2005).

Bibliography

Mullis, A. K., R. A. Mullis, S. J. Schwartz, J. L. Pease, and M. Shriner. "Relations Among Parental Divorce, Identity Status, and Coping Strategies of College Age Women." *Identity: An International Journal of Theory and Research.* Vol. 7, No. 2, 137–154, 2007.

Mummendey, A. "Positive Distinctiveness and Social Discrimination: An Old Couple Living in Divorce." *European Journal of Social Psychology.* Vol. 25, 657–670, 1995.

Nair, Anitha. *Understanding Infertility.* Retrieved from http://www.doctoroz.com/fertility-videos/understanding-infertility, 2010.

Nelson, Annabelle, Charles McClintock, Anita Perez-Ferguson, Mary Nash Shawver, and Greg Thompson. "Storytelling Narratives: Social Bonding as Key for Youth at Risk." *Child & Youth Care Forum.* Vol. 37.3, 2008.

Ngewa, S. "Principles of Interpretation" in *Africa Bible Commentary.* Editor Adeyemo Tokunboh. Nairobi: World Alive Publishers, 2006.

Nouwen, Henri J. M. *The Wounded Healer.* New York, New York: Doubleday, 1972.

Oates, W. E. *The Bible in Pastoral Care.* Philadelphia: Westminster Press, 1953.

O'Connor, M. "Bereavement and the Brain: Invitation to a Conversation Between Bereavement Researchers and Neuroscientists." *Death Studies.* Vol. 29, 905–919. DOI:10.1080/07481180500299063, 2005.

Oden, Thomas C. *Classical Pastoral Care,* Vol. 3, Grand Rapids: Baker Books, 2001.

Olmstead, S. B., T. G. Futris, and K. Pasley. "An exploration of married and divorced, nonresident men's perceptions and organization of their father role identity." *Fathering,* Vol. 7, No. 3, 249–268. doi:10.3149/fth.0703.249, 2009.

Parrinder, G. *West African Religion.* Epworth Press, 1961.

———. *West African Psychology: A Comparative Study of Psychological and Religious Thought.* Cambridge: James Clark & Co., 2002.

Pederson, P. B. *Hidden Messages in Culture-Centered Counseling—A Triad Training Model.* Thousand Oaks, CA: Sage Publications, Inc., 2000.

Penner, M. *Hope and Healing For Kids Who Cut.* Grand Rapids, MI: Zondervan, 2008.

Peoples, Feruson. *Experiencing Infertility: An Essential Resource.* New York, New York: W.W. Norton & Company, Inc, 1998.

Phinney, J. S. Ethnic Identity in Adolescents and Adults: Review of Research. *Psychological Bulletin.* Vol. 108, No. 3, 499–514, 1990.

Pohl, Christine D. 'Bioethics and the Future of Medicine' in *A Christian Appraisal, Abortion: Responsibility and Moral Betrayal,* editors Kilner, John F., and Cameron, Nigel M de S., and Schiedermayer, David L. Carlisle, United Kingdom: Paternoster Press, 1988.

Purnell, Douglas. *Conversation as Ministry Stories and Strategies for Confident Caregiving.* Cleveland, Ohio: The Pilgrim Press, 2003.

Reardon, David C., *Aborted Women: Silent No More.* Chicago: Loyala University Press, 1987.

Reich, Ellen Judith. *Waiting: A Diary of Loss and Hope in Pregnancy.* New York: The Haworth Press, 1991.

Resolve. *Fast Facts on Infertility.* Retrieved from http://www.resolve.org/about/fast-facts-about-fertility.html, 2011.

Rizzuto, Ana-Maria. *The Birth of the Living God: a Psychoanalytic Study.* Chicago: University of Chicago, 1979.

Schwartz, A. *Complicated Grief.* Retrieved June 23, 2010, from http://www.mentalhelp.net./poc/view_index.php?idx=119&w=5&e=28572&d=1, 2006.

"Scientist Make Curing of HIV a Priority" http://www.msnbc.msn.com/id/48308434/ns/local_news-anchorage_ak/t/scientists-make-curing-hiv-priority/#.UBbF-RyKu1Y.

Segovia, F. F. "Biblical Criticism and Post-Colonial Studies: Toward a Postcolonial Optic," in *The Postcolonial Biblical Reader*. Editors R. S. Sugirtharajah. Malden: Blackwell Publishing, 2006.

Seltzer, Dr. Leon F. "From Parent-Pleasing to People Pleasing: The Journey Away From Self . . . And Back." Retrieved from http://www.psychologytoday.com/blog/evolution-the-self/200807/parent-pleasing-people-pleasing-the-journey-away-self-and-the-way-ba-0, July 24, 2008.

Shaffer, D., and B. Waslick. *The Many Faces of Depression in Children and Adolescents*. London: American Psychiatric Publishing, Inc., 2002.

Shapiro, J. *Applications of Narrative Theory and Therapy to the Practice of Family*. 96–100, February, 2002.

Sigley, Thomas. "Evangelism Implosion: Reaching the Hearts of Non-Christian Counselees," in *Journal of Biblical Counseling*. Vol. 17, No. 1, 7–14, 1998.

Smoke, J. *Growing Through Divorce*. Eugene, OR: Harvest House Publishers, 1995.

Smokowski, Paul R., and Kelly Holland Kopasz. "Bullying in School: An Overview of Types, Effects, Family Characteristics, and Intervention Strategies." *Children & Schools*. Vol. 27, No. 2, 101–110, April 2005.

Speckhard, Anne C., and Vincent M. Rue. "Post-Abortion Syndrome: An Emerging Public Health Concern." Journal of Social Issues, April 14, 2010.

Stamm, B. H. editor. *Secondary Traumatic Stress: Self-Care Issues for Clinicians, Researchers, and Educators, 2nd Edition*. Lutherville, MD: Sidran Press, 1999.

Sundermeier, T. *The Individual and Community in African Traditional Religion*, New Brunswick: Transaction Publishers, 1998.

Suter, E. A. Discursive Negotiation of Family Identity: A Study of U.S. Families with Adopted Children from China in *Journal of Family Communications. Vol. 8*, 126–147. doi: 10.1080/15267430701857406, 2008.

Swetland, Kenneth L. *Facing Messy Stuff in the Church, Case Studies for Pastors and Congregations*. Grand Rapids, MI: Kregel Publications, 2005.

Syed, M., and Azmitia, M. A Narrative Approach to Ethnic Identity in Emerging Adulthood: Bringing Life to the Identity Status Model in *Developmental Psychology. Vol. 44, No. 4*, 1012–1027. doi: 10.1037/0012-1649.44.4.1012, 2008.

Tajfel, H. *Human Groups and Social Categories*. New York: Cambridge University Press, 1981.

Thompson, Janet. *Dear God, Why Can't I Have a Baby? A Companion Guide for Couples of the Infertility Journal*. Abilene, Texas: Leafwood Publishers, 2011.

Thurneysen, E. *A Theology of Pastoral Care*. Richmond: John Knox Press, 1962.

Ukpong, J. "Development of Biblical Interpretation in Africa: Historical and Hermeneutical Direction." In *Bible in Africa*. Leiden, Boston: Brill, 2000.

———. "The Problem of God and Sacrifice in African Traditional Religion." In *Journal of Religion in Africa*, Vol. 14, No 3, 185–203.

———. "Inculturation Hermeneutics: An African Approach to Biblical Interpretation." In *The Bible in a World Context: An Experiment in Contextual Hermeneutics*, editors Walter Dietrich & Ulrich Luz. Grand Rapids: Eerdmans, 2002.

Walker, F. David. *Thomas Birch Freeman: The Son of an African*. London: Student Christian Missionary Movement, 1929.

Bibliography

Waruta, D. W. *Caring and Sharing: Pastoral Counseling in the African Perspective.* Nairobi: AITEA Publications, 1995.

Webb Willyn Solutioning. *Solution-Focused Interventions for Counselors.* Philadelphia, PA: Accelerated Development, 1998.

West, G. O. *Biblical Hermeneutics of Liberation: Modes of Reading the Bible in the South African Context,* 2nd Edition. Pietermaritzburg: Cluster Publication, Maryknoll: Orbis, p. 131, 1995.

White, C., and D. Denborough. *Introducing Narrative Therapy: A Collection of Practice-Based Writings.* Adelaide, South Australia: Dulwich Centre Publications, 1998.

White, Michael. *Reflections on Narrative Practice: Essays and Interviews.* Eugene, Oregon: Wipf & Stock, 2000.

White, M., and D. Epston. *Narrative Means to Therapeutic Ends.* New York , NY: W.W Norton & Company, 1990.

Williams, Michael, and John Winslade. "Co-Authoring New Relationships at School Through Narrative Mediation." *New Zealand Journal of Counseling.* Vol. 30, Issue 2, 62–74, 2010.

Williams, W., and A. Caldwell. *Empty Arms.* Chattanooga, TN: AMG Publishers, 2005.

Willimon, William. *Pastor: the Theology and Practice of Ordained Ministry.* Nashville: Abingdon Press, 2005.

Winslade, John, and Lorraine Smith. "Countering Alcoholic Narratives" in, *Narrative Therapy in Practice: The Archaeology of Hope,* edited by Gerald Monk, John Winslade, Kathie Crocket, and David Eston. San Francisco: Jossey-Bass, 158–192, 1997.

Wimberly, Anne E. Streaty. "Narrative and Personhood," in *Journal of the Interdenominational Theological Center.* Vol. 25, No. 3, 231–257, 1998.

Wimberly, Anne. S. *Soul Stories: African American Christian Education.* Nashville: Abingdon Press, 1994.

Wimberly, Edward P. *Moving From Shame to Self-Worth: Preaching and Pastoral Care.* Nashville, Tennessee: Abingdon Press, 1999.

———. *Using Scripture in Pastoral Counseling.* Nashville: Abingdon, 1994.

———. *Recalling Our Own Stories.* San Francisco: Jossey-Bass, 1997.

Wise, Carroll A. *Psychiatry and the Bible.* New York: HarperCollins, 1956.

Worden, W. *Grief Counseling and Grief Therapy.* New York: Springer Publishing Company, 1982.

Wright, N. T. *The Last Word: Beyond the Bible Wars to a New Understanding of Scripture.* New York: HarperCollins, 2005.

Yai, O. B. "The Path is Open: The Herskovits Legacy in African Oral Narrative Analysis and Beyond," in *Program of African Studies,* Working Paper 5. Evanston: Northwestern University, 1999.

Yarhouse, Mark A. and et al. *Modern Psychopathologies: A Comprehensive Christian Approach,* Downers Grove: InterVarsity, 2005.

———. *Family Therapies: a Comprehensive Christian Appraisal.* Downers Grove, IL: InterVarsity Press, 2008.

Zimmerman, J., and M. Beaudoin. "Cats Under the Stars: A Narrative Story." *Child and Adolescent Mental Health, Vol. 7.1,* 2002.

Zimmerman J., and Dickerson. *If Problems Talked: Narrative Therapy in Action.* NY: The Guilford Press, 1999.